*f*P

BIRTH OF THE COOL

BEAT, BEBOP, AND THE AMERICAN AVANT-GARDE

Lewis MacAdams

THE FREE PRESS
New York   London   Toronto   Sydney   Singapore

THE FREE PRESS
A Division of Simon and Schuster, Inc.
Rockefeller Center
1230 Avenue of the Americas, New York, NY 10020

Designed by Douglas Riccardi and Lara Harris,
Memo Productions, NY

Manufactured in the United States of America

10 9 8 7 6 5 4 3 2 1

Library of Congress Cataloging-in-Publication Data

MacAdams, Lewis, 1944–
    Birth of the cool : beat, bebop, and the American
        avant-garde / Lewis MacAdams.
        p. cm.
    Includes filmography, discography, bibliography, and index.
    1. Bop (Music)—United States—History and criticism.
    2. Avant-garde (Aesthetics)—United States—History—
        20th century. I. Title
ML3508 .M23 2001
700'.973'09045—dc21   00-048253

ISBN 0-684-81354-8

Page 288 constitutes an extension of the copyright page.

FOR OCEAN, WILL, TORII, AND NATALIA—

so they'll know where I was coming from

ACKNOWLEDGMENTS

I'd like to give thanks to my agents, Betsy Amster and Angela Miller; and to my editor, Bill Rosen; as well as to Sharon Gibbons, Anne Yarowsky, and Janice Easton, who did immense amount of work on various stages of this book; and to Andrea Au, who helped boot it home.

Jon Taplin gave me the original idea for *Birth of the Cool* one day over lunch. John Heiden of S.M.O.G. Design in Los Angeles gave me a way to look at it. RJ Smith made early editorial suggestions that allowed the writing to proceed. Joan Cohen of Legwork has been much more than a photo researcher (though she's great at that): she's collaborated on this project every step of the way. Douglas Riccardi and Lara Harris of Memo designed the interior of the book as if they were reading my mind. Philip Metcalf, Matt Shine, and Robert Legault made this a much better and stronger book through their copyediting and proofreading.

The writing of this book benefited mightily from interviews and conversations with David Amram, Amiri Baraka, Jim Carroll, Clark Coolidge, Fielding Dawson, Larry Fagin, Ed Fancher, Jules Feiffer, Charles Henri Ford, Gordon Onslow Ford, Jack Gelber, Lelia Goldoni, Gary Goodrow, Allen Ginsberg, James Grauerholz, Shirley Hayes, Thomas Hines, Herbert Huncke, Jane Jacobs, Ivan Karp, Dr. Norman Kelman, Ed Koch, Jackson Mac Low, Clarence Major, Gerard Malanga, Judith Malina, Maurice "Moe" McEndree, Jackie McLean, Jonas Mekas, Dan Morgenstern, Mary Perot-Nichols, Lewis Porter, David Ritz, Pete Rugolo, Barney Rossett, Peter Schjeldahl, Gary Snyder, Peter Stearns, Robert Farris Thompson, Quincy Troupe, Philip Whalen, Dan Wolfe, and Seymour Wyse.

Laura Kuhn of the John Cage Trust allowed me to read the "Cage and Zen Buddhism" chapter from her doctoral dissertation. Julie Lazar, who curated "Rolywholyover," the 1991 John Cage retrospective at the Los Angeles Museum of Contemporary Art, shared her vast collection of Cage's music. Marcia Westkott, professor of women's studies at the University of Colorado, let me read her paper "Karen Horney's Encounter with Zen." Marta Vega at the Caribbean Cultural Center in New York let me wander around and ask questions. Michael Hotez at the First Zen Institute talked to me for one whole, mesmerizing evening about the history of Buddhism in New York. Ramon Rodriguez at Boys Harbor School for the Performing Arts in Manhattan allowed me to study his massive archive of Latin music.

Psychohistoran Peter J. Swales, who exhumed and translated the German-language case file of Dr. Paul Federn's 1944 analysis of William Burroughs, generously shared with me relevant pieces of his lecture "Burroughs in the Bewilderness," which he presented in 1995 at New York's Payne-Whitney Hospital. Bob Dobbs, formerly of the Center for Culture and Technology at the University of Toronto, helped clarify some of Marshall McLuhan's ideas. Lisa Phillips, curator of the 1995 "Beat Culture and the New America" show at the Whitney Museum in New York, kicked my ass.

I would especially like to acknowledge the help of the librarians at the Los Angeles Central Library; the New York Public Library's Humanities and Social Sciences Library, Lincoln Center Performing Arts Research Collection, and Schomberg Center for Research in Black Culture; the Museum of Television and Radio in New York and Los Angeles; the Institute of Jazz Studies at Rutgers University's Newark, New Jersey, campus; the UCLA Film and Television Archive; Phil Runkle of the Catholic Worker Archive at the Marquette University Library in Milwaukee; and Wendy Chmielewski, the curator of the Swarthmore College Library Peace Collection.

Along the way, I've had help from Michael Attias at Librairie de France in New York, Sanford Bardwell, Gordon Baldwin, Garrick Beck, the Dark Bob, Paul Body and the staffs at Video Journeys and Vidiots in Los Angeles, Peter Case, Scott Cohen, Wanda Coleman, Victor Hernandez Cruz, Anthony de Curtis, Michael Cuscuna, Steve Davis, Kirby Dick, Jeff Dietrich of the *Catholic Worker*, Big Greg Edwards, Rick Fields, Jonathan Gathorne-Hardy, Brett Goldstone, Woody Haut, Immy Humes, Jonathan Hyams at the Michael Ochs Archives, Sarah Kernochan, Ki-gen at the Mt. Baldy Zen Center, Asako Kitaori, Josh Kun, JoAnne Kyger, Eric La Prede, Craig O'Rourke, Dr. Bernard Paris, Renate H. Patterson, Pierre Picot, Paul Prince, Kyle Roderick, Laurie Sanger, Tensho David Schneider, Matthew Spender, Nick Taplin, Steven Taylor, Rita Valencia, Dr. Marianne Von Eckardt, Jerome Weeks, Eli Wolf at Blue Note Records, Angus Wynne, and many others. Thank you all.

Most of all, I want to thank the entire Klabin family for their incredible generosity and support over the years; most especially, I thank my wife, JoAnne, the only one who knows what this book really cost.

CONTENTS

PREFACE

A COOLER WORLD

In 1949 and 1950, a black, twenty-one-year-old trumpet player from East Saint Louis named Miles Davis, and a white, thirty-seven-year-old big-band arranger from Toronto named Gil Evans, working out of Evans's windowless basement apartment behind a Chinese restaurant on Fifty-fifth Street in Manhattan, created a new kind of music—brass accented and smooth; then suddenly jagged and cut-to-the-chase, with in-a-hurry titles like "Boplicity" and "Move." The music wed the sophistication of Duke Ellington with the break-neck tempos of bebop. It melded the blues with the intellectual advances of the black avant-garde. It was "slow and strange," admitted big-band leader Count Basie, whose music was formed in an earlier era, but it was "good, real good."

Davis and Evans brought in some of the best and most innovative young players in town, including Gerry Mulligan, Lee Konitz, and Max Roach, for a trio of recording sessions, which were released as a series of 78s. In 1957, eight of the tunes were reissued by Capitol Records as one of the first wave of twelve-inch LPs. Titled *Birth of the Cool*—the phrase came from Capitol arranger-conductor Pete Rugolo, who'd overseen the original sessions—the collection was, as jazz critic Pete Welding pointed out, "anything but cool. As anyone familiar with the music can attest, it possesses an abundance of focused emotional power." *Birth of the Cool* came to symbolize the style and attitude of an era. And Miles Davis, with his "clean as a motherfucker" custom-tailored suits, his Picasso-like "cold flame," his "take no prisoners" approach to the work, came to epitomize its art.

I think I heard the word "cool" for the first time when I was about eight years old—roughly 1952—while tuning in to *Cat's Caravan*, a rhythm 'n' blues show on WRR radio that came on after the Dallas Eagles baseball games. The host of the show was the old "coffee-drinkin' nighthawk," Jim Lowe, the "Cool Fool." Every night, when Buddy Morrow shouted "All abooard for the night train!" I embarked on a journey into the life I wanted to live.

In November 1959, my sophomore year at St. Mark's School of Texas, *Life* magazine published a story about "beatniks," a term that had only

Miles Davis live in New York City, 1958.

13

recently been coined by San Francisco gossip columnist Herb Caen. The word combined "beat"—beatific, so beat-down as to be forced to give one's ego, one's pretensions of control, up to the flow—with *Sputnik*, the name of the first earth-orbiting satellite, which the Russians had launched in 1957. The *Life* profile was meant as a hit piece on William Burroughs, Allen Ginsberg, Gregory Corso, and Jack Kerouac, the beats' best-known literary practitioners. "Undisciplined and slovenly amateurs," the magazine sneered, "who have deluded themselves into believing that their lugubrious absurdities are art." But to me, they seemed very cool.

Even in high school I could see through the corny media image that was already spreading about the idea of the "cool." To me, the July 1960 *Mad* magazine parody "'Beatnik': The Magazine for Hipsters," featuring brooding, bearded, huarache-shod bongo players at a coffeehouse poetry reading (*snap, snap*) was the exact opposite of what Kerouac and Ginsberg meant by "cool." Decades later, Ginsberg was still putting down the so-called cool scene for being so negative that it didn't even bother to create works of art. "They became junkies or businessmen," he told me once. What did I mean, then, when I thought that the beats were cool? I had no idea. I just liked the feeling I got when I said the word. "Cool" meant not only approval, but kinship. It was a ticket out of the life I felt closing in all around me: it meant the path to a cooler world.

THE ESSENCE OF COOL

Where does "cool" come from? *The Random House Dictionary of American Slang* points to an 1825 reference in the English satirical publication *Spy*. A young Etonian is referred to as "a right cool [hence impudent, insolent, or daring] fish." Most scholars point to an African-American derivation. In his pioneering African-American dictionary, *Juba to Jive*, Clarence Major finds the root of cool in the Mandingo word for "gone out" or, as we might say, "trippin'," linking it to the hippies' "far out" and the hipster's "gone, man, gone."

Gil Evans, 1956.   "Cool" was in use among African Americans in Florida as early as 1935,

the year in which the flamboyant African-American folklorist and author Zora Neale Hurston published her book *Mules and Men*. In it, Hurston tells of a marathon hoedown that welcomed her back home to Eatonville, Florida, from Columbia University in New York, where she'd been studying with the great anthropologist Franz Boas. As Hurston and her friends pile into a jalopy that will haul them from one party to another, someone asks a guy named Johnny Barton if he's got his guitar with him. "Man, you know Ah don't go nowhere unless Ah take my box wid me," replied Barton, who, Hurston notes, was wearing cream-colored pants with a black stripe down the side, a starched blue shirt, and a collar pin with heart bangles on each end. "And what makes it cool, Ah don't go nowhere, unless I play it."

As a calling card for his Cotton Club Orchestra, bandleader Cab Calloway in 1938 published *Cab Calloway's Cat-ologue: A Hepster's Dictionary*. Described as "the first glossary ever compiled of the colorful and unique words, phrases and expressions employed by Harlem musicians and performers on Lenox Avenue," it contained two hundred words favored by the "hep cats . . . when they talk their jive." In Calloway's book, "hip" means wise or sophisticated. Anyone unhip is "square" or a "Jeff." And even in 1938, **Calloway and company were already using such terms as "groovy," "dig"—as in "I'll plant you now, and dig you later"—and "mellow." A "viper" was a dope-smoker, a "drape" was a suit of clothes, and a "gate" was a "cat," as in "Greetings, gate." He doesn't mention the word "cool."**

Following Calloway's *Cat-ologue* came a much more ambitious effort from Dan Burley, a columnist for New York City's leading African-American weekly newspaper, *The Amsterdam News*. At the urging of his friend Langston Hughes, Burley in 1944 published a two thousand-word "Negro-American lexicon," *Dan Burley's Original Handbook of Harlem Jive*. Burley included street-corner conversations from the heart of Harlem's "Stroll," the corner of 126th Street and Seventh Avenue, between mythical hipsters Joe Q. Hipp and Sam D. Home ("Just here from Rome"); as well as jive rewrites of Hamlet's soliloquy, "The Night Before Christmas," and Joyce Kilmer's "Trees" ("I think that I shall never dig/A spiel as righteous as a twig"). "Cool" isn't in Burley's vocabulary, either.

The brilliant tenor-saxophone player Lester Young was a fabulous wordslinger. He hung the name "Sweets" on candy-loving trumpeter Harry

Zora Neale Hurston, 1950.

Edison, pinned rotund jazz singer Jimmy Rushing with "Mr. Five-by-Five," and dubbed Billie Holiday (whom Duke Ellington pronounced "the essence of cool") "Lady Day." In the documentary *Song of the Spirit*, a Young biographer, Douglas H. Daniels, claims that Young coined the phrase "that's cool." Jackie McLean, the great bop alto player, agrees: "Anyone who tells you otherwise is bullshitting," he warned me. "Lester Young was the first."

An intensely private, solitary man, so cool he wore crepe-soled shoes, Young's Fu Manchu mustache and trademark porkpie hat were pieces of a mask that hid many things. To most of the world, Young appeared unruffled and fastidious. He always came in a moment after the beat, just to remind you that you were on Lester's time. Even when he was sitting in the window of his final room, across the street from Birdland at the Alvin Hotel, knocking down his daily quart of hundred-proof, cool remained Lester Young's unassailable castle, his signature.

Anybody trying to define "cool" quickly comes up against cool's quicksilver nature. As soon as anything is cool, its cool starts to vaporize. To Carnegie Mellon emotionologist Peter Stearns, cool symbolizes "our culture's increased striving for restraint" to better blend into the social fabric. In his *American Cool: Constructing a Twentieth-Century Emotional Style*, Stearns says to be cool means "conveying an air of disengagement, of nonchalance, and using the word is part of the process of creating the right impression." We can "lose" or "blow" our cool, Stearns points out. Cool, he goes on, "has become an emotional mantle, sheltering the whole personality from embarrassing excess."

In her book *What Is Cool?: Understanding Black Manhood in America*, Marlene Kim Connor says, "*Cool is perhaps the most important force in the life of a black man in America* [italics Connor's]. Cool is the closest thing to a religion for him, and it is easily his most basic method of determining manhood. Cool cannot be taught, or handed down from generation to generation." For black men, "Cool essentially defines manhood." Only one's peers can bestow cool.

"Cool for us, was to be there without being into nothing dumb," the poet Amiri Baraka writes in his *Autobiography*. In Newark, New Jersey, "where I was comin from, the brown side, we just wanted to keep steppin. The black had shaped us, the yellow had taunted us, the white had terrified and alien-

Lester Young, mid-1950s.

Amiri Baraka,
holding his new-
born daughter,
Kellie, 1959.

ated us. And cool meant, to us, to be silent in the face of all that, silent yet knowing." Later, cool meant well dressed: "dap," "clean," "down," "hooked up." To Baraka, just being from New York was cool. The coolest guy in his Howard University set was "Smitty from the city." Bop was cool. The original *Birth of the Cool* 78s came out when Baraka was a senior in high school. "For me, Miles was what *cool* meant."

Clarence Majors traces cool back to the first rebellious slave submerging his emotions in irony and choking back his rage. "Black cool," adds Dr. Richard Majors, a psychologist and senior research associate at the Urban Institute in Washington, "is better understood as a complex system of coping mechanisms, a technique for black survival in America." "I play it cool," Langston Hughes wrote, "And dig all jive/That's the reason/I stay alive."

Marlene Kim Connor posits that cool arose when male slaves were forced to maintain an outward calm while their wives and mothers and daughters were raped by white men. For an African-American male, "being cool" meant that he had harnessed his anger. Indeed, as Connor writes, **"A man's ability to protect himself is at the very core of cool." Cool, then, became the ultimate revenge of the powerless. Cool was the one thing that the white slaveowner couldn't own. Cool was the one thing money couldn't buy. At its core, cool is about defiance.**

For a white hipster like Garry Goodrow, an actor in New York's Living Theater throughout most of the 1950s, "to be cool was to be in charge, unfazed by the bullshit of life. . . . The outward signs of cool had everything to do with an appearance of easy competence. . . . To be cool was to be not frantic, not overblown." In Goodrow's world, black people had the keys to cool, "to many beautiful, life-affirming things—like jazz, like relaxation, like general enjoyment of life outside the commercial pressure cooker. Any white who felt a healthy disgust for the ridiculous society around him gravitated in that direction."

The poet and critic Peter Schjeldahl sees cool as transcending race, citing the unemployed aristocracy disenfranchised by the French Revolution as one likely source of the cool. "Cool is one of the consolations for the aristocracy's loss of power—[cool is] an inborn excellence that you don't have to prove."

Cool can be extremely negative. Cool can refuse to get involved or to take a stand. Cool may reject all feeling and become, as William S. Burroughs put

it, an "Ugly Spirit." Before Burroughs understood that he could use writing to exorcise his demons, he shot his wife, rejected his parents' love, and would live to see his only son kill himself with alcohol and drugs. In the '30s, American gangsters said "to cool" when they meant "to kill." To say "he's cool" of someone meant that he wasn't a cop. In *Naked Lunch*, William Burroughs described a character called the Rube whose need for heroin was absolute. "The Mark Inside was coming up on him and that's a rumble nobody can cool."

The birth of the cool took place in the shadows, among marginal characters, in cold-water flats and furnished basement rooms. Most midcentury Americans were defined by their role in World War II, but cool wasn't drafted; and cool didn't serve. Cool was too young, too weird, too queer, too black, too strung out, too alien to take part. Cool wasn't part of the victory celebration.

The history of cool is a history of a shiver in the human heart. In the face of the atomic bomb, everybody felt powerless. After 1945, the idea that history was a steady progression toward perfection began to seem naïve. Absolutes were shaken; relativity entered the world. As the World War victory euphoria gave way to the paranoia and conformity of the Cold War, artists were forced to turn inward and go underground in search of ways to express the powerful new realities. Before, there had been many individual acts of cool. Now Cool—a way, a stance, a knowledge—was born.

A COOL REVOLUTION

Cool could not remain at the culture's cutting edge forever. In January 1945, as tanks from General George S. Patton's Third Army sliced into the German heartland, Jean-Paul Sartre, philosopher (*Being and Nothingness*), novelist (*Nausea*), playwright (*No Exit* and *The Flies*), hero of the intellectual underground and young France, was climbing out of an American military transport plane in New York after a twenty-hour flight from freshly liberated Paris. He brought with him an idea: existentialism. "God is dead," the diminutive, pipe-smoking Sartre announced, therefore the universe is

Gerry Mulligan,
1956

Jean-Paul Sartre
in his trademark
sheepskin jacket in
Paris, late 1940s.

absurd. The only thing we know is that we exist. We alone are responsible for our destinies.

Wrapped in a battered sheepskin jacket and peering through Coke-bottle-thick eyeglasses, Sartre lectured up and down the East Coast and was the subject of adoring articles in New York newspapers and magazines. "One is free to act," he told reporters, "but one must act to be free." Beboppers like trumpeter Dizzy Gillespie and pianist Thelonious Monk picked up on him, appropriating the Left Bank café-intellectual style—the black beret, the horn-rimmed glasses, the wee goatee. **Gillespie claimed to wear berets because they were the only hats that he could stuff into his pocket, but there was more to it than that: the beret was his, and other musicians', way to signify that they were no longer to be looked at as clowns and entertainers, but as artists. The jazzmen's adoption of the philosopher's trappings was a merger of two potent stances—bebop and existentialism.**

In Paris, the existential crowd, or "les rats," hung out in "caves" along the Boulevard St.-German-des-Pres near the Sorbonne. In those tiny cellar nightclubs like Le Tabou, Le Mephisto, and La Rose Rouge, the scene's reigning young chanteuse was Juliette Greco. Wearing a beret atop straight black hair that hung down over the turned-up collar of her loosely tied raincoat, whispering the songs of the poet Boris Vian into a microphone with an air of studied indifference, she expressed the world-weariness of young people who had lived through a war. In 1949, Miles Davis made his first trip to Paris to play the inaugural post-Occupation jazz festival; he and Greco met and fell in love. As Davis would later tell his amanuensis, the poet Quincy Troupe, Juliette Greco was "probably the first woman that I loved as a human being." The offspring of their three-year, long-distance liaison—of the marriage of bebop and existentialism—was the birth of the cool.

As the Cold War deepened, the seeds were planted for what Robert Thurman, in his book *Inner Revolution*, calls "a cool revolution." In 1950, Buddhist scholar D. T. Suzuki arrived from Japan to teach at Columbia University. The composer John Cage was one of his first students. Cage spread zen teachings through classes and performances at the two most important schools of cool, the New School for Social Research on the uptown edge of Greenwich Village, where an eighteen-year-old bongo-playing, blue jean–wearing Midwestern rebel named Marlon Brando was

kicked out of his first drama class, and at tiny Black Mountain College in North Carolina.

Juliette Greco on stage at La Rose Rouge, Paris, 1950.

By the late 1950s, cool could even claim its own turf; the denizens of Greenwich Village rose up to preserve Washington Square from the bulldozers of the master city planner Robert Moses, who tried to ram a highway through the middle of the park. **This victory marked the first successful neighborhood revolt against urban renewal, and in the course of the battle, the first alternative newspaper, *The Village Voice*, emerged into its own. Cool signaled it would not be overrun by "progress," the mainstream ideology. By the late fifties cool was capable of holding its own.**

During the few years that separate Jackson Pollock and Andy Warhol, between the heydays of Woody Guthrie and of Bob Dylan, cool spread quickly from the edge to the cultural mainstream. By the 1960s, as Thomas Franks writes in *The Conquest of Cool: Business Culture, Counterculture, and the Rise of Hip Consumerism*, cool had become a commodity—something money could buy. By the mid-1990s, there were, like, cool malls. Allen Ginsberg and Miles Davis appeared in Gap advertisements. Jack Kerouac's *On the Road* speech celebrating "the mad ones, the ones who are mad to live, mad to talk, mad to be saved," had become a Volvo advertisement.

In his 1995 book *I Sing the Body Electronic: A Year with Microsoft on the Multimedia Frontier*, Fred Moody writes that, on the Microsoft campus, "cool" could mean any one, or combination, of the following, depending upon context and tone of voice: "perfect, phenomenal, awesome, ingenious, eye-popping, bliss-inducing, pretty clever, enchanting, fine or adequate, acceptable, okay." That same year, I heard my three-year-old daughter say "cool" when she saw an ad for *Scooby-Doo* reruns on the Cartoon Network. Today, cool is everywhere. This book illustrates the theory and practice of cool—and shows how we got to where we are.

THE CAPITAL OF THE WORLD

Other cities may lay claim to being the birthplace of the cool. In late '40s and '50s, San Francisco was the center of American poetic style, and the tiny night-spot Jimbo's Bop City in the Fillmore was one of cool's cradles. In the 1950s, years before Jean-Luc Godard, François Truffaut, Claude Chabrol, and the rest of the "Nouvelle Vague," Paris gave birth to filmed cool when director Jean-Pierre Melville dropped *Bob le Flambeur*, a film about a Parisian con man who drives only the coolest American muscle cars and wears Ted Lapidus suits inspired by American gangster cool. But cool as we know it was made in New York.

New York has always been the home of the American avant-garde. In 1775, as Martin Shefter writes in *Capital of the American Century: The National and International Influence of New York City*, New York agreed to host the General Magazine of Arms and Military Stores for all of British North America. In exchange for agreeing to stockpile munitions that could be used against the anti-British mobs of Boston and Philadelphia, the London Board of Trade made New York the western terminus for the first regular transatlantic postal route. **As a result, Shefter argues, New York's newspapers were the first to get the political, economic, and cultural news from abroad. Ever since, the United States has seen the world through New York City's eyes.**

In the latter half of the nineteenth century, every major U.S. newspaper chain owned a New York daily. The wire services—the Associated Press (founded in the offices of the *New York Sun* in 1848) and the United Press (founded 1907)—were New York–based. By 1880, most large book and sheet-music publishers had moved to New York from Boston, Philadelphia, and other cities. Sheet-music publishing evolved into the recording industry, which also came to be based in New York. The mass circulation–magazine business has been based in New York since the 1890s.

The modern advertising industry came into existence in the 1920s in New York, to service the mass magazines. Then, in the '30s, advertising helped create the radio networks, which in the '40s evolved into the four national television skeins: ABC, CBS, NBC, and DuMont, all of them live from New York. Until the coast-to-coast coaxial cable was completed in the early '50s, all network-television programming in the U.S. originated in New York. In 1945, there were 6,000 television sets in America. By 1951, there were ten million, all receiving their entertainment from New York.

In 1945, Europe was exhausted, and its intellectual and financial capital fled to New York. The "liberty ships" bringing home our troops steamed through the Narrows into what had become the world's largest port. By war's end, the United States, with just 6 percent of the world's population, boasted two-thirds of the world's economic capacity. The United Nations secretariat going up on Rockefeller-donated land along the East River only confirmed what everybody already knew: Washington may have been the capital of the world's richest nation, but New York was the capital of the world.

Growing up in a series of minty-fresh suburbs following the bulldozers north from Dallas, Texas, I knew only a few people besides myself who had any desire to bail out. My friends who were smart rednecks knew that they were pointed toward the greedy energy of Los Angeles. But Judy Marcus and Eloise LaGrone and I always knew—I felt as if we knew it in our genes—that our destinies were tangled up with New York's.

At that time in Texas, one could still get a driver's license at age fourteen and a half, and I did. On one of the first occasions that I borrowed the car, I drove it downtown, just so that I could stand at the only corner in Big D—probably the only such corner within five hundred miles—where the buildings were tall enough to form a canyon, and imagine how cool it would be to be in New York. It would not be saying too much to say that this book is the product of that dreaming.

THE UN-COOLEST THING IN THE WORLD

"BIRD WAS BEBOP'S SPIRIT...

Charlie Parker was just nineteen when he left Kansas City on a freight train headed for Chicago in the fall of 1939. In the Windy City, he had to pawn his alto sax—his only possession—so that he could hitch a ride on a band bus to New York City. An old K.C. cohort, tenor player Prof Smith, bumped into Parker on a Manhattan street corner shortly after his arrival. "He sure did look awful when he got in," Smith recalled. Parker was dressed in rags, and noted Smith, "he'd worn his shoes so long that his legs had swollen up." It was an inauspicious beginning for a man whose name would become synonymous with cool.

When Charlie Parker was eleven his father was stabbed to death by a hooker in a drunken brawl. Parker hardly knew him. When he was fifteen, he asked his doting mother for a saxophone. Working the graveyard shift cleaning a local Western Union office, she scraped together forty-five dollars for a threadbare, twenty-year-old pawnshop sax held together by rubber bands.

His mother said Charlie was a bright child, but the only thing he ever worked at was music. He got his first horn when he joined the Lincoln High School marching band. During the Prohibition-era mayoral reign of a musclebound liquor vendor named Tom Pendergast, the nightclubs and dance halls of Kansas City's red-light district, the lawless Combat Zone, featured African-American jazz bands 'round the clock. Night after night, Parker saw his momma off to work on the trolley car, then lied his way into the Club Reno or any one of a dozen other nightspots to drink in the saxophone glories of his heroes: "the Rabbit," Johnny Hodges, from Duke Ellington's Orchestra; "the Hawk," Coleman Hawkins; and Parker's main man, "the President," Lester Young. Parker acquired a phonograph with a setscrew that allowed him to slow down the turntable so he could steep himself in Young's blues-drenched nuances. When people heard Charlie Parker play, they said he sounded like Lester Young, only twice as fast.

When Parker was fifteen, a girlfriend, Rebecca Ruffin, a woman four years his senior, moved in with him and his mother. Parker and Ruffin had a son the next year. If Parker's mother hoped the birth of her first grandchild

Charlie Parker at Capitol Records, Hollywood, January 17, 1946.

would straighten out her unruly son, she was surely disappointed. When she was three months pregnant, Rebecca discovered her husband in their bedroom with the blinds drawn, shooting heroin. Calmly rewrapping around his neck the tie he'd just used to raise a vein, Parker came over, kissed her goodnight, and said that he had to go to work.

The jam session, Ralph Ellison writes in *Shadow and Act*, is a school where "it is more meaningful to speak, not of a course of study, of grades and degrees, but of apprenticeships, ordeals, initiation ceremonies." The first session Charlie Parker ever got into was at Kansas City's High Hat Club, which featured a gong like the one Ted Mack used on his network radio show, *The Original Amateur Hour*. When he got mixed up while playing the chorus of Coleman Hawkins's hit "Body and Soul," Parker was gonged. He spent the next two years woodshedding in the backwaters of the Ozarks before making his way to New York. One night in December 1939, during a jam session at Dan Wall's Chili House, an all-night restaurant on Seventh Avenue and 139th Street in Harlem, he experienced a sudden epiphany: "I could play the thing I was hearing. I came alive!"

"...DIZZY WAS ITS HEAD AND ITS HANDS"

One day in 1940, Dizzy Gillespie, a trumpet player in Cab Calloway's horn section, was in Kansas City for a show at the Booker T. Washington Hotel when a local musician friend "pulled his coat" about a saxophone player named Charlie Parker. In his memoir, *To Be or Not to Bop*, Gillespie remembers that first encounter. Though he was only twenty-two, Gillespie had played around New York with saxophone giants like Benny Carter, Coleman Hawkins, and Lester Young.

Charlie Parker wasn't interested in how he looked. The suit he was wearing looked like it had been slept in, his tie like it had been tied with a pair of pliers. But the fastidious Gillespie was "astounded" by what Charlie

Dizzy Gillespie, 1948.

Parker could play. "Those other guys I had been playing with weren't my colleagues," he remembered. "But the moment I heard Charlie Parker, I said, *there* is my colleague." Miles Davis explained the relationship to Quincy Troupe like this: "Bird was bebop's spirit, Dizzy was its head and its hands."

Dizzy Gillespie was born John Birks Gillespie on October 21, 1917, into a large and poor family in Cheraw, South Carolina. His mother was a homemaker and his father a bricklayer who also played piano in a weekend band. The youngest of the seven siblings who survived long enough to be christened, the young Gillespie was, by his own estimation, a "tough little rebel"—"a devil," according to his brother. If he didn't practice music, his daddy whipped him with a strap. At fourteen, Gillespie was a good enough trumpet player to get a band scholarship to Laurinburg Technical Institute in North Carolina. In 1935, after his dad died, Gillespie's mother moved the family to Philadelphia. There, he began playing music for money.

No single tale accounts for how John Gillespie became Dizzy. Some people say that it was because he was just funny. He played practical jokes, like hot-footing an unsuspecting bandmate or covering a sleeper's chest with cellophane and setting it aflame. **He wore goofy hats, like his famous bearskin busby, and he smoked elaborate meerschaum pipes. But everybody who knew Gillespie knew he was dizzy like a fox, focused and determined to make a living by playing music, from the day he arrived in New York, twenty years old, carrying his trumpet in a paper sack.**

According to Big Jay McShann, the bandleader who hired Parker for a brief, tumultuous stint when he was nineteen, Bird earned his nickname on the way to a date in Lincoln, Nebraska. The car he was riding in hit a couple of chickens, and Parker told the driver, "Man, go back—you hit that yardbird." By the time Parker had transported the deceased fowl to Lincoln and presented them to the lady of the house, he had his name. "Bird" eventually came to refer not only to Parker the man but also to his spirit, the way he played, and the realization that Bird's spirit needed to escape its body to truly sing.

In the late 1930s, no black bandleader save perhaps Duke Ellington ran a tighter business than Cab Calloway. Calloway paid his musicians as well as Ellington did. He could afford to: they were booked up three years in advance. And like Ellington's, Calloway's band sidestepped Jim Crow laws by

Cab Calloway in full zoot, 1943.

traveling in their own private railroad car. In 1939, Calloway gave Gillespie his first steady gig. With that secured, Gillespie went out and married his ever-loving Lorraine, a blunt, outspoken chorine from the Apollo Theater. The Gillespies rented a three-room apartment at 2040 Seventh Avenue, one of the best blocks in Harlem at the time, in the heart of Strivers' Row. Lorraine hung up her dancing shoes to manage her husband's affairs, and they stayed together for the rest of his life.

Cab Calloway's thing was corny—chanting "hi-de-hi-de-hi," then cupping his hand to his ear as his band chanted back "hi-de-hi-de-ho"—but as a singer-dancer, he could drive a crowd wild, dancing himself into such a frenzy that his 'do would collapse across his eyes. Though the band was good, Gillespie soon wearied of the act, of popping up from the trumpet section to vamp "I'm Diz the Whiz, a swingin' hip cat, swingin' hip cat, I'm Diz the Wiz" three hundred nights a year. After he and Parker hooked up and began pushing each other to experiment with flatted fifth chords and odd-ball harmonies, it was inevitable that Gillespie and Calloway would clash. Finally, one night, Calloway stopped the music suddenly and screamed at Dizzy, "I don't want you playing that Chinese music in my band!"

Even sporting a cream-colored zoot suit with a padded-shouldered, wide-lapeled double-breasted jacket draped to his knees over extrawide high-waisted trousers with tourniquet-tight pegged cuffs, a floppy bow tie, a foot-long watch chain, and a hat with a brim so broad it encircled his head like the yolk of a fried egg, Cab wasn't cool, because, musically, he was standing in the way of the future. One night, in September 1941 he was conducting the band but facing the audience, and somebody hit the back of his conk with a spitwad. Calloway accused Gillespie of the deed, precipitating a fight that ended with Gillespie pulling a carpet cutter out of his trumpet case and stabbing Calloway in the butt. Calloway took ten stitches and Gillespie was out of there.

For most of 1942 Gillespie bounced from band to band, while Charlie Parker played for tips in uptown after-hours spots. In January 1943, Gillespie and Parker finally got the opportunity to play together regularly when they both became members of the "bebop incubator," the band that backed the great piano player Earl "Fatha" Hines. "Father [was] so cool," Dizzy wrote, "the epitome of perfection." Hines says that while on tour, Parker and

Billy Eckstine,
1945.

Gillespie practiced together constantly during the intermissions between the band's four daily shows, even trading sax and trumpet exercise books so that each could learn the other's music. In a photo of Hines's band onstage at the Apollo Theater in Harlem in 1943, Gillespie and Parker are seated at opposite ends of the band, and opposite ends of the life-style spectrum. Gillespie is on Hines's extreme right, and looks earnest and clean-cut. Parker, on the extreme left, is the only guy in the ensemble wearing dark glasses.

"I don't think it came as easy with John [Gillespie] as it did for Bird," mused Billy Eckstine, the honey-baritoned "Sepia Sinatra" who was Hines's male vocalist (Sarah Vaughan handled the distaff chores). Could anybody have been cooler than "Mr. B."? I don't think so, not from the stitched edge of his softly rolled shirt collar to the crepe soles of his suede shoes. When Billy Eckstine left Hines at the beginning of 1944 to go out on his own, he hired Gillespie to put together what history would remember as the first bebop band. The first person Dizzy brought aboard was Charlie Parker. "Bird was responsible for the actual playing of it," Eckstine explains, "and Dizzy put it down." In *To Be or Not to Bop*, Gillespie says that "Charlie Parker was the other side of my heartbeat."

MINTON'S UNIVERSITY OF BEBOP

Until Henry Minton took it over in 1938, the space was an unused dining room off the lobby of the Hotel Cecil. Standing at 118th Street between St. Nicholas and Seventh Avenues in Harlem, the Cecil housed many black musicians when they were in New York. Henry Minton was a saxophone player and a community leader, and the first African-American delegate to the American Federation of Musicians Local 802. In *Shadow and Act*, Ralph Ellison remembers Minton as someone you could always go to for a small loan, and a man who "loved to put a pot on the range." It was Minton who transformed the Cecil's old dining room's battered bar, its discolored mirrors, and its postage-stamp dance floor into Minton's Playhouse, a supper

Kenny "Klook" Clarke, 1955.

Thelonious Monk
playing at Town
Hall, New York,
1958.

club with white linen tablecloths and flowers in little glass vases, a "first-class place," Miles Davis told Quincy Troupe, "with a lot of style."

Minton's Playhouse functioned mainly as a hangout for Minton and his friends until the end of 1940, when Minton put Teddy Hill in charge of music. Although he'd fired him from a band the year before for "playing too modern," Hill hired Kenny "Klook" Clarke to assemble a trio to back the club's after-hours jam sessions. The first player that Klook—short for "klook-a-mop," one of his trademark percussion figures—hired was piano player Thelonious Monk.

Thelonious Sphere Monk grew up on the Upper West Side of Manhattan, in a neighborhood, San Juan Hill, long since obliterated by Lincoln Center. The area's name probably commemorates the First Negro Cavalry's capture of the height above the Puerto Rican capital just ahead of Teddy Roosevelt's Rough Riders during the Spanish-American War. San Juan Hill became the pre-Harlem heart of black New York after the denizens of the city's first Little Africa were driven north from what is now Greenwich Village by razor-wielding Italian immigrants. Monk lived in the same fourth-floor walk-up apartment at 243 West Sixty-third Street for fifty years, first with his mother and sister after his dad moved back to North Carolina because of his asthma, then with Nellie Smith, the neighborhood girl who would become his wife and the mother of his two children.

Monk learned to play the piano by listening to his older sister, Marion, take lessons on the family's old upright piano. When he was eleven the teacher figured out it was Thelonious who had the talent. Monk took lessons, but he soon figured out that no school was going to teach him to play like the musicians he loved—Duke Ellington, Fats Waller, and especially James P. Johnson, the great stride pianist who lived in the neighborhood when Monk was growing up. Monk began showing up every Wednesday for the Amateur Night contest at the Apollo Theater until he won so often that he was barred from the competition. By the time he was fourteen, he was playing at Harlem rent parties. Two years later, he quit high school to go on the road as a faith healer's pianist.

A gruff "Solid" or "All reet!" was about the most conversation most people ever got out of Monk. But by the time he was in his early twenties, he

was already the supreme chordal architect of his generation, the visionary creator of spare, soulful, classics like "Round Midnight" and "Ruby, My Dear." Late one fall night in 1941, Monk and Kenny Clarke went over to Clark Monroe's Uptown House—which hosted the other great Harlem after-hours jam session—to listen to Charlie Parker, who was playing there for tips. Klook, who'd in the past been fired by such swing titans as Louis Armstrong and Ben Webster for dropping bass drum "bombs" into their suddenly old-fashioned 4/4 time, was flabbergasted. "Bird was playing stuff we never heard before," he recollected. "He was running the same way we were, but way ahead." Clarke and Monk pooled their meager dollars, got Parker a place to stay and something to eat, then steered him to Minton's.

At Minton's, Monday night—most club musicians' off night—was "Celebrity Night," when Teddy Hill's guests of honor usually included the stars of the current show at the Apollo. The food was down home—barbecued ribs with Creole sauce, pan-fried chicken, collard greens, candied yams, and sweet potato pie, and it marked an occasion when Diz and Bird (along with nearly every other hungry young vanguard musician in town from Art Blakey and Max Roach to wraithlike guitarist Charlie Christian, Fats Navarro, and Bud "Little Monk" Powell) ambled up to the buffet—and the stage. Sometimes twenty people would be waiting to climb up and jam. When Miles Davis, fresh out of Lincoln High School in East Saint Louis, hit New York in September 1944, his first stop was Minton's. According to Miles, fistfights erupted over the seats close to the bandstand whenever Charlie Parker and Dizzy Gillespie were in the house.

To keep from getting blown away by the musicians at Minton's, a player not only had to possess great skill and taste, but also be so completely grounded in music theory that he could play a song in almost any key. The pressure was intense. "If you got up on the bandstand at Minton's and couldn't play," Miles told Quincy Troupe, "you were not only going to be embarrassed by people ignoring you or booing you, you might get your ass kicked." Minton's was an institute of higher learning, maintains Miles, where "We was all trying to get our master's degrees and Ph.D.'s from Minton's University of Bebop under the tutelage of Professors Bird and Diz."

Nobody knows who invented the word "bebop." One school claims that it began with a Kenny Clarke drum figure, an onomatopoetic take on two quick, evenly accented quarter notes. Charlie Parker didn't like the word. In reply to a reporter's question about it, he said that bebop was just "trying to play clean and look for the pretty notes." Parker's favorite drummer, Max Roach, said he never heard the word "bebop" until he came downtown to play on Fifty-second Street toward the end of 1944. Up at Minton's, Roach remembers, if they ever called it anything, they called it "modern" music. Thelonious Monk says that he actually called the music "bip-bop," but "everybody must've misheard."

Bebop was a code, and its phrase fragments themselves were the only clues to its meaning. As Dizzy, who started doing a tune called "Bebop" in 1942, once told a reporter, "If you're doing *boom-boom*, and you're supposed to be doing *bap* on a *boom-boom*, that's just like *beeping* when you should have *bopped*."

Beboppers were the first generation of thoroughly schooled black musicians. Unlike many of their predecessors, most could read music and understood music theory. Some had gone to college, and they knew what was going on. Even the way bebop presented itself— with berets and goatees and horn-rimmed glasses—signaled not only the musicians' personal rejection of their own often all-too-recent rural roots, but an affinity with the European cultural avant-garde. One of the reasons why beboppers gave their tunes names like "Tautology" and "Ornithology" was because they knew that they had something to teach.

Beboppers "refused to accept racism, poverty, or economic exploitation," says Kenny Clarke. "If America wouldn't honor its constitution and respect us as men, we couldn't give a shit about the American way." The beboppers saw black soldiers dying for their country yet still coming home to the "colored" sections of everything—to segregated schools and the backs of the buses and "white only" water fountains—and they said "fuck this."

Very few beboppers joined the armed services during America's most popular war. Charlie Parker, Dizzy Gillespie, Thelonious Monk, and Miles Davis were all rejects, happily classified 4-F. To them, Lester Young was a prisoner of war: He'd managed to avoid the army until 1944, when a friendly zoot-suiter ("big chain down to his knees like Cab Calloway," recalled Young) turned out to be an FBI agent who served him with a draft notice. Soon after he was inducted, Young was arrested for boiling up a gallon of muscatel wine and dental cocaine, and he spent the rest of the war in the brig.

Long before he got his "greetings from Uncle," Dizzy Gillespie wrote in *To Be or Not to Bop*, "I already had in mind what I would do if they called me. I wasn't going to make it if I could." He arrived for his physical with his horn in a paper sack under his arm. "When they told me to take off my clothes I did, but I kept my horn." Dizzy told the shrink that white America was just as much his enemy as white Germany. "At this stage of my life, whose foot has been in my ass? The white man's foot has been in my asshole buried up to his knee!"

What the Cabaret Voltaire in Zurich meant to dada during World War I, Minton's was to bebop in Harlem during World War II: compared to the rest of the United States, Harlem was almost neutral territory, and Minton's was the nursery where the new artistic movement met the world. **Bebop was its music and its attitude was cool. Cool joined the aesthetic to the political. Cool was a militant act, a way of staying below the radar screen of the dominant culture without losing the respect of one's peers. Before bebop there was cool, but it was individual cool. For the first time, at Minton's, cool became an allegiance, a code that only those who knew could break into or share.**

In his 1952 masterpiece, *Invisible Man*, Ralph Ellison's nameless black hero represents an entire race invisible to the white world. The beboppers needed to be similarly invisible so as to avoid the whole crushing apparatus of world war. They had to stifle their rage and fear or hide it in their music. They had no choice but to be cool. They were a cabal. But like Shakespeare's Coriolanus telling those who would send him into exile, "I'll banish *you*. There is a world elsewhere," they traded their invisibility in the known world for the enhanced power of vision and exploration in an as yet undiscovered but more compelling world of their own invention.

In the afternoons, the beboppers would gather round the upright piano in Dizzy and Lorraine Gillespie's apartment and work out weird, unprecedented chord progressions that eventually turned into tunes with names like "Klactoveesedstene" and bebop chants like "Ooh-Bop-Sh-Bam (Klook-a-Mop)" and "Salt Peanuts" in a language that no outsider could understand. In the evenings, up on a stage barely big enough for a piano and a drum kit, Kenny Clarke would suddenly call a tune in some strange key, and after a chorus or two, the less-talented players on the stand would begin to, as they used to say, "feel a breeze."

One of the very few white people who got a glimpse of the action at Minton's was Jack Kerouac who, at age seventeen in 1939 and 1940, was making the academic transition from Lowell (Massachusetts) High School to Columbia University via Horace Mann School in the Bronx. At Horace Mann, Kerouac had fallen in with Seymore Wyse. Wyse, who Kerouac later described as a "strange English kid who stumbled along with Lester Young in his head," had been evacuated with his mother to New York when the Germans started bombing the English countryside; he and Kerouac shared their status as lonely aliens and lovers of jazz. The two hooked up a with a hemp-smoking jazzbo named Jerry Newman, owner of a tiny record store and jazz label in Greenwich Village called Esoteric Records.

Because of a shellac shortage and a three-year recording ban imposed on the record companies by the American Federation of Musicians in an effort to make them pay into a musicians' health and pension fund, very few records were released in America during World War II. As a result, the birth of bebop is shrouded in mystery. Newman's Esoteric Records released some of the only commercially available music ever recorded at Minton's. In those days, to say that recording equipment was "portable" meant that three people could wrestle it into a taxi. Newman asked Wyse and Kerouac to help him lug his bulky amplifier, turntable, and glass-based acetate discs uptown.

Kerouac, who claimed that Lester Young turned him on to reefer for the first time at Minton's in 1941, invoked those late-night hours a decade later in his "Fantasy: The Early History of Bop." In his eyes, Dizzy Gillespie, Charlie Parker, and Thelonious Monk were like "12th Century monks," street-corner "witch doctors" with their "backs to each other, facing all the winds—bent. miserable and cold." The only way their genius could survive was by becoming less visible. The straight-forward handshake gave way to the palm and finger brush. The "put-on" replaced the "put-down" in dealing with "squares." In the process, the ultimate outsider became the ultimate insider, able to neutralize the oppressor by creating a style.

Overleaf:
52nd Street at
night, 1948.

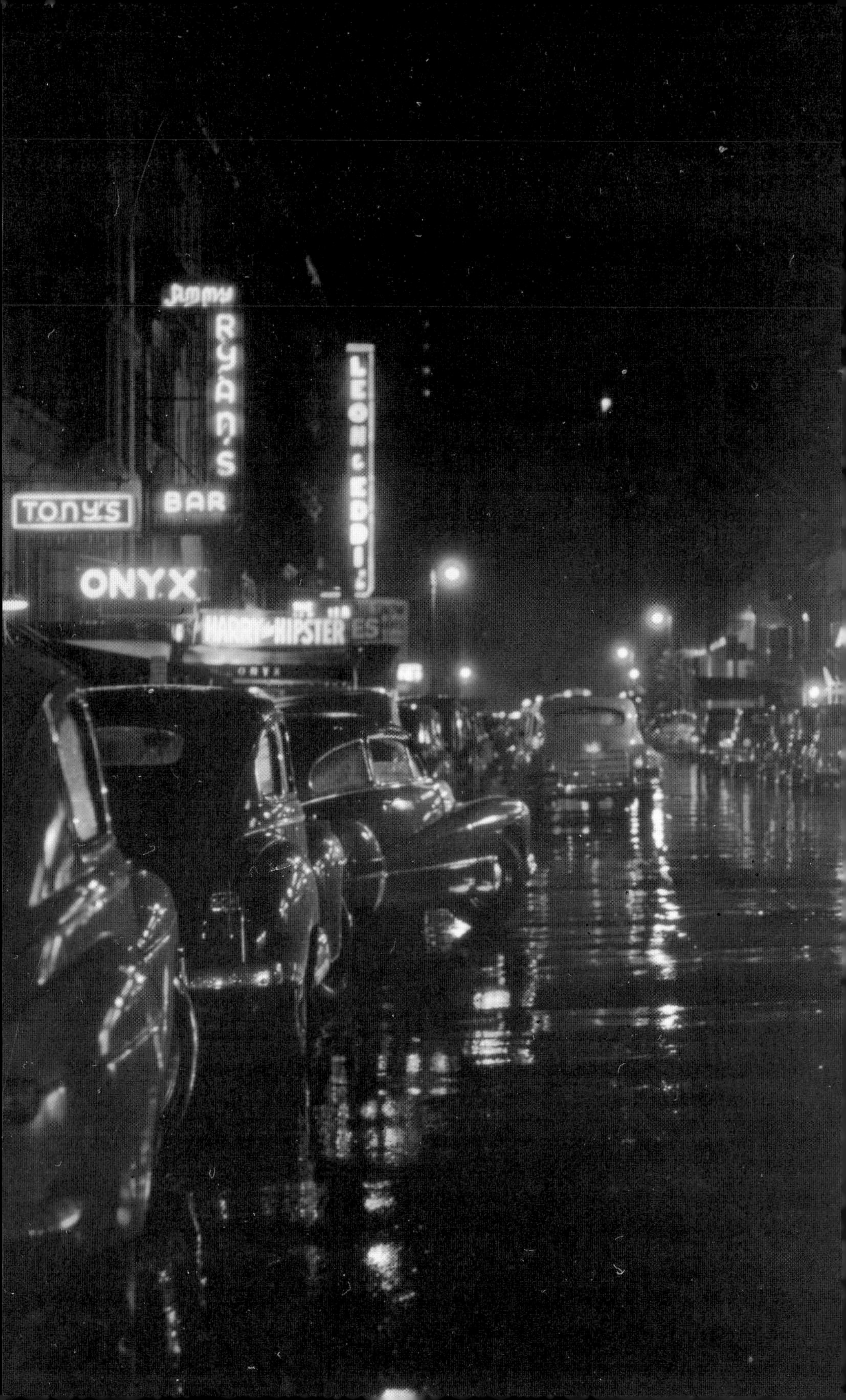
Jimmy
RYAN'S
BAR
LEON & EDDIE'S
TONY'S
ONYX
HARRY the HIPSTER

CLUB SAMOA
Club CAROUSEL
3 DEUCES
FAMOUS DOOR
B.S. PULLY
GARNER
J.C. HEARD
OSCAR PETTIFORD
THREE DEUCES
CLUB CAROUSEL

GROOVIN' HIGH

Today, Fifty-second Street between Fifth and Sixth Avenues is crowded with fifty-story media high-rises. At twilight on a wintry evening with all the lights on in the offices at *Newsweek* and *Rolling Stone*, as steam billows from beneath the streets, in the honking traffic and the rumble of the D train, the air is humming "Lester Leaps In" as I walk past a sign that reads "Swing Street," on the side of a loading dock.

Before World War II, when Fifth Avenue in the Fifties was still known as Millionaire's Row, this block of Fifty-second Street was lined with brownstones. The upper stories, which earlier in the century had housed upwardly mobile, middle-class families, now provided shelter for fringe denizens of Broadway—sign-painters and private detectives and the freelance "shooters," who, their pockets stuffed with flashbulbs, prowled the neighborhood nightclubs looking for a picture that they could sell.

Encouraged by the thousands of servicemen flooding through the neighborhood on their way to war, the ground floors and damp basements had been converted into tiny night spots—the Downbeat, the Spotlite, Kelly's Stables, the Yacht Club, the Famous Door, and half a dozen more—some no bigger than apartment living rooms, charging stiff prices for watered-down cocktails. On any night, you could hear virtually the entire history of jazz from New Orleans and Dixieland to swing and bebop as you walked up and down the street—"The Street." "Unquestionably, the most exciting half a block in the world," tenor player Dexter Gordon called it in Ira Gitler's *Jazz Masters of the '40s*. "Everything was going on—music, chicks, connections—so many musicians working down there side-by-side."

In the late fall of 1944, Gillespie and Parker cut the first bebop "sides" for Savoy Records in Newark: "Groovin' High," "Dizzy Atmosphere," "Salt Peanuts," "Hot House." The following May, they took a quintet into the 3 Deuces. Many of the clubs along Fifty-second Street were controlled by shady operators, but the Deuces was different. It was run by Sammy Kaye, a tough Jewish kid from Brooklyn who'd been to Minton's and dug the music and didn't try to tell the musicians how to play it. "The height of the perfection of our music," Gillespie wrote, "occurred in The 3 Deuces with Charlie Parker." The music was jerky and dissonant. Its jaggedy rhythms and breakneck tempos reflected wartime's fractures and dislocations, but it was cocky and struttin', the first indication of what life might be like after the war.

Using a no. 5 reed, the thickest available, Bird could make his alto sound like it was coming from the center of the earth. Dizzy raised his eyes to heaven as he blew, the goatish tuft beneath his lower lip bobbing as he unfurled cascades of eighth- and sixteenth-note trumpet blasts that rose high above the traffic outside. The run at the Deuces was the first time that white critics and the culture at large got to hear the new music, and Dizzy's reputation began to soar. It was Diz who won the *Esquire* jazz poll, Diz who got the profile in *The New Yorker*, not Bird. **Blowing musicians all considered Charlie Parker to be the fountainhead of the new music, bebop's soul. In his book *To Be or Not to Bop*, Gillespie defines "hip" as "in the know," "wise," or "one with the 'knowledge' of life." To the outside world, Dizzy Gillespie was cool's first ambassador; but the insiders knew better. Dizzy was hip. Charlie Parker was cool.**

Dizzy exploited his newfound celebrity with his own line of bebop clothes, manufactured and marketed by the Fox Brothers out of their shop on Roosevelt Road in Chicago. "Order YOUR leopard skin jacket as worn by Dizzy Gillespie—Now!" demanded a Fox Brothers ad, "Just $39.50!" The heavy, horn-rimmed glasses that Dizzy wore became known as "bop glasses" or simply "bops." Likewise, his floppy polka-dot bow ties became "bop ties"; berets became "bop caps." "Bop in here," trumpeted the ads, "and let Fox build you a crazy box!"

Fox Brothers had been founded by Harold Fox, a former big-band leader whose father operated a piece-goods woolens business in Chicago. In the late 1930s, the younger Fox started noticing zoot suits being worn by what Meyer Berger of the *New York Times*, possibly the first life-style reporter, called "the hep-cats and swing-mad kids." Though he was quick to credit the zoot suit's inspiration to the ghetto, Fox took credit for giving it and its components—the "reet-pleat," the "reave-sleeve," the "ripe-stripe," the "stuff-cuff," and the "drape-shape"—their names, through which he paid tribute to the rhyming slang employed by many of his black customers.

Fox came up with the word "zoot," he claimed, because it started with the last letter of the alphabet, the coolest, most laid-back letter of them all.

"HEROIN WAS OUR BADGE"

The end of the war was bad news for Fifty-second Street. The soldiers were going home. After a few servicemen got mugged, the military made The Street off-limits. The few joints that weren't padlocked had to turn to strippers to survive; the brownstones themselves began falling to the wrecking ball. By the end of 1945, even Diz and Bird were looking at Swing Street in the rear-view mirror. The Parker-Gillespie band took a six-week booking at Billy Berg's club in Hollywood.

L.A. wasn't ready for bebop. The local papers nixed the music, the audiences were openly hostile, and Billy Berg sided with his customers. He told Gillespie and Parker to start playing more-familiar music. They reacted in very different ways. Diz wasn't about to compromise what he was doing, but he knew how to make people laugh. "If you want to make a living at music," he wrote in *To Be or Not to Bop*, "you've got to sell it."

Diz tried hard to woo Billy Berg's crowd, announcing that he was going to introduce the band, then introducing them to each other, wiggling his butt in time to the music, directing the band with his trumpet as he duck-waddled across the stage. To Bird, what Diz was doing was "Tommin'." To Diz, Bird was falling apart—shooting dope, gobbling handfuls of Benzedrine, staying up for four or five days at a time, missing shows. When he did show up at Billy Berg's, Parker nodded out on the bandstand. He named a tune after his heroin connection, a crippled shoeshine-stand operator named Moose the Mooch, then signed over the ownership of the tune to its namesake for fifty bucks' worth of H. Ross Russell, who would later become one of Parker's biographers (*Bird Lives*), owned a Hollywood Boulevard record shop and Dial Records, which released some of Charlie Parker's greatest music, including "Cool Blues." Russell says that Bird loved the word "cool." To him, "it denoted all good qualities and situations under control." Bird told people he'd shot heroin since he was twelve years old. Now, at twenty-five, heroin had become his world. When he had enough to shoot, he was cool.

With everything that was going on, the rest of the band couldn't wait to get back to New York. When Gillespie handed out the airplane tickets, Bird cashed his in and disappeared. On the morning that the band was scheduled to leave, drummer Stan Levey spent twenty dollars racing around L.A. in a cab in a futile effort to find Bird.

Once the band left, Parker moved into a cheap hotel on the edge of Little Tokyo and started playing at a club called the Finale. One night, he set his bed on fire. Another night, he came down to the lobby to make a phone call, naked except for his socks. He ended up handcuffed to a bed in the psychiatric ward of the Los Angeles County jail, and was ultimately remanded to the state hospital in Camarillo, where he was hit with multiple shock treatments. Once, according to Miles Davis, he almost bit off his tongue.

Joseph Bayer called his elixir *heroisch*, German for heroic, because that's how it made him feel: calm, powerful, detached, cool. **Introduced in 1898 and aggressively marketed by the Bayer drug company, heroin was soon widely prescribed by doctors for the suppression of coughs. By the time the American medical establishment realized that heroin was addictive and sought to criminalize it, thousands of ordinary, law-abiding citizens were strung out.** According to Jill Jonnes's history of drug use in America, *Hep-Cats, Narcs, and Pipe Dreams*, after the Harrison Act went into effect in 1915, as many as fifty American cities opened clinics to supply heroin to those who'd been inadvertently addicted—with the aim of gradually weaning them from their habits.

When more than a thousand people a day began queuing outside the Worth Street clinic in Manhattan, it attracted the attention of Arnold Rothstein—"A.R.," the man suspected but never convicted of fixing the 1919 World Series—a gambler, rumrunner, financier, and real-life inspiration for Jay Gatsby's shadowy friend Meyer Wolfsheim in *The Great Gatsby*. The idea that junkies would kick heroin voluntarily turned out to be wishful thinking. Less than a third of Worth Street's nearly eight thousand clients went on the program, and the last of the clinics was shut down within a year. Rothstein, who had been one of the first gangsters to exploit the economic opportunities presented by Prohibition, recognized a market. He started

Lucky Luciano, accompanied by an Italian policeman, leaves Genoa for his native Sicily, 1947.

buying heroin in Europe, where it was still legal, smuggling it into the United States in hollowed-out bowling balls, and distributing it through his network of bootleggers.

Rothstein was murdered in 1928. By the mid-1930s, one of his foot soldiers, a Sicilian-American thug named Charles Lucania—better known as Lucky (so named in honor, people said, of his having beaten nineteen consecutive criminal indictments) Luciano—had clawed his way to the top of the American heroin trade. Luciano lived a life of lurid celebrity, with his own private plane and a suite in the Waldorf Towers, until he was toppled by New York State Attorney General Thomas Dewey, who succeeded in having Luciano and some three hundred other Sicilian-American gangsters deported to their home island in the late '30s.

The Sicilian Mafia was no friend of Mussolini's Fascisti, whom they regarded as interlopers on their turf. Thus, in the months preceding the 1943 Allied invasion of Italy, the U.S. Office of Naval Intelligence approached the Mob for help. The undercover role actually played by the exiled gangsters has never properly been documented, but after the war, Thomas Dewey, by now governor of New York, pardoned Luciano, and Lucky returned to the States. Heroin began flooding into America's black ghettos while American police authorities looked the other way. In the mid-1950s, the FBI's New York office had four hundred agents battling communism, and just four investigating organized crime. Yet between 1947 and 1950, heroin-related admissions of African Americans to the federal prison hospital in Lexington, Kentucky, quintupled.

Jazz historian Lincoln Collier estimates that as many as 75 percent of bebop musicians in the 1940s and '50s experimented with heroin. Billie Holiday spent the war years on Fifty-second Street, she said, wearing white gowns with white shoes, "and every night they'd bring me the white gardenias and the white junk." Miles Davis got hooked when he came back from Paris in 1949 after he and Juliette Greco fell out of love. Junk destroyed the great trumpet player Fats Navarro. Denzil Best, the drummer on *Birth of the Cool*, overdosed and died. The list goes on and on. "In the end," says Gerry Mulligan, who got hooked while he was playing saxophone on *Birth of the Cool*, "the carnage was immense."

Poet Amiri Baraka calls heroin addiction "one-upsmanship of the high-

est order." He argues that heroin's popularity among African-Americans derives from the drug's ability to "transform the negroes' normal separation from the mainstream into an advantage" by creating a clique in which only the most alienated are welcome. Junkies *have* to be cool, because junkies can't afford to attract attention. Everything has to be understated, circuitous, metaphorical, communicated in code. Loud voices are uncool. Hurried, overstated behavior is "too frantic, Jim," as the junkies used to say.

"Heroin was our badge," said Red Rodney, a trumpeter who toured with Bird and was one of the few white musicians on the bepop scene. "Hipsters used heroin. Squares didn't. Heroin gave us membership in a unique club, and for this membership we gave up everything else in the world. Every ambition. Every desire. Everything."

Of all of the junkies in jazz, Charlie Parker was supreme. He was, in Miles Davis's estimation, the greatest saxophone player of all time, yet nevertheless "a selfish motherfucker" whose profligate genius lent "horse," as it was called then, its first cachet. Though he was always telling people in the pursuit of cool not to do what he did, many musicians and others became junkies just to emulate Bird.

"For urban black people of his generation, Charlie was a genuine culture hero," writes Ross Russell. **"The revolutionary nature of his music was explicit. Implicit in his lifestyle was defiance of the white establishment." A survival mechanism that had been passed down from the days of slavery, cool in the form of studied indifference was the only way in which a hip African American could stifle rage at the same time that he or she was expressing it.**

One night, in the middle of a set at the Argyle Lounge, the hippest club in Chicago at the time, Bird came down from the bandstand, walked right past the bathroom door to the telephone booth, unzipped his fly in full view of the club's owner and patrons, and relieved himself before returning to the stage to blow. At a time when even looking at a white woman could get a black man killed in many parts of the country, Parker was going out with two at once: Doris Sydnor, an unassuming hatcheck girl at the Spotlite Club, and Chan Richardson, a pretty ex-dancer raised on the fringes of New York showbiz, with whom he moved to the Lower East Side and had a couple of kids.

Billie Holiday,
circa 1945.

Miles Davis told a story of a time when he was nineteen, coming down-

town in a cab with Bird to play on Fifty-second Street. "Bird had this white bitch in the back seat of the taxi with us," Davis remembered. "He'd done already shot up a lot of heroin and now the motherfucker's eating chicken— his favorite food—and drinking whiskey and telling the bitch to get down and suck his dick," which she did. Then, between bites of chicken, Bird start- ed eating her out. After a time, Bird asked Miles if the scene was bothering him, and Miles admitted that it was. Bird told Miles to turn his head and look out the window.

People followed Bird around everywhere, analyzing his moves. A white saxophone player named Dean Benedetti even tried to become Charlie Parker, dressing like him and talking in Bird's husky baritone, transcribing Bird's solos and imitating them note for note. Eventually he gave up playing the sax altogether to play the role of Bird's majordomo, pimping for him, scoring drugs, driving him to gigs, lugging an immense tape recorder around the country on Greyhound buses to places Bird's band was playing, and taping only Bird's solos.

After his L.A. breakdown, Bird spent late 1946 and early '47 at the State Hospital, or, as he put it in the title of a piece written while there, "Relaxin' at Camarillo." He returned to New York in April 1947, cleaned up and look- ing better than he had in years. With a new band featuring Miles Davis, who replaced Dizzy Gillespie on trumpet, and Max Roach on drums, Parker stormed into the 3 Deuces. On the stand, they barely spoke to each other, Miles remembers, except to argue about money; but when he and Bird were playing together, "it was like hearing music for the first time."

Parker and Gillespie didn't reunite until September 29, 1947, the night Dizzy's big band played to a sold-out, high-styling, black and white audience at Carnegie Hall, and bebop broke through to a wider audience. Though he said that he'd play the date, Bird's name didn't appear in the ads, because nobody trusted him to show up. By the time he finally made it to the con- cert, it was already intermission, and Bird was hurt, pissed off, and stoned.

He walked on stage "casually, almost indifferently," wrote Ross Russell, who was there, "his eyes heavy-lidded, a sly smile on his face, badly dressed in an unpressed suit." When the band kicked in, Bird flung Dizzy's music right at him. Once they'd played like a single heartbeat. Now, as the hall of hipsters went agog, they dueled their way through "A Night in Tunisia" and "Dizzy Atmosphere" while the rest of the band scrambled to keep up. One last time, Dizzy Gillespie, that most brilliant and wholly conscious of technicians, rose to meet Bird's challenge.

In *To Be or Not to Bop*, Dizzy is very cool about what went down that night, discounting reports of any rifts between him and Bird. During one number, Gillespie points out, Bird walked up and handed him a long-stem rose—"He'd probably spent his last quarter to buy it"—then "kissed me right on the mouth" and walked off the stage. Bird's connection was waiting right outside the stage door. Parker and Gillespie would play again over the next few years, but their real work together was done.

In 1948, *Metronome* magazine's readers voted Charlie Parker best jazz saxophonist for the first time. **In '49, Bird signed his first major label deal and made his first trip to Paris, where he was greeted as a celebrity on the Left Bank and treated by the press as a great artist. Through it all, he was cool. Responding to an interviewer's question about his religion, Parker replied, "I am a devout musician." When another writer asked him the "purpose" of his music, he replied, "I am aiming at beautiful tunes."** At Le Tabou, a club in St. Germaine-des-Pres, the poet, singer, and songwriter Boris Vian, Juliette Greco's frequent collaborator, introduced Charlie Parker to Jean-Paul Sartre. "I'm very glad to have met you," Parker told the philosopher. "I like your playing very much."

Yet even as his reputation soared, and the music that he pioneered was coming of age, Parker's health and music were collapsing. He gained fifty pounds, developed ulcers and heart problems, and his erratic behavior was wearing thin on everybody around him.

By the early fifties, the Swing Street dives had given way to Broadway jazz palaces like the Royal Roost, a former fried-chicken shack now equipped with bleachers from which, for ninety cents, underage kids could listen to bebop without being hassled to buy cocktails, and Birdland, where the gravelly rasp of "Symphony Sid" Torin could be heard live over WJZ from midnight until four every morning. In a depressing, embarrassing debacle, Bird's band—featuring Art Blakey on drums, Charlie Mingus on bass, and Bud Powell, still reeling from shock treatments, on piano—broke up onstage, and Bird was banned from the club he'd lent his name.

Late one evening, outside the Open Door in Greenwich Village, Parker, shuffling along in a pair of old carpet slippers, bumped into Jackie McLean. Parker had no doubt heard that the talented young saxophone player from Harlem was fooling around with junk. "I want you to kick me in the ass, Jackie McLean, for letting me get myself in this position," Bird commanded, bending over. McLean couldn't bring himself to do such a thing to his idol. Bird insisted, and a crowd began to gather. McLean, embarrassed, nudged Parker's behind with his foot. Parker demanded McLean put some boot in it. Mortified, McLean did. "Jackie McLean," Bird warned, "don't you ever let this happen to you." A few days later, Parker borrowed McLean's sax to make an out-of-town gig, a sax McLean had himself borrowed from a friend; Parker pawned it.

They say there was thunder and lightning over New York on March 12, 1955. That night, in a suite at the Stanhope, a Fifth Avenue crash pad leased to the "Jazz Baroness," "Nica" Von Koenigswarter, the estranged wife of a French diplomat, Charlie Parker died of liver failure while laughing at a clown on the Tommy Dorsey television show. Before the stormy night had passed, the scrawled phrase BIRD LIVES began appearing on walls across urban America, and the myth of tragic cool, the idea that cool was a caged thing waiting to be freed, had begun to spread across the land.

THE VERY ARCHITECTURE OF COOL

After the war, the nucleus of bebop began to disintegrate. After mysteriously disappearing the night before an important recording session with Dizzy Gillespie (a session that Savoy Records would later trumpet as "the greatest jazz recording session of all time"), Thelonious Monk withdrew into himself. When in 1946 Diz put together his first big band, it featured a thunderous arrangement of one of Monk's bluest tunes, "'Round Midnight," but there wasn't much room in the band for Monk himself. Knowing he hadn't been Diz's first choice, Monk infuriated Diz by showing up late for every gig. Monk was gone after three months. In July 1946, he was replaced by the future founder of the Modern Jazz Quartet, John Lewis. About his decision to fire Monk, Gillespie was uncharacteristically blunt, "We needed a piano player to stay out of the way." He didn't want a genius with his own wholly idiosyncratic vision of modern music.

After that, Gillespie and Monk maintained a cool formality. **"Thelonious, you murder me,"** a *New Yorker* **journalist heard Diz tell Monk when the two ran into each other on a Manhattan street corner in the late 1940s. "You're it. You're a killer." "Dizzy, you're real crazy," Monk replied gravely. "You knock me out." Then they went their separate ways.**

From the 1940s until the early 1960s, New York City required that everybody who worked more than three days in a place where liquor was sold had to be fingerprinted, have mug shots taken, and purchase a two-dollar cabaret card, proceeds to benefit the police pension fund. Monk's card was canceled in 1949 when the cops found some drugs in a car he was riding in with Bud Powell. For Monk, the road was equally problematic. Driving to a gig in Baltimore in 1958, Monk, a hulking, silent, six-foot-two, two-hundred-pound black man, freaked out the desk clerk at a motel in Delaware just asking for a glass of water. Monk retreated to his car when the white cops arrived; when he wouldn't let go of the steering wheel, they smashed his hands with their clubs. After that Monk entered into what his wife, Nellie, would later call the "un-years," withdrawing into himself and refusing to play publicly. So distanced was he from the scene, he even had to pay to get into Birdland.

Supported by a loyal wife who took care of their kids and held down two jobs, and by occasional gifts from Baroness von Koenigswarter, Monk spent his time lying on his bed in a twilight world, hovering on the edge of mental illness, staring up at a picture of Billie Holiday tacked to the ceiling, praying to the essence of cool. He watched television, smoked cigarettes, took long walks, or sat at the baby grand piano that filled his living room and half the kitchen as the darkness settled in around the Upper West Side, composing immortal tunes like the urbane, teasing, beautiful tribute to his wife, "Crepuscule with Nellie."

One of Monk's very few connections to the outside world was the team of Alfred Lion and Francis Wolff, a pair of German-Jewish refugees who ran Blue Note Records. If there was ever such a thing as a cool record label, it

OUT!

STEREO
THE FINEST IN JAZZ SINCE 1939
84165 BLUE NOTE

Grachan Moncur III | *Bobby Hutcherson* | *Larry Ridley* | *Roy Haynes*

DESTINATION...
JACKIE MC LEAN

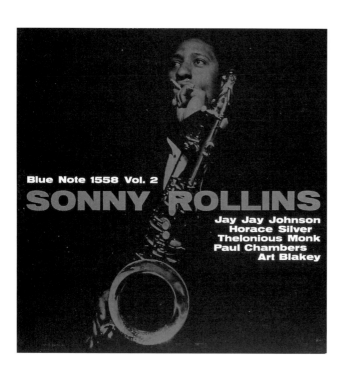

Blue Note 1558 Vol. 2
SONNY ROLLINS
Jay Jay Johnson
Horace Silver
Thelonious Monk
Paul Chambers
Art Blakey

was Blue Note during the twenty-eight years that it was owned and operated by Lion and Wolff, who'd been friends ever since their years as teenaged jazz fiends in Berlin.

Lion and Wolff were "more like jazz musicians than record producers," according to vibist Bobby Hutcherson, an early Blue Note artist. "They loved to hang out and have a good time." They also had a feel for the players. They scheduled recording sessions for 4:30 in the morning after the clubs closed in order to get that intimate, bluesy, after-hours feel that they sought to capture on vinyl. And, unlike other independent jazz labels of the day, they actually paid musicians to rehearse. "The difference between Blue Note and every other jazz label," the old saying went, "is two days' rehearsals."

Frank Wolff had been a commercial photographer in Berlin, and in New York he began documenting Blue Note recording sessions. Moving unobtrusively through the darkened studio, Wolff captured thirty years' worth of intimate portraits of jazz artists creating their music. In 1953, Lion and Wolff hooked up with recording engineer Rudy Van Gelder, an odd-duck audio goof who had built a recording studio in his parents' Englewood Cliffs, New Jersey, living room and always put on white gloves before he touched a microphone. Together, Lion, Wolff, and Van Gelder created what record producer and Blue Note historian Michael Cuscuna calls "a warm, clear, big sound that would forever redefine the way jazz was heard."

With the invention of first the ten-inch then the twelve-inch long-playing record in the early 1950s came the opportunity to create great album art. In 1956, Blue Note discovered a young designer, a classical-music lover named Reid Miles, working in the art department at *Esquire* magazine. For the next eleven years, Miles, working with Wolff's black-and-white photos, designed more than five hundred severely geometrical, radically simple, two- or three-color, no-budget album covers that indelibly shaped the look of the 1950s.

Though nothing the company ever released sold more than five thousand copies, Blue Note put out some of the coolest records ever made, including John Coltrane's *Blue Trane*, Miles Davis and Cannonball Adderley's *Somethin' Else*, Lee Morgan's *The Sidewinder*, Eric Dolphy's *Out to Lunch,* and Jackie McLean's *Destination Out!*, to name just a very few. Nothing they did, however, mattered more than recording the work of Thelonious Monk.

Two Blue Note album covers designed by Reid Miles: Jackie McClean's Destination Out! and Sonny Rollins, Vol. 2.

Alfred Lion had been inspired to start a record label by the boogie-woogie piano playing of Albert Ammons and Meade Lux Lewis at the famed 1938 "Spirituals to Swing" concert at Carnegie Hall. Accordingly, Blue Note in its early years was dedicated to swing music. The label's earliest releases were all-star sessions featuring great traditional players like soprano saxophonist Sidney Bechet, who gave Blue Note its first bona fide hit with a cover of "Summertime." During the war years, Blue Note had a string of minor successes with blues honker Ike Quebec, but by '46, Lion and Wolff had begun to realize that something new was happening in jazz. They decided to take a year off from recording just to listen.

When Ike Quebec turned Lion on to Thelonious Monk, Lion, in his own words, "keeled over" with excitement. Blue Note brought Monk into the studio in October and November 1947 and recorded everything that he had composed up to that time: fourteen sides—a then unheard-of number for the indie jazz world—including much of the music we know him by today. Issued on 78 RPM records between 1947 and 1952, and currently available as *The Best of Thelonious Monk: The Blue Note Years*, Monk's first recordings under his own name add up to less than ninety minutes of music. Nevertheless, it was, and remains, the ur-shit, the root of all jazz art that followed, filled with silences as resonant as the notes that created them, an art of implication, which is the very architecture of cool.

THE UNCOOLEST THING
IN THE WORLD

As heavily as Bird's departure must have weighed on Dizzy Gillespie, the defection of Kenny Clarke, his close friend and drummer, must have been worse. For a decade, Gillespie had relied on Clarke's timekeeping and sense of rhythm. But terminally sick of American racism, Clarke, one of the few beboppers to see World War II combat, decided to stay in the Paris he'd just helped liberate. When the war ended, he applied immediately for French citizenship, and he was soon directing his own hugely popular band. Deprived of rhythm support, Diz had to reconsider his place in music. "It's funny," Gillespie would muse later in his life, "but I don't consider myself a blues man. Blues is my music, the music of my people, but I'm not what you call a blues player." After Clarke's departure, he remembered, "I worked on developing modern jazz of a different kind."

As a teenager brand-new to New York, Gillespie had gotten to know the Cuban trumpet player Mario Bauza, who was the musical director of Cab Calloway's band. It was Bauza who called in sick one night so that Dizzy could sit in and be heard for the first time by Calloway. With Calloway, Dizzy was playing a watered-down version of Latin music, but, as he wrote in *To Be or Not to Bop*, "I've always had that Latin feeling."

The "Latin feeling" that swept New York in the 1940s was the result of both the 1917 Jones Act, which granted Puerto Ricans U.S. citizenship; and World War II, which cut the United States off from Europe, encouraging closer ties with Latin America. Between 1917 and 1955 the Hispanic community in New York grew from less than a thousand Cubans and Puerto Ricans to 450,000 Puerto Ricans alone. Every midnight flight from San Juan and Havana that touched down at La Guardia or Idlewild Airport (which opened in 1948) brought Nueva York more Creole culture with its drums.

Puerto Rican bandleader Noro Morales, a particular favorite of Walter Winchell, the famed and feared Broadway gossip columnist of the *New York Daily Mirror*, starred at the Stork Club and the Copacabana; but until Frankie "Macho" (his manager eventually convinced him to soften his nickname to "Machito") Grillo came along in the early 1940s, most successful Latin band-leaders in the United States were on the order of Xavier Cugat, the former *Los Angeles Times* editorial cartoonist who'd become—thanks to a string of movie appearances—a wildly popular bandleader specializing in polite dance music played by musicians of Spanish descent. The only Cuban drums that had insinuated their way into the music were high-pitched little bongos. The groin-high congas, with their booming evocations of Africa, were considered too primitive for American popular music, too black. But in 1940, when Bauza left Cab Calloway to become musical director for Machito, that began to change.

When they took the stage at La Conga at Fifty-second and Broadway in the summer of 1943, Machito's Afro-Cubans with Mario Bauza became the

Overleaf: Frank "Machito" Grillo and Graciela: mambo at the Savoy, late 1940s.

first black Latin band to play a midtown club. The Afro-Cubans, in fact, served as La Conga's house band for four years, and their live-at-midnight broadcasts from the club were heard from coast to coast. The Afro-Cubans had their first hit in 1944 with their theme song, "Tanga." *Tanga* was Afro-Cuban slang for pot.

In the summer of 1947, Machito and Bauza took over the Alma, a moribund dime-a-dance studio at Fifty-third and Broadway. There they staged a spectacular series of "Latin Nights on Sunday Afternoons," which they hyped by handing out thousands of flyers and blasting ads all over New York's first Spanish-language radio stations. **On the afternoon of the first show, the line waiting to get in stretched around the block. Spanish Harlem had come to Times Square. Within a few weeks, the Alma had changed its name to the Palladium, gone strictly Latin, and given birth to the mambo.**

Dizzy Gillespie had already sat in with Machito at the Royal Roost and Bop City, and he could see what was going on. "When Dizzy and me got to bullin'," Mario Bauza recalled years later, "we always said jazz was a great thing but the rhythm was very monotonous." When he was putting together his big band, Dizzy stated, "I told Mario I wanted a 'tom-tom' player. I didn't even know it was called a conga." In the fall of 1947, Mario Bauza told Dizzy that he had just the *conguero* Diz had been looking for.

Chano Pozo was born January 17, 1915, in a *solar*, a Havana neighborhood of one-room apartments built around a communal water tap, a place so tough that the police left it alone. By the time he was a teenager, he had a reputation as a *guapetón*, a tough guy, who spent his time ricocheting between reform school and dancing in the streets—drinking, chasing women, and playing his conga drum. A feared battler with brick-hard calluses from pounding on his two-and-a-half-foot-long wooden drum, Pozo had a nasty reputation for chasing every woman who caught his eye, whether she was with somebody or not.

Like Machito, Pozo was a product of Carnival, with its parade of neighborhood *conjuntos*, or music crews. His songs took the top cash prizes year after year. By the late 1930s, Pozo, dressed in white top hat and tails, was choreographing Havana's hottest nightclub revues, and spending everything he had on jewelry and fine clothes. Though he was a celebrity, he never moved away from his *solar*, parking his gold Cadillac outside his two-hundred-year-old former slave dwelling, a figure of pride and awe in the community, wrapped in a red satin robe washing at the communal water tap.

Word began to trickle back to Pozo that some of his compositions had become hits for Machito and other Latin bands in New York. Previously unaware that others were playing—and making money from—his music, Pozo went loco, tearing up his music publisher's office and promising to come back the next day and shoot the publisher if he didn't hand over some royalties. When Pozo returned, he got into a gunfight with the publisher's bodyguard, who shot him in the stomach. A bullet lodged so near Pozo's spine that it could never be removed. For the remainder of his brief life, the *conguero* couldn't sit for more than five minutes without pain.

After the shooting, Pozo ran into Mario Bauza at a Havana musicians' hangout, and asked Bauza if he thought that he could become famous in New York. "New York is ready for you," Bauza replied. To pay for his trip, Pozo is reputed to have stolen money from one of the secret societies charged with maintaining particular African tribal spiritual and cultural links; and, later, with pooling resources to buy each other out of slavery.

Chano Pozo was in New York for a year and a half, even dancing briefly with Katherine Dunham's Afro-Caribbean dance company, before Mario Bauza hooked him up with Dizzy Gillespie. "When we shook hands," Gillespie writes, "it felt like I was being crushed by cinderblocks!" At the press conference where Gillespie, who didn't speak Spanish, announced that Pozo, who didn't speak English, was joining his orchestra, a reporter asked Pozo how they planned to communicate. "We speek Africa!" Pozo replied with a big grin.

September 29, 1947: On the same night at Carnegie Hall that Dizzy Gillespie and Charlie Parker were saying good-bye, Gillespie and Chano Pozo were world-premiering Dizzy's "Afro-Cuban Suite." Naked to the waist, his upper body oiled to an ebony glow, Chano strutted the stage barefoot, pounding out rhythms, chanting in Yoruba, and driving the audience wild.

Yoruba is a language spoken by many of the people of what is now Eastern Nigeria. Fleeing civil unrest in the early eighteenth century, they were captured by coastal people who sold them into slavery. Many of the Yorubas who survived the Middle Passage ended up working on Cuban

Chano Pozo,
conguero,
1947–48.

sugar plantations. In the New World, slave owners hated and feared the Africans' drums, because the drums embodied a life force that the slavers were determined to suppress. Possession of a drum by a slave could be punished by death, for, as Dizzy Gillespie put it, "they figured you could foment revolution with the drums." However, expansion of the sugar industry in the late eighteenth century required an even greater number of slaves in Cuba. As a result, the Spanish slave owners were soon so outnumbered that they had to let their slaves keep their drums. In the relative freedom of Sunday afternoon get-togethers, Afro-Cubans kept alive the traditional African faiths through drumming. Each of the four main branches of their religion—the Abakuá, the Iucumí, the Kongo, and the Arará—was responsible for particular rhythms. Chano Pozo was schooled in all the traditions.

From the beginning, Chano Pozo employed Afro-Cuban rhythms in his collaboration with Dizzy Gillespie. Their 1947 "Cuban Be, Cubana Bop" was based upon a Nanigo rhythm that Pozo taught the band on a bus ride to a Symphony Hall date in Boston. Their other Afro-Cuban hits, "Tin Tin Deo" and "Manteca," evolved from sacred chants as well. Pozo didn't seem to acknowledge any line between secular music and his religious tradition. In late 1948, for example, Gillespie writes that Pozo came to him with a rhythm and an idea for the name. In Spanish, "*Manteca* means grease, lard, or butter. Everybody at that time was saying 'gimme some skin.' 'Manteca' is something greasy. 'Manteca' was his way of saying 'Gimme some skin!'" Released in late 1948, "Manteca" became the biggest-selling record Dizzy Gillespie ever had.

Gillespie called Chano Pozo "the Master" because, according to Gillespie, he could play in one rhythm, sing in another, and dance in a third. "He'd give me a drum, Al McKibbon a drum, and he'd take a drum. Another guy would have a cowbell, and he'd [Pozo] give everybody a rhythm. We'd see how all the rhythms tied into one another, even though everybody was playing something different. We'd be in a bus, riding down the road, and we'd sing and play all down the highway."

Robert Farris Thompson, a professor of African art history at Yale, specializes in the living connections between Africans and their New World descendants. His work has often turned on questions of cool. In what may have been the first paper ever written about cool, his 1966 "An Aesthetic of the Cool," Thompson writes that traditional Yoruba dances "express a phi-

losophy of cool: patience and collectedness of mind." Thompson underlines cool's political nature: cool, he asserts, is "an expression of community," part of the mutual relationship between a drummer and his dancers that helps to reinforce the Yoruba social fabric. For the Yorubas, according to Thompson, drumming is uncool if the drummer is too self-involved.

In *Flash of the Spirit*, his classic study of African and African-American art and philosophy, Thompson quotes one Yoruba explaining that **"Coolness of character is so important to our lives. Cool is the correct way you represent yourself to a human being." Cool is one of the essential elements of Yoruba style. It is high praise for a Yoruba to say of someone that his or her "heart is cool." The cool heart, however, is not exclusive to the Yoruba.** For example, the anthropologist John Miller Chernoff writes in *African Rhythm and African Sensibility* of a Dagomban drummer living in what is now Western Nigeria who told him that music is served best when cool: "Unless you cool your heart, your drumming will not stand." Dagombans told Chernoff that one who has learned well "has cooled his heart."

In 1947, Dizzy Gillespie defied the odds and hit the road with an avant-garde bebop big band. Even with Chano Pozo igniting the audience, a European tour was a roller coaster that lurched from one city to another making great music but plagued by amateurish production. The next autumn, Gillespie booked a tour of the American South. The one white guy in Gillespie's band, piano player Al Haig, refused to go.

Chano Pozo hated Dixie. He hated riding filthy Jim Crow railroad cars. He hated going through the back door. He hated that Diz had to keep the band's best arrangements locked away in the music trunk because the local concert promoters wouldn't let people dance. In November 1948 in Raleigh, North Carolina, somebody stole his congas, and Pozo decided to go back to New York to buy new ones. "I drove him to the train station," Gillespie recalled. "I saw the train leave. I didn't know that would be the last time I would see him alive."

Once he got back to Spanish Harlem, Pozo decided not to rejoin the band until it left the South. Meanwhile, he bought fifteen suits in every color of the rainbow and doused himself with expensive cologne. When he needed money, he went to his record company, got a box of 78s on credit, and sold them for fifty cents each on the street. According to Miles Davis, Pozo was a heavy cocaine user. "He was the baddest conga player on the scene," Davis told Quincy Troupe. "But he was a bully. He used to take drugs from people and wouldn't pay them. People were scared of him because he was a hell of a street fighter and would kick a motherfucker's ass in a minute."

Simon Joub's restaurant on Lenox Avenue near 116th Street was noted for its fine Cuban pastry, its strong black coffee, and its conga drums. After Pozo bought his new congas, he hung around Joub's, stretching his drum-skins with hot wax. As he did, he attracted a crowd that included a deco-rated World War II *veterano* and influential neighborhood bookie who called himself Cabito. Cabito sold Chano Pozo twenty-five *pitos*, or joints. At first, everything was *chevere* (Afro-cuban for "cool"). But that night, Pozo turned his friends on—and they didn't get high. So, Pozo went looking for Cabito. He found him hanging out at a restaurant with friends. Pozo berated the dealer for selling him such low-grade *tanga*, and one thing led to another. Pozo knocked Cabito out, took five dollars from his wallet, then walked out.

The next morning, December 2, 1948, the early morning sun was glint-ing through the windows of El Rio, a bar at 111th Street and Lenox Avenue, as Chano Pozo, dressed in the same black pinstripe suit he'd been partying in all night, eased a nickel into the jukebox. "Manteca" was playing when Cabito walked in. Cabito and Pozo tried to stare each other down, and Cabito split. When he returned a minute later, Pozo and a barmaid were dancing. Cabito called out Pozo's name. Pozo turned his back and walked toward the bar. Cabito emptied his *pistola* into Pozo, who collapsed backward, his eyes rolling up and his arms splayed outwards as if crucified. Cabito laid his gun down on the bar and asked the barmaid to call the police.

At his trial, Cabito told the judge that he couldn't live with the embar-rassment of having had his butt kicked by Chano Pozo in front of his friends, so he was left with no choice but to take him out. The judge must have understood, because he gave Cabito only five years. Chano Pozo's body was shipped back to Havana, and poor people turned out by the thousands to welcome it home. Legends have swirled around the death of Chano Pozo ever since. Many say he died because he'd done the uncoolest thing in the world: he'd offended the gods by turning their secret rhythms into pop hits.

BREAKING
THE ICE

THE RANK OUTSIDER

Dig Jackson Pollock in the August 8, 1949, issue of *Life* magazine: in paint-spattered blue denims, his arms folded across his chest, and his sleeves rolled up like he's ready to change your oil. An unfiltered cigarette dangles from the right corner of his mouth. He leans back, poised like a coiled spring against a wall on which he's tacked his eighteen-foot-long painting *Summertime*, which he's just finished. His head is at a cocky, fuck-you-and-the-horse-you-rode-in-on angle.

His eyes, though, look puzzled; his brow is furrowed. He squints through the cigarette smoke as if he can't believe that anybody could possibly want to know where he's coming from or what he's gone through to get to where he is now: in color when color was special, on page 42 of *Life*, his well-worn work boots crossed between the words "greatest" and "living" in the headline IS HE THE GREATEST LIVING PAINTER IN THE UNITED STATES?

In the Los Angeles Central Library half a century later, staring down at his frayed and yellowing image in Arnold Newman's photo, I can still feel the kundalini crawling up my spine as I study Pollock. As I turn the pages of the magazine, studying the images in the articles and advertising, Jackson Pollock is the only one among them all who looks cool.

In 1949, Jackson Pollock, at thirty-seven, was making some of his greatest paintings—gigantic, gorgeous drip masterpieces like *Lavender Mist* and *Autumn Rhythm*—infinitely intricate webs of color, rhythm, and line so far beyond the realm of language that in some cases, Pollock could only give them numbers, like *Number 28, 1949*.

In 1949—four years after his first one-man show at Peggy Guggenheim's gallery, Art of This Century—the debate over Pollock's work was raging, spreading from the Waldorf's Cafeteria on Sixth Avenue—the all-night eatery where the painters gathered to unwind—to the mass media and the culture at large. Clement Greenberg, already the leading theoretician of American action painting, had declared Pollock "the most powerful painter in contemporary America." On the other hand, in a *Life* magazine "Round Table" on modern art, Pollock had been denounced by Alfred Frankfurter,

Jackson Pollock at the Springs, Long Island, New York, 1947.

the editor and publisher of *Art News*; and Leigh Ashton, the director of London's Victoria and Albert Museum, who sniffed that Pollock's painting *Cathedral* "would make a most enchanting printed silk." *Time* magazine dubbed Pollock "Jack the Dripper."

Though Pollock showed little interest in defending his technique—"Technique," he once grumbled, "is just a means of arriving at a statement"—he didn't shy from discussing what he was really doing. What he claimed for painting was a sacred ground—both a trancelike state and an actual space around a canvas on the floor—where his visions could unfold with the relentlessness of nature. "When I am in my painting," he once told documentary filmmaker Hans Namuth, "there is no accident."

In the United States, 1949 was the year of the Great Heat, the year of the clampdown. That year, the Soviets blew up their first atomic bomb, which they had constructed with the help of blueprints stolen from Los Alamos and the Manhattan Project, and Mao marched into Beijing to declare the People's Republic of China. In America, the federal government started making its employees take loyalty oaths. "Communists are everywhere," Attorney General J. Howard McGrath warned the American people in '49, "in factories, offices, butcher stores, on street corners, in private businesses; and each carries within himself the germ of death for society." Ninteen forty-nine was the year the phrase "Cold War" entered the lexicon.

In 1949, the first fully air-conditioned, fluorescent-lit office buildings opened in midtown Manhattan, permitting more and more people to be packed into what Lewis Mumford in *The City in History* called "vertical human filing cases." That same year, twenty miles from midtown, in the spinach and potato fields of Hempstead, Long Island, William Levitt broke ground for the seventeen thousand cookie-cutter houses of Levittown. The year was one of unparalleled American economic expansion, yet at the same time every incoming message for America said to hunker down, pull back, buckle up, and conform.

Was America feeling guilty for A-bombing Japan? Paranoia was erupting from the American unconscious. A 1949 *New York Times* article addressed the citizens of America's major cities: "If war is declared, you, your home, and your place of business will disappear in the next second." The next year, *Life* magazine's biggest rival, *Collier's*, published "Hiroshima U.S.A.," a detailed description of what a devastating nuclear attack on the United States would be like. Accompanying the story was a lurid illustration of a cratered, incinerated Manhattan a few minutes after the A-bombs rained. In a poll, 73 percent of the American people said that they would turn in neighbors whom they considered to be communists. Nineteen forty-nine was also a peak year for film noir with new films from Jules Dassin (*Thieves Highway*), Nicholas Ray (*They Live by Night*), and Robert Wise (*The Set-Up*).

In such a dark moral and intellectual climate, the only uncorrupted man would have to be a rank outsider, a virtual untouchable. Enter Jackson Pollock. Pollock was so alienated from even his fellow outsider artists, themselves clinging by their fingernails to society's fringes while trying to make their still virtually unknown paintings, that when Willem de Kooning, Franz Kline, Ad Reinhardt, and three dozen other denizens of New York's nascent modern-art world decided in 1949 to contribute twenty dollars apiece to rent a fifth-floor walk-up on Eighth Street (which came to be known, for lack of a better name, as the Artist's Club), Pollock wouldn't have anything to do with it.

The other artists drank coffee or cheap wine and debated whether to call what they were doing "action painting," "School of New York," or "abstract expressionism"—a term Pollock particularly loathed. Pollock—on the occasions he did leave his isolated farmhouse refuge in Springs, at the eastern tip of Long Island, to come into town to see his psychiatrist—preferred getting smashed a few blocks away at the Cedar Tavern, a smoky neighborhood gin joint with green paint peeling off the walls and a clock that sometimes ran backwards.

In 1947, writer Tennessee Williams, director Elia Kazan, and twenty-four-year-old actor Marlon Brando, a bongo-playing midwestern refugee in Greenwich Village with no fixed address, created the character of Stanley Kowalski in their hit Broadway play *A Streetcar Named Desire*. As portrayed by Brando in a tight, torn T-shirt, Stanley was a brute, but a brute with the heart of an artist, a "hoodlum aristocrat" as Elia Kazan wrote in his stage notes, a cool character. But Stanley Kowalski was a fiction. Jackson Pollock was the real thing. Even Robert Motherwell, perhaps the best-educated of the New York School, compared Pollock to Brando in Streetcar, "only Brando was much more controlled than Pollock." When Hans Hofmann, the painter

Overleaf: Chesley Bonestell's painting Atom Bombing of New York, *which appeared in* Collier's *magazine, 1950.*

Chesley Bonestell

and teacher, criticized Pollock for not painting from nature, Pollock shot back, "I am nature."

In his book *How New York Stole the Idea of Modern Art*, Serge Guilbaut asserts that Pollock, in his painting, was the one American capable of meeting the Atomic Age head-on. "The effect," Guilbaut writes of Pollock's work, "is one of bedazzlement, such as can be caused by staring too long at the sun." But it is "not the sun," he goes on, "but its equivalent, the atomic bomb, transformed into myth."

Life magazine helped make Pollock its first art star. But *Life's* readers weren't as interested in Pollock's work as in Pollock himself. That's why *Life* posed him in front of his painting. To the faceless strivers described in *The Organization Man, The Man in the Grey Flannel Suit*, and *The Lonely Crowd* (to cite only three middle-class-skewering tomes of the period), Pollock must have looked like an agent of survival, the rebel artist who could face down the Bomb and the world of paranoia, guilt, and fear that it had helped create. But they didn't actually want to rebel themselves—not yet, because they could see from Pollocks's picture in *Life* what it still cost to become cool.

A HARD LESSON IN THE COOL

The first time Jackson Pollock ever laid eyes on Arshile Gorky was in 1931, in a lunch room at the Art Students League on Fifty-seventh Street, soon after Pollock had blown into town from Los Angeles. Just turned twenty, with blond hair down to his shoulders, Pollock, busy busing tables, was craning to overhear the dialogue boiling up from a table where Gorky and Stuart Davis were the center of attention. The subject was modern art.

The Art Students League was the place where New York's most ambitious young artists came to test themselves. Long ensconced on West Fifty-seventh Street by the time Pollock got there, the League had operated for *John Graham and* half a century on the principle that, as painter John Sloan put it, a student *Arshile Gorky,* could "choose his studies much as he can choose his food at the automat." *circa 1934.* There were no required courses, no attendance taken, no efforts to regulate

the instruction of the thousand or so students. Many of the city's best artists, from George Bellows to Edward Hopper, were on the faculty.

Arshile Gorky stood six feet four inches tall with stooped shoulders, deep, dramatic accent, thick mustache, and an otherworldly pallor. A shock of pitch-black hair fell across his enormously sad, dark, haunted eyes. He wore a ragged, ankle-length overcoat buttoned up to his chin. One winter he went without electricity so he could spend $75 on an art book about Pieter Breughel. Gorky taught at the League briefly during the late 1920s, but now he only came around in the afternoons with a pair of Russian wolfhounds to troll for girls and talk art with Davis, who was teaching there.

No one in the swirling lunchroom crowd could have known the extent to which Gorky was a creation of his own imagination. He wasn't Russian, as he told people, and Arshile Gorky wasn't his name. He was Vosdanik Manoog Adoian, from a long line of local priests and tradesmen in rural Turkish Armenia. When he was fifteen, his mother died of starvation in his arms during the Turkish siege of Yerevan; he and his beloved sister fled to America. During a two-year stint spent working in a Watertown, Massachusetts, factory, he took on his new identity. "Arshile," his biographer, Matthew Spender, speculates, may have been derived from the Armenian word for "evil spirit"; "Gorky" is Russian for "bitter." In 1925, at the age of thirty, he moved to New York to become an artist.

Unlike Gorky, who frequently *implied* he'd sojourned there, Stuart Davis had actually been to Paris, which was still the center of the art world. **Dapper and hip, politically engaged, Davis was one of the first American artists to reflect the influences of America's undergrounds. Davis's artist parents had exposed him to black culture, black clubs, black music from the time he was a kid.** "He talked out of the side of his mouth like a gangster," one artist remembered. Writing about him as a much older man, a reporter noted Davis's "hipster" vocabulary. Davis had already begun to sell paintings, the jittery, jazz-driven, raucously colored celebrations of American products he'd become known for.

John Graham was tall and powerfully built. At sixty, he could still do a headstand without using his hands. Graham claimed to be an ex–White Russian cavalry officer and to have met Picasso, but no one knew for sure if

Stuart Davis at the piano, circa 1926.

either story was true. Graham was an ironist and an art theorist, a ladies' man and thrift-store Beau Brummel who marched in the 1936 New York City May Day Parade, one chamois-gloved fist thrust into the air, chanting "We want bread!"

Gorky, Davis, and Graham were known around New York as "The Three Musketeers," an international art squad that haunted the secondhand bookstores of lower Fourth Avenue in search of color Kandinsky reproductions, pored over the latest issue of *Cahiers d'Art* as if they were trying to crack a code, and held the still-provincial New York art world up the highest world standards.

Gorky worked out of an enormous, moldering attic room at 36 Union Square East. At the time, the Square was home to the national headquarters of both the American Communist and Socialist Parties, as well as the left-wing International Ladies Garment Workers Union. Although Gorky liked to linger over coffee at the left-wing Co-op Cafeteria on Union Square beneath banners celebrating the role of the working class, he had little patience with proletarian or populist art, contemptuously dismissing it as "poor art for poor people."

Gorky and his friends particularly despised Jackson Pollock's mentor, the painter Thomas Hart Benton, who also taught at the Art Students League. Benton was, as they used to say, a "man's man"—a short, powerfully built, hard-drinking, argumentative, overbearing raconteur who claimed to have become an artist on a dare from a whore at the House of Lords, a bordello in Joplin, Missouri. Benton specialized in highly sentimental portrayals of small-town working people's everyday lives, and he preached a surly nativism that infuriated Gorky and his pals. "There are no artists in Paris," Benton would tell anyone who'd listen—this at a time when Picasso, Matisse, and Braque were all hard at work—"none at all." He once claimed that nonobjective art was part of a communist plot to defraud the American people.

Jackson Pollock came to the Art Students League because his brother Charles, ten years his senior and long considered the real artist among LeRoy and Stella Pollock's five sons, was Benton's star pupil. In New York, Jackson Pollock had been sleeping on his big brother's couch since his expulsion from

L.A.'s Manual Arts High School for working on a newspaper that published an anonymous newsletter denouncing the school's overemphasis on athletics, proposing that it issue varsity letters to "our scholars, our artists, our musicians," then getting into a fistfight with a gym teacher over the issue.

Despite his social awkwardness and his rudimentary artistic skills, Jackson soon began to supplant Charles as Benton's favorite. Benton appointed the brawny, rawboned younger man his classroom monitor, responsible for collecting the other students' twelve-dollars-a-month tuition. Jackson Pollock was the only student whom Benton regularly invited back to his place on Hudson Street, where Pollock baby-sat Benton's kid and half–fell in love with Benton's wife, Rita, an Italian-born earth mother who played the guitar and sang folk songs and cooked spaghetti dinners for fifty people at a time.

Born in Cody, Wyoming, on January 28, 1912, Jackson Pollock grew up in a family that rambled all across the West in search of a better life that never quite panned out. The family was going broke managing a hotel in Janesville, California, when Jackson's father, Roy, in a drunken rage, beat the eight-year-old Jackson and two of his brothers with a barrel stave before deserting the family for the last time. Even while a student at the League, Pollock continued to roam, piloting a stripped-down Model T over the still-primitive system of transcontinental roads, hitchhiking, hopping freights, living hand-to-mouth alongside hundreds of thousands of other men washing back and forth across the country looking for work in the Depression. Benton's was very likely the only warm, loving household that Jackson Pollock had ever known. Benton got Pollock his job in the Art Students League cafeteria.

Brooding, inarticulate, and choking with emotions he couldn't begin to express, Pollock tried to come on like Benton in cowboy boots and a ten-gallon hat, but he secretly envied Gorky, Davis, and Graham not only for their ability to sling contemporary art jargon and their accepted place in the world of artists, but for their prowess with women as well. Pollock had to get drunk before he could even ask a woman at a party to dance. Any woman who said yes could expect to be mauled and crudely propositioned before Pollock staggered away, threw up, and passed out.

One day while busing dishes at the cafeteria, Pollock overheard Gorky brag that he planned to convince Matisse to give a lecture at the League during his upcoming visit to New York. As the other students listened in awe, Pollock walked over to the table and blurted out, "What do we need those Europeans for?" Gorky became furious and started screaming at him, "Where do you think the Renaissance came from?"

Pollock didn't know what to say. Sweeping coffee cups and doughnut crumbs onto a tray to cover his embarrassment, Pollock went blank. He'd been slapped down by the modern art club, the only club he'd ever wanted to belong to, but he couldn't show any emotion. He couldn't reveal his feelings to anybody. He had to channel them so deep into his work that his art became his very being. He had just learned a hard lesson in the cool.

"LET PARIS COME TO ME"

In his essay "Are Black People Cooler Than White People?" the journalist Donnell Alexander writes, "cool was born when the first plantation nigga figured out how to make animal innards—massa's garbage—taste good enough to eat." Cool, now, he goes on, is "an inclination to make something out of nothing. . . .Cool is all about trying to make a dollar out of fifteen cents."

Like Gorky and Graham, Jackson Pollock was forced to create himself out of inferior materials. Unlike them, Pollock couldn't see Paris as his model. Pollock had no idea of the sort of training that his genius required.

Rejecting the European tradition, Pollock began to turn himself inside out, opening up to every form of "primitive" art from Navajo sandpaintings to Gabonese sorcerers' masks.

If Pollock hadn't known about surrealism after the 1932 "New Super Realism" show at the Wadsworth Atheneum in Hartford, or from photographer Man Ray's erotic fashion spreads in *Harper's Bazaar*, or through Salvador Dalí's tabloid misadventures in New York—Dalí had nearly decapitated himself shoving a fur-lined bathtub through a plate glass window at Bonwit Teller after discovering that someone had tampered with one of his displays—he certainly had learned about it by the end of 1936, when the Museum of Modern Art produced its blockbuster exhibition "Fantastic Art, Dada, and Surrealism."

The nineteenth-century French poet Arthur Rimbaud wrote that the true function of a poet is not to express an existing reality but to discover a new one. Similarly, in the superheated political atmosphere of interwar Europe, the surrealists had acted on the messianic principal that the artist was a seer who could lead the way to political and cultural revolution. From the beginning, the surrealist movement saw itself as more than an avant-garde art movement. It was a philosophy, a way of life, the culmination of advances in art, philosophy, psychology, and politics. To its founders, surrealism offered a way to reconcile the century's two most dominant yet seemingly irreconcilable ideas: the interior Freudian world of the unconscious and the exterior dialectical world of Karl Marx.

Although three of Jackson Pollock's brothers were in the Communist Party and his father was a card-carrying member of the Industrial Workers of the World, Pollock had little interest in surrealism's political dimension. For him, surrealism was personal—a tool for accessing his subconscious. Considering the teeming horrors that awaited him there, critic Meyer Schapiro's claim that what Pollock and his contemporaries learned from the surrealists was not just automatism, but "how to be heroic," seems more than justified.

Surrealism—the name derives from "surreality," a phrase that poet Guillaume Apollinaire coined to mean "absolute reality"—advocated the Freudian technique of free association; "free," the movement's chief spokesman and theoretician, André Breton, underlined, "of moral or aesthetic considerations." Automatism—automatic painting and automatic writing—was a major tenet of surrealism, a way, in Meyer Schapiro's words, of achieving "total liberation of the mind." Hence, surrealists celebrated the violent and the arbitrary. "The simplest Surrealist act," André Breton declared in the *First Surrealist Manifesto* in 1924, "consists of dashing down the street, pistol in hand, and firing blindly." As Breton wrote in his surreal novel *Nadja*, "Beauty will be CONVULSIVE or it will not be at all."

Frustrated by his inability to come to grips with his inner demons through his art, Pollock's life was spiraling downhill. A series of violent binges had left him weak, filthy, and incoherent, and landed him in Bellevue Hospital in 1938. Pollock was now sleeping on his brother Sande's couch, but his stay was precarious: Arloie, Sande's wife, had become so terrified by Jackson's drinking that she told her husband that she wouldn't get pregnant until Jackson moved out. After his release from Bellevue, Pollock tried to dry out by voluntarily committing himself to New York Hospital in White Plains, a private asylum outside the city known as "Bloomingdale's" to its mostly affluent clientele. He got drunk again as soon as he left. At twenty-six, he was broke, practically homeless, and had never sold a single painting. One of the only times he'd even shown his work was on a sidewalk during the Washington Square Outdoor Art Show, where a few oils had gone begging at five to ten dollars apiece.

Pollock was drowning, and John Graham, Gorky's old friend, came to his rescue. Graham was *too* cool, the kind of guy who was swallowed up by his pose. Though twenty-three years older than Pollock, Graham had admired Pollock profoundly from afar. According to Graham's fourth wife, Constance, Graham saw Pollock as the kind of artist Graham wished he could be: a man determined to manifest his own vision at whatever cost. The first time Graham came to Pollock's studio, he asked if Pollock had ever been to Paris and Pollock shot back, "Let Paris come to me."

Graham started coming around Pollock's studio every week, encouraging him, and introducing him to recent intellectual developments.

Graham turned Pollock on to the writings of psychiatrist Carl Jung, which were published for the first time in English in the early 1940s. In an attempt to figure out why he couldn't stop drinking, Pollock started seeing Dr. Joseph Henderson, a psychiatrist who'd apprenticed with Jung. But neither Henderson nor the parade of Jungians who followed could help Pollock give up drinking for long, though they did introduce Pollock to the ideas of archetypes and of a universally shared collective unconscious, a world soul.

In the process of assembling a collection of African fetishes and masks—which Graham considered "the greatest of all art" because he believed that tribal people had a readier access to the universal unconscious—for Frank Crowninshield, the publisher of *Vanity Fair*, Graham put together a collection of his own. Pollock saw African art for the first time at Graham's apartment.

Graham guided Pollock through the Museum of Modern Art's Picasso retrospective in 1939, the first time that Picasso's vast body of work, including the just completed *Guernica*, had ever been shown in America. He also took Pollock to MOMA's 1941 American Indian show, which marked Pollock's exposure to sand painting, the spiritual craft of squeezing a fine stream of powdered rock or colored charcoal on the earth to create a mandala, a visual prayer, which must inevitably be blown away. For Graham, it must have been a thrill to pass along a lifetime's research in practices outside the western intellectual tradition to such a willing student. In her book *What Is Cool?*, Marlene Kim Connor says **cool can't be handed down from generation to generation, but rather bestowed, as a recognition of manhood by one's peers. John Graham was the first artist who understood what Pollock was trying to do. Through Graham's eyes, Pollock began to see that his search was meaningful, that he could be cool.**

THE TECHNICIAN OF SHOCK

André Breton had always steered Surrealism's erratic political course, aligning it briefly with the Third International Communist Party, only to break with the party after a few tumultuous months over the 1935 Moscow show trials. In 1938, Breton paid a very public visit to the exiled Soviet Leon Trotsky in Mexico, only months before the old Bolshevik had his skull cleaved by an ice pick–wielding Stalinist agent. After their confab, Breton and Trotsky, together with left-wing Mexican painter Diego Rivera, issued a communiqué proclaiming the responsibility of artists in their time to make revolution. Two years later, when the Nazis entered Paris, Breton had to run.

The boat tickets out of intrigue-wracked Marseilles for Breton, his wife Jaqueline Lamba—a former "aqua-dancer" in a Parisian fish-tank bar—and their daughter Aube were paid for by Peggy Guggenheim, the fun-loving, art and artist-collecting American heiress. She too would soon be winging her way from France to the New York Marine Terminal on a Pan Am Clipper with an entourage that included her future husband, the great German-born Surrealist painter Max Ernst, her past husband, the painter Laurence Vail, and his present and former wives, and their seven children.

The New York that greeted them was, in painter-writer Robert Motherwell's fine phrase, "a strange mixture of Cole Porter and Stalinism"— soldiers in transit, billboards screaming out pleas for blood drives and war bonds, and the doom-ridden voice of *The March of Time*'s Westbrook Van Voorhis with the news. In wartime New York, cool was an alien presence. In a time of world war, you had to be invisible if you were cool. Single and twenty-nine when the United States entered the war, Pollock managed to avoid the service by badgering his analyst to get him a psychological deferment. Reluctantly, she did so. Her description of Pollock as having "a certain schizoid disposition" got him reclassified 4-F—"unqualified."

For Peggy Guggenheim, however, her art collection swollen by dozens of new paintings she'd purchased at fire-sale prices from artists desperate to leave Europe, New York during wartime was a glittering stage. On October 20, 1942, on the top floor of a building on Fifty-seventh Street just off Fifth Avenue, only four blocks away from her aging copper tycoon uncle Solomon Guggenheim's Museum of Non-Objective Art, Peggy Guggenheim opened her gallery and museum, Art of This Century, with a gala benefit for the American Red Cross.

Art of This Century was nearly as well known for its design, courtesy of Romanian-born sculptor Frederick Kiesler, as it was for the work it showed. The unframed paintings (a practice theretofore unheard-of in the U.S.) in the windowless surrealist wing were mounted on baseball bats and protruded a foot from the gallery's curved gum-wood walls. In the gallery's abstract and cubist wing, the paintings—suspended from the ceiling on taut strings and lit by individual spotlights that went on and off at three-second intervals, making them almost impossible to see—seemed to float in space in the middle of the room. Every few minutes the atmosphere was rent by the tape-recorded roar of an onrushing train. For Art of This Century's opening night, Guggenheim wore an Alexander Calder mobile in one ear and a little painting of a pink desert by the surrealist Yves Tanguy in the other, to signal the melting pot of European and American art that her gallery would become.

André Breton in America, circa 1945.

No one knows for sure who turned Peggy Guggenheim on to Jackson Pollock, but it was probably John Graham, who was telling everybody about his discovery. "It was hard for other artists to see what Pollock was doing.

Peggy Guggenheim sitting on her Frederick Kiesler–designed bed in her palazzo on the Grand Canal, Venice, 1950.

Their work was so different from his," Willem de Kooning explained many years later. "But Graham could see it." Guggenheim was not an immediate convert, though. Asked to judge a Pollock for inclusion in an Art of This Century group show in 1942, the great Dutch painter Piet Mondrian corrected Guggenheim when she made a disparaging comment about Pollock's painting: "You must watch this man," he told her. Guggenheim was soon repeating the comment as if it were her own.

In the spring of 1943, Peggy Guggenheim's life was in an uproar. Max Ernst, who'd only recently become her husband, had run off to Sedona, Arizona, with Dorothy Tanning, a pretty young Surrealist painter thirty years his junior. Now Guggenheim was trying to decide whether to give Jackson Pollock his first one-man show, the first solo show she'd ever given an American. She knew that such a show would mean trouble from André Breton and the rest of the surrealists, who liked neither Pollock nor his work.

In public, the Surrealists condescended to Pollock. Max Ernst, for example, called him "a wild man, like our Soutine." In private, they mocked his caveman antics and his uncouth demeanor. Guggenheim too had experienced the dangerously belligerent, falling-down drunken Pollock on numerous occasions. Still, her gallery manager, the perceptive Howard Putzel, wanted to do the show; but with her husband on the lam, Guggenheim wasn't sure what to do—the Surrealists were, after all, the backbone of her social life—so she called in her old friend and now-and-then lover, Marcel Duchamp.

Marcel Duchamp, dubbed by André Breton "the Technician of Shock," was probably the only living artist to whom Breton deferred. **The Surrealists had long claimed Duchamp as one of their own—Breton declared *In Advance of the Broken Arm*, Duchamp's "ready-made" snow shovel, to be the first surrealist object—but Duchamp never called himself a surrealist.** Dada—the name taken from a German toddler's word for a rocking horse, chosen for its meaninglessness—like surrealism, had been spawned by revulsion at the meaningless butchery of World War I, and it too claimed Duchamp. Dada embraced Duchamp's *Fountain*, a porcelain men's urinal he signed "R. Mutt," but Duchamp never embraced dada. The only organization Duchamp ever belonged to was the Society of Independent Artists, from which he resigned when the group rejected *Fountain* from its 1917 exhibition. Still, he retained the respect of every camp of the avant-garde.

Marcel Duchamp was spare, brilliant, detached, ascetic, easygoing, incorruptible, and great looking. Two years before his painting *Nude Descending a Staircase* scandalized the 1913 New York Armory Show, the first international exhibit of modern art ever held in the United States, and brought him fame in America far beyond that of any other modern painter, Duchamp had already given up painting for an art that was rigorously cerebral and completely radical; a lifelong assault on the forces of ordinary logic. His 1926 short film, *Anemic Cinema*, dared to suggest with its spinning disc that art was entirely retinal. His shattered, dust-encrusted *Large Glass* of the same year was the ultimate collaboration with chance. **With his intellectual clarity, his physical bravery, and his studied indifference to the vagaries of fate, Duchamp was a paragon and progenitor of cool before cool had a name.**

As a person who had long lived by his wits, Duchamp understood that the people treated best by Peggy Guggenheim were the ones who needed her the least. Duchamp's principal solution to the problem of earning a living was to suppress his needs. He ate very little, drank almost no alcohol, and bought his clothes off pushcarts on Orchard Street on the Lower East Side of Manhattan. In Man Ray's famous 1920 photograph of Duchamp and the painter Joseph Stella, the pale, closely cropped Duchamp has the appearance of a cool monsignor, manifesting by cool example.

When the Germans invaded, Duchamp had been in France putting together his *Box in a Valise*, a briefcase containing miniature versions of all his major works of art. For the next two years Duchamp repeatedly risked his life as he slipped in and out of France's occupied zones disguised as a cheese merchant, completing his project. When he finally made it back to New York in June 1942, Duchamp reconnected with Peggy Guggenheim. It was then that Guggenheim asked him to take a look at Jackson Pollock's work.

The fifty-six-year-old Duchamp and the thirty-year-old Pollock had met once before. Pollock had heard Duchamp didn't like *Stenographic Figure*, the sexually charged painting Pollock had finished the year before when he was just getting it together with his wife-to-be, Lee Krasner. Krasner was an art student from Brooklyn who'd showed up one day at Pollock's Eighth Street apartment to check out his painting and stayed to help him make sense out of his life. When Duchamp ran into Pollock at Art of this Century, Pollock

Marcel Duchamp (top) with painter Joseph Stella, 1920.

exploded in his face, ripping a copy of a poster for a Duchamp show off the gallery wall and shoving it at him, snarling, "You know where this goes."

But Duchamp was cool. In early July 1943, on assignment from Peggy Guggenheim, he came over to check out Pollock's studio. At the time, Duchamp was doing hardly anything but playing chess and studying chess problems, telling anyone who asked that he'd run out of art ideas. What did he think of Pollock, so frantically wound up in trying to create paintings that were "true"? **Duchamp saw a man as singular as he, a man who'd staked everything on his ability to make art that had to change the world in order to be understood. Duchamp reported back to Peggy Guggenheim that Pollock's work was "pas mal." Coming from the oracular Duchamp, "not bad" was cool. Pollock got his show.**

"IT WAS A STAMPEDE"

For an American artist, the offer that Peggy Guggenheim made to Jackson Pollock was unprecedented: she would pay him $150 a month against sales from his November 1943 Art of This Century show just to paint. Pollock leaped at the opportunity and went feverishly to work, keeping three or four paintings in motion at once. Around that same time, Robert Motherwell worked with Pollock on some collages. Motherwell, a twenty-seven-year-old Harvard-educated philosophy major with French tastes and very little experience as an artist, was shocked by Pollock's "attack on the material." Motherwell reported that Pollock tore the collage paper, spit on it, and burned the edges with kitchen matches. "I can still remember watching him with a mounting tension, fearing I don't know what."

Three times in 1943 Pollock returned to the same subject, which he called *Guardian of the Secret*: a group portrait of his shattered family sitting around a dinner table, with everybody on hand but the artist himself. At five feet high by eight feet long, the third of the canvases was the largest of his career and in the words of Pollock's biographers Steven Naifeh and Gregory White Smith, "a painting of furious, exploded imagery, filled with figures caught between two worlds." At each end of the table is a ghostly figure, one male and dark, the other lighter and female. The other diners are less distinct. The table itself is covered with glyphs and wild swirls of paint. Pollock was still caught in the shadowlands between abstraction and representation.

It wasn't a large crowd that showed up at Art of This Century that unseasonably mild night of November 8, 1943, mostly friends and fellow painters. Peggy Guggenheim only sold one painting, She-Wolf, out of the show, but it went to the Museum of Modern Art. "I wasn't bowled over at first," remembered Clement Greenberg, the Partisan Review art critic who would soon become Pollock's most articulate champion. "I didn't realize what I'd seen until later." In the weeks and months that followed, in the columns of the little magazines and art reviews, the critics chose sides.

At the same time that she commissioned Pollock's show, Guggenheim had contracted him to paint a mural for the massive ground-floor entrance hall of her new duplex on East Sixty-first Street. Pollock had promised to deliver the mural in time for his Art of This Century opening, but nearly two months after the opening, the canvas was still blank. Guggenheim threatened to cut off Pollock's stipend if he didn't get the mural done in time for a party that her friend and supporter Jean Connelly, the art critic for The Nation, was giving in the apartment in January 1944. The day before the party, just before nightfall, Pollock began to paint.

His canvas was huge: eight by twenty feet. Pollock didn't work from drawings or color sketches. He came to the painting like a boxer stepping into the ring or a priest approaching a ritual—fully prepared, instinctually aware. Sande Pollock had recently visited his brother, and this visit had conjured up a childhood memory of the Grand Canyon and wild horses on the run. With bold black strokes, then, Pollock set out to capture figures of animals and men as they hovered at the borders of his consciousness. As he painted, the horses were transformed into rough-hewn cave portraits of bulls, which then became antelope, buffalo, and every animal of the American West. As the night wore on, the beasts became swirling bands of teal and raspberry and yellow, a frenzied, swarming force field of color and light. By the next morning, the "Guggenheim Mural," as it would become known, was finished. "I had a vision," Pollock would tell people over the years. "It was a stampede."

As soon as the paint was dry to the touch, Pollock took the canvas uptown to Guggenheim's apartment to install it. When he got there, however, he realized that it was almost a foot too long for the wall. Knowing him too well, Guggenheim had hidden her whisky before she left for the gallery. Still, Pollock found it. In response to his increasingly drunken calls for help, Guggenheim dispatched Marcel Duchamp and sculptor David Hare to her apartment, and it was Duchamp who solved the problem: he cut off eight inches from one end of Pollock's mural. In this kind of painting, Duchamp explained to Hare, it wasn't needed. Pollock seemed cool with Duchamp's mandate. The mural thus installed, Pollock wandered, completely naked, into Jean Connolly's already-in-progress party, and peed in the fireplace—a dog staking out a bigger territory than art had ever claimed before.

"From then on until I left America in 1947," Guggenheim wrote, "I dedicated myself to Pollock." She advanced him enough money to buy an old farmhouse in Springs, then still a tiny, inbred community of potato farmers and fishermen on the eastern tip of Long Island. There, during the winter of 1946–47, in a freezing-cold barn on the edge of a potato field facing into the gales smashing in off Long Island Sound, Pollock rolled out canvas after canvas, tacking them to the floor. "When I am in my painting," Pollock would later write in a magazine called *Possibilities,* as if to say "when I am in my trance," "I'm not aware of what I'm doing . . . I have no fears about making changes, destroying the image, etc. because the painting has a life of its own. It is only when I lose contact with the painting that the result is a mess."

Circling, Pollock began to drip quick-dry lacquer paints from sticks and brushes, covering canvas after canvas with webs of color that evolved into enormous, gorgeous, sweeping visionary masterpieces like *Shimmering Substance, Lavender Mist, Blue Poles,* and *The Deep.* In 1948, he completed thirty-two paintings that also incorporated sand, broken glass, screws, and cigarette ashes—whatever was at hand. Pollock was as possessed by his art as shamans are by their spirits, and in as complete control. In late '48, he stopped giving his paintings names because "it would only confuse things."

Yet even though Pollock was fast becoming the best-known American painter of his generation, his work still wasn't selling. In 1947, Peggy Guggenheim unloaded Art of This Century's curved gum-wood walls to the Franklin Simon department store, assigned her Pollock contract and her huge cache of his paintings to art dealer Betty Parsons, and relocated to one of the largest palazzos on Venice's Grand Canal.

Betty Parsons was a high-strung, hard-drinking, lesbian daughter of New York high society, and a great good friend of Eleanor Roosevelt, Greta Garbo, and Martha Graham. Though she had excellent connections and represented Mark Rothko, Barnett Newman, and several other of Pollock's most brilliant peers, Parsons actually harbored an aversion to business. "I give the artists the four walls," she once said, "and they do the rest." Pollock's first show at Betty Parsons Gallery in 1947 was panned by every critic except Clement Greenberg, despite the presence of such future Masterpieces as *Cathedral* and *Full Fathom Five*. Pollock's 1948 show at Parsons, featuring numbered and dated paintings like *November 4, 1948*, was a second commercial dud.

More galling than his own show's lack of success, from Pollock's point of view, was the success of Willem de Kooning's first one-man show only a few months later. Highlighted by a series of voluptuously rich, all-black and all-white paintings done with cheap, easy-to-use housepaints, de Kooning's show also scored a sale to the Museum of Modern Art, a triumph which put Parsons's Fifty-seventh Street rival, the Egan Gallery, on the map.

Pollock and the then forty-four-year-old de Kooning were natural rivals. Both had been mentored by John Graham, who, in the late 1930s, had introduced de Kooning around as "the greatest young painter in the United States." De Kooning looked up to Arshile Gorky, sometimes referring to him as "the boss."

Pollock's differences with de Kooning could be seen as the natural struggle between two ambitious, immensely talented, and vastly dissimilar men. Pollock just thought he was a better painter than de Kooning, but Pollock *hated* Gorky. One time, Pollock showed up drunk and hostile at Gorky's Union Square studio, and Gorky threatened to throw him down a flight of stairs. At a party after de Kooning's opening at Sidney Janis Gallery, Pollock, drunk, insulted Gorky again and wouldn't back down—even after Gorky put a knife to Pollock's throat. It was as if Pollock had never recovered from his put-down by Gorky at the Art Students League, a riveting illustration of how desperately one can need to be cool.

Overleaf: Willem de Kooning, 1937.

Since jumping ship in New Jersey in 1926 and making his way to New York, knowing only a single word in English, "yes," the Rotterdam-born de Kooning had become a central figure in the New York avant-garde. Widely respected for his artistic intelligence and his refusal to exhibit his work until he felt ready, de Kooning was the center of a wide circle of admiring art-world friends. Pollock, by contrast, was alone. De Kooning understood his work in the grand tradition of Rembrandt and Vermeer. Pollock was a mongrel, a weed.

With his carpentry skills and his keen craftsman's eye, de Kooning was one of the first New York artists to illegally transform a factory loft into a studio and living space. When de Kooning met his future wife, Elaine Fried, in 1936, the studio he was living in at 143 West Twenty-first Street had one table, four chairs, one bed, one painting on one easel, and one fantastically good phonograph, which cost eight hundred dollars at a time when its owner was making twenty-two dollars a week painting display windows for the A.S. Beck shoe company. At a time when Pollock was still sleeping on his brother Sande's couch, de Kooning was painting his floors gray, his walls white—the flagship colors of cool.

By the late 1940s, while the outside world was beginning to see Pollock as a hero, Pollock himself must have sensed de Kooning was a much cooler character. Though his work never left the easel, de Kooning was every bit as physical a painter as Pollock: art collector, gallery owner, and shirt manufacturer Sidney Janis told of de Kooning paintings sometimes arriving at his gallery with ragged holes in the canvas where the artist had rammed his brushes through as he worked. Nevertheless, Pollock dismissed de Kooning as "nothing but a French painter"—meaning, perhaps, that he was interested ultimately in effect. Pollock said of himself that he wanted to express his feelings, not illustrate them. "You *know* more," Pollock once sneered at de Kooning, in a classic summation of the difference between intellectual cool and emotional heat, "but I *feel* more."

"BREAKING THE ICE"

In 1949, just as television was beginning to spread, *Life* magazine, guided by its founder Henry Luce, was approaching the peak of its influence. It would be difficult to overstate the role played by *Life* magazine in midcentury American culture: *Life* was the place where masses of Americans discovered the modern world. In 1949, more than 6 million copies of *Life* were sold each week, and they were read by more than a third of all American families. *Life* was the world's first mass-produced magazine organized around photographs, and the finest photojournalists in the world, from Margaret Bourke-White to Robert Capa to Alfred Eisenstadt, passed through its One Rockefeller Center doors.

Born in China to a Presbyterian missionary couple, Henry Luce was twenty-four and fresh out of Yale when he cofounded *Time*, the first successful news magazine, in 1923. He was thirty-one when he founded *Fortune*, the first mass-market magazine devoted to business. In 1949, 18 million Americans listened to Luce's *March of Time*, a weekly compilation of news events on the radio; the film version was seen on all four fledgling television networks and in 13,000 theaters in the U.S. and abroad. Dynamic, aggressive, ambitious, rich, and deeply devoted to Christianity, country, capitalism, and his second wife, the playwright, and future congresswoman Clare Boothe Luce, the fortunate Luce held a deep belief in the possibilities of human progress.

Life had always featured art—the magazine's art section was one of the first of its kind to employ color—and particularly American art. In an early memo, Luce urged his staff to concentrate on American artists, "especially those who delight in painting the American scene with some degree of sympathy," but cautioned that "we want to avoid artists that are too bizarre." In the introduction to *Life*'s first issue, November 23, 1936, Luce wrote, "the editors are particularly pleased that art is represented not by some artfully promoted Frenchman, but by an American," in this case John Steuart Curry, the Kansan best known for his painting of a farm family fleeing an onrushing tornado.

In 1940, Luce had written an editorial entitled "The American Century." America was not only becoming the world leader in free trade, Luce argued, but the world's guarantor of freedom: "We must accept whole-heartedly our duty and our opportunity as the most vital nation in the world to exert upon the world the full impact of our influence." From the short interview Robert Motherwell did with Jackson Pollock in the February 1944 *Art and Architecture*, Pollock's attitude dove-tailed nicely with Luce's vision. "Would you like to go abroad?" Pollock is asked. "No," he replies. "I don't see why the problems of modern painting can't be solved as well here as elsewhere." By 1949, the Jackson Pollock phenomenon had finally reached the *Life* offices in midtown Manhattan. The photographer *Life* sent to shoot Pollock's portrait was, naturally, Arnold Newman.

In 1949, Arnold Newman was among the most active magazine photographers in New York, a *protégé* of Alexey Brodovitch, *Harper's Bazaar*'s innovative art director, who'd also given Richard Avedon his start. Newman had come a long way since his first New York visit in 1941, when he'd met Alfred Stieglitz, the pioneer American art photographer, and Beaumont Newhall, the photographic historian and Museum of Modern Art curator. By 1949, Newman had already made many of the most memorable artist portraits of his time with shots of figures like Grandma Moses, Marc Chagall, Piet Mondrian, and Fernand Leger, and had nine assistants working for him full-time.

Arriving at Pollock and Krasner's farm house on Fireplace Road in Springs in a rented car with an assistant and a driver, Newman was clearly the star. Despite his newfound fame, Pollock hadn't sold a painting in a year, and he was eager to cooperate with Newman, giving him the whole day, taking him around to meet the locals, even setting up a simulated painting session for Newman to shoot. When they finished, Pollock, like an American Indian hinting awkwardly that a tourist ought to pay for shooting his picture, dragged a painting out of the barn and tried to sell it to Newman for one hundred fifty dollars. Newman refused.

Judging from the outtake of Pollock's *Life* portrait that Deborah Solomon uses on the cover of her Pollock biography, Newman must have posed Pollock in front of the painting *Summertime* and ordered him to cross his hands over his chest. It worked. Pollock still looks, in the words of

Pollock's first monographer, the poet and Museum of Modern Art curator Frank O'Hara, like an artist "who was totally conscious of risk, defeat, and triumph. He lived the first, defied the second, and achieved the last"— pinned like a butterfly to a wall.

When the August 8, 1949, issue of *Life* hit the stands, Pollock's life changed forever. Fan mail started coming in from all over. In Springs, neighbors who'd previously avoided him as a drunken madman now stopped him on the street to give him their congratulations. **When he came into New York, he was deluged by women who wanted to fuck him, and by artsy college boys trying to make his scene. Pollock himself pretended to be embarrassed by all the attention, but secretly he arranged to have a hundred copies of the magazine delivered to his door.**

Though plenty was laid on him by a generation craving a rebel artist to believe in, Pollock—like Jack Kerouac ten years later—would bring most of the heat down on himself. The defiant, rebel artist with the cool stance was nothing against the power of the press, which could twist his cool into a caricature, transform him into a beautiful loser—which is the dark, vampiric, shadow side of cool. Cool was still too weak. Cool was still about trying to *deflect* attention. Cool couldn't survive the light of day.

Ahead for Pollock lay greater and more terrible celebrity, a river of whiskey, money, and a torrent of anxiety and self-doubt. It all would end for him seven years later, at age forty-four. On August 10, 1956, drunk, with his voluptuous young girlfriend Ruth Kligman at his side, Pollock lost control of his Oldsmobile convertible going eighty miles an hour on his way to a concert near his home. Kligman survived, but Pollock died behind the wheel.

But as he stood before Arnold Newman's camera, all that was still to come. The immediate result of the *Life* article was that the crowd at the opening of Pollock's November 1949 show at Betty Parsons encompassed more than just the artist and his friends, and the paintings flew off the walls. When Willem de Kooning and his friend the painter Milton Resnick arrived at Pollock's opening, they were astonished to find that they could barely wedge themselves through the door. "What's all this about?" a shocked Resnick asked de Kooning as they contemplated the madhouse. "Look around," de Kooning replied. "These are the big shots. Jackson has finally broken the ice."

SOMEWHERE WHERE IT'S COOL

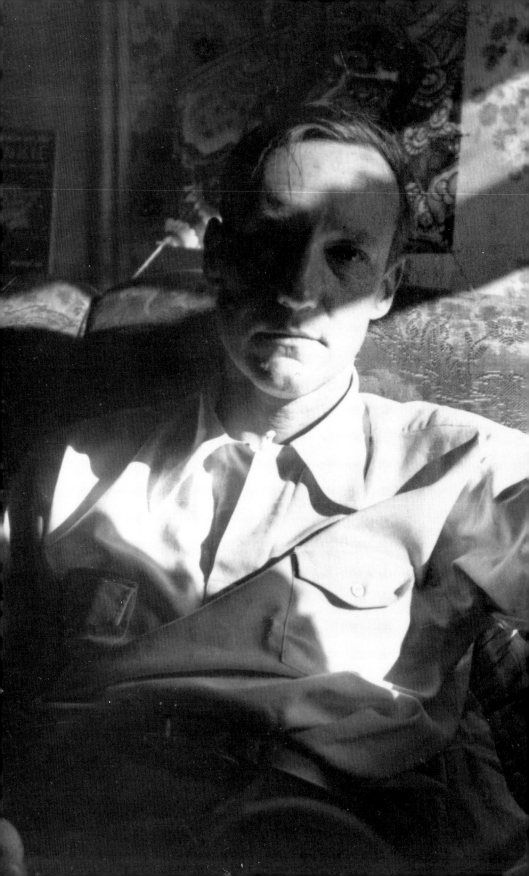

"THIS GUY IS THE HEAT"

The first time Herbert Huncke laid eyes on William Burroughs was in early January 1946. Huncke was living in a railroad flat on Henry Street underneath the Manhattan Bridge with a couple of other heroin addicts, a statuesque hooker named Vicki Russell, and Phil White, a thief they called "the Sailor." The walls of the place were painted black and yellow, the ceiling was red. The windows were covered with thick yellow drapes. Huncke heard a knock, and opened the door. Standing there in a Chesterfield coat, a gray snap-brim fedora, and gray gloves was a tall, pallid stranger, carrying a package and looking down his nose. "Jesus Christ," Huncke remembers thinking to himself as Burroughs slipped into the apartment, "get him out of here, man. This guy is the heat!"

A PARALLEL UNIVERSE

No white boy ever wanted to be cool more than William S. Burroughs did. Born weird into genteel St. Louis upper-middle-class society in 1914 and raised at in a comfortable suburb on Pershing Avenue, "a street of red-brick houses with slate roofs," his was a smothering, privileged upbringing with a cook, a maid, a gardener, and a nanny.

William S. Burroughs was a lonely child who, early on, sensed that he was different. Others saw it too. A parent of a friend said that Burroughs looked "like a sheep-killing dog"; another described him as "a walking corpse." The boy found a refuge in fiction. He wrote his first book, *The Autobiography of a Wolf*, when he was eight. "You mean *Biography of a Wolf*, don't you, son?" a friend of his mother's chided him gently. No, insisted Burroughs, "autobiography" was precisely what he'd meant. In 1925, when he was thirteen, Burroughs's family enrolled him in the exclusive John Burroughs School (no relation). When he fell in love with a classmate named Kells Elvins, who was straight, Burroughs realized that he was gay.

William S. Burroughs in New York, fall 1953.

As an adolescent, Burroughs read and reread *You Can't Win,* the autobiography of a yegg, a turn-of-the century western safecracker named Jack Black. *You Can't Win* introduced Burroughs to a world as far away as he could get from Pershing Avenue. It was still a world that in 1925 St. Louis was almost tantalizingly near. There were plenty of people around who could remember the closing of the frontier, when that icon of American cool, the lone gunslinger, began to recede into myth.

In the laconic drawl that Burroughs would take as his own, Jack Black described a fugitive world: "We jumped from one state to another, kept away from the cities, lived almost entirely on the road." Arrayed against them were the "suckers and the saps" of mainstream society. "Society represented law, order, discipline, punishment," wrote Black. "Society was a machine geared to grind me to pieces. Society was an enemy." He called his friends "Johnsons." A Johnson was "good people"; and even though Johnsons "did wrong things," as Jack Black was quick to admit, "they always tried to do them in the right way." Because cool and style are inseparable, "right things" as well as "wrong things" must always be done in "the right way."

A Johnson knew that if you lived outside the law, you had to be cool about it. "Do you want everybody to look at you? Do you want everyone that looks at you to remember you?" Black asked. "You do not. You want as few people to look at you as possible, and you want those few to forget you as soon as possible." Only a Johnson can recognize another Johnson. A Johnson knows immediately if somebody else is cool.

More than fifty years later, living in Lawrence, Kansas, Burroughs was still influenced by Jack Black. In a trio of novels culminating in his *The Place of Dead Roads,* William Burroughs constructed a Johnson universe around a gay gunfighter named Kim Carsons. In the story, Kim is a born assassin, a lonely, late-nineteenth-century St. Louis boy who decides to head west and become a shootist, a lonesome gunman looking for others of his own kind.

In *The Place of Dead Roads,* the Johnsons are so cool they inhabit a parallel universe, the scourge of shits everywhere. For Jack Black, "shits" are synonymous with "citizens"—those who haven't lost the right to vote because of felony convictions. Shits are not cool. The mark of a shit is that he or she always has to be right. Johnsons settle in and around little nowhere prairie towns with names like Johnsonville or Lawrence, Kansas—"Potential America," as Kim Carsons refers to it, "P.A."—a nearly invisible, all-male, free association of highwaymen.

"I was fascinated by gangsters," Burroughs recalls in an autobiographical essay, "The Name Is Burroughs," "and like most boys at the time, I wanted to be one. I would feel so much safer with my loyal guns around me." Growing up in the Midwest during the crime wave of the 1920s and '30s provided him with plenty of role models.

The mainstreaming of the American gangster in the 1920s was a direct result of the passage of the Eighteenth Amendment to the U.S. Constitution, which forbade the sale and distribution of liquor—Prohibition—and of the hypocrisy that accompanied it. Less than one hour after Prohibition officially began, on January 17, 1920, six masked men invaded a Chicago railroad yard and hijacked a hundred thousand dollars' worth of so-called medicinal liquor, inaugurating a wave of lawlessness that wouldn't end until Prohibition's repeal in 1933.

Almost overnight, a gangster class sprang from the big-city slums. Al Capone; Lucky Luciano; the "Little Man," Meyer Lansky; Frank Costello; Lepke Buchalter; Dutch Schultz—these immigrant Italians and Jews clawing their way out of their ghettos were the inspiration for the raffish Times Square mobsters Damon Runyon created for magazines like *Collier's, The Saturday Evening Post,* and *Cosmopolitan,* all of which were part of the Burroughses' milieu.

Big-city crime was exciting, but Burroughs was turned on by more familiar figures—trigger-happy country boys like the gay bank robber Alvin "Creepy" Karpis (who picked up his moniker after a plastic surgeon's unsuccessful attempt to alter his appearance left his eyeballs sagging), the Barker brothers, and Charles "Pretty Boy" Floyd—hell-bent country boys with imaginations fueled by the exploits of Jesse James, Cole Younger, and the rest of the late-nineteenth-century western badasses celebrated in the lurid paperback "penny dreadfuls" of their time. Spawned by Depression and Dust Bowl, these wild-eyed desperadoes acquired a populist tinge. Pretty Boy Floyd, for instance, was celebrated in song for his delight in burning farmers' mortgage papers as he looted small-town banks.

Even their violent outlaw deaths exuded a heartless cool, a gob in the face of the ones who gunned them down, turning their inevitable demises

into acts of defiance. John Dillinger, "Public Enemy No. 1," a shrewd Indiana farm boy, made his name synonymous with bank robbery in the early 1930s by robbing small-town banks, and screeching away in a Hudson Terraplane, submachine guns blazing. He died under a Chicago movie marquee in a hail of FBI gunfire, a midwest Götterdämmerung so inspiring that Burroughs dedicated *Tornado Alley*, a 1989 collection of story fragments and "routines," to Dillinger "in hope he is still alive."

Left: Alvin Karpis, Public Enemy Number 1, 1935. Right: John Dillinger shortly before he was killed, a Colt .38 in one hand, a submachine gun in the other, 1934.

In 1929, at fifteen, Burroughs was sent off, against his will, to the Los Alamos Ranch School in New Mexico, because his mother was worried about his sinus condition. He hated Los Alamos, with its Boy Scout attitudes, its relentlessly positive thinking, its push-ups in the snow. Located on a remote mesa overlooking the Rio Grande, forty miles of dirt road northwest of Santa Fe, Los Alamos was so isolated the United States War Department took over the school in 1943 for its top-secret Manhattan Project to build the first atomic bomb.

At sixteen, Burroughs altered his mind with drugs for the first time, ingesting a near-lethal dose of chloral hydrate that sent him wobbling in to see the school nurse. Trapped in a Boy Scout world, he aspired to decadence, burning incense in his room and reading Baudelaire and the Comte de Lautréamont, who once walked a lobster on a velvet leash down the Champs-Elysée. Utterly powerless himself, Burroughs felt a visceral link to the gangster's ability to smash and grab, to effect the most basic power over life and death. Burroughs wanted badly to be cool, hard, remorseless.

Two months before he was scheduled to graduate, Burroughs convinced his mother to let him drop out of school by admitting to her his first brief dormitory homosexual experience. She had him out of there so fast he didn't have time to pack a bag.

SOMEWHERE WHERE IT'S COOL

In 1932, Burroughs enrolled at Harvard, because that was what young men of his social position did in those days. In Cambridge, he was known for keeping a live ferret in his room and as a collector of "sleazy characters," as Richard Stern, a gay friend of Burroughs from Kansas City, recalls. Burroughs graduated in 1936 with a degree in American literature. There's a blank rectangle where his yearbook photo was supposed to be. It's not unlikely that on the day they took yearbook pictures, Burroughs was in New York, prowling Greenwich Village and Times Square with Stern.

In the mid-1930s, Times Square was the epicenter of the American news and entertainment businesses. Mainstream newspapers like the *New York Times*, the tabloid *Mirror*, and the *Daily News*, trend-setting culture magazines like *Vanity Fair* and *The New Yorker*, and show-biz bibles *Variety* and *Billboard* were all headquartered there. Shubert Alley, the center of the American theater, was just off the square. Restaurants like Astor's and Sardi's, clubs like the Friars and the Lambs all catered to a theatrical crowd. The sporting types, the fun-loving criminals immortalized by Damon Runyon, went to prizefights at Madison Square Garden, which at that time was at Broadway and Fiftieth Street.

In the 1930s, the Fifties east of the square had been speakeasy streets, organized crime–dominated islands of glamour in the sea of depression. While thousands squatted in wretched Hoovervilles like the one on Central Park's Great Lawn, a few blocks away at the Stork Club on East Fifty-third Street, Oklahoma bootlegger Sherman Billingsley was introducing the first champagne cocktail at America's first contoured bar.

With Prohibition came Cafe Society, where an intoxicating mixture of upper crust glamour and lower class bravado created a new, national, egalitarian theater at places like Jack and Charlie's '21,' and The Stork Club, "New York's New Yorkiest Place," where "Broadway's Boswell," Walter Winchell, the *New York Mirror*'s all-powerful syndicated columnist, held court.

In the mid-1930s when William Burroughs was prowling Times Square, it was the breeding ground of a new national "slanguage," to use Winchell's term, a confluence of argots from theater, journalism, sports, and the underworld employed by Winchell as he broadcast over the NBC Blue radio network to millions of people from coast to coast every Sunday night. Burroughs was fascinated by the "drug lingo and jive talk," writes Ann Douglas in her introduction to *Word Virus*, a Burroughs compendium. "He

was fascinated by their mutability, their fugitive quality, the result of the pressure their speakers were under to dodge authority and leave no records behind." It was a subversive tongue, a language that only an insider could decode. As Neal Gabler writes in his biography of Walter Winchell, "to know which words were in vogue, to know what 'scram' meant, and 'palooka' and 'belly laughs' and 'lotta baloney' and 'push-over,' was like being part of a secret society."

The 1930s marked the heyday of the gangster movie. With the advent of "talkies" in 1928, audiences could for the first time hear the "pineapples" exploding, the *rattatat* of submachine guns, the shattering glass, the squealing tires of the Stutz-Bearcat getaway cars. In 1930 alone, three movies were produced based on the real-life, up-from-the–Brooklyn Navy Yard saga of Al Capone. One of them, Howard Hawks's *Scarface*, penned by the godfather of the gangster movie, the former newspaper journalist Ben Hecht, and starring Paul Muni as the hulking Capone clone Tony Camonte and George Raft as his lethal sidekick, provided two of the most critical moments in the history of cool: Muni whistling a sextet from the opera *Lucia di Lammermoor*, "Che mi frena in tal momento?" ("What restrains me in such a moment?"), as he moves in for a kill, and Raft flipping a quarter again and again as he studies his next victim.

The adolescent Burroughs had been drawn to gangster cool by its allure of power. If he were more like the gangsters he emulated, he'd be able to fight his way out of the hypocritical universe he felt pressing down on him. But as gambling replaced whiskey as the gangsters' primary criminal enterprise, the wild freelancers of the Prohibition era who had so inspired the young Burroughs began to organize.

Frank Costello, a gambler, bootlegger, and murderer who spoke in a sinister whisper (courtesy of a slipshod childhood tonsillectomy), became known as the prime minister of the underworld for his ability to link "the combination" with Tammany Hall politicians. Lucky Luciano virtually became a corporate executive, living large as "Mr. Ross" in a twenty-ninth-floor suite at the Waldorf Towers. At the 1932 Democratic convention in Chicago, New York's Tammany Hall machine made the decision to support Franklin Roosevelt, and thus assure him the Democratic Party nomination,

Paul Muni in Scarface, 1932.

in Lucky Luciano's suite at the Drake Hotel. It all turned Burroughs off. To him, the criminals had become indistinguishable from the businessmen. By the late 1930s, Burroughs had left the gangsters behind to seek his cool in the lower depths.

THE FURTHEST THING FROM COOL

For the first fifteen years after his graduation, Burroughs drifted slowly downhill, buoyed by a two-hundred-dollar-a-month trust fund. He spent six months studying psychiatry in Vienna, where he picked up boys in ancient steam baths and observed Hitler's rise to power. In 1937, Burroughs shocked his family by marrying Ilse Klapper, the doyenne of his circle of gay young men, so she could escape from Hitler. The pair parted quickly when he got back to New York.

Burroughs took psychology courses at Columbia, then went to live in Cambridge with his childhood friend and crush Kells Elvins, then moved to Chicago to attend lectures by the father of the theory of general semantics, Count Alfred Korzybski. Korzybski confirmed Burroughs's belief in a relativistic universe with conditional notions of right and wrong. "What is just for the judge," as Burroughs once explained it to me, "is not necessarily just for the criminal." Back in New York in the fall of 1939, he was studying anthropology at Columbia when he fell for a handsome lowlife named Jack Anderson.

After being kicked out of the respectable Taft Hotel when the hotel detective found them naked in bed together, Burroughs followed Anderson downtown to Bedford Street in the Village, where he took a room next door to Anderson in a boarding house. Much to Burroughs's dismay, Anderson frequently brought partners, both men and women, back to his room for sex. At night, Burroughs could hear them fucking, and it drove him over the edge. He cut off the last joint of his left little finger with a pair of poultry shears and presented it wrapped in a handkerchief to his psychiatrist, Dr. Wiggers, who persuaded him to commit himself to the Payne-Whitney clinic, where he stayed for a few days before returning to St. Louis with his parents.

He was soon scooped up by the machinery of war. Burroughs was drafted into the infantry after Pearl Harbor, then cashiered when his psychiatric history came to light. He applied unsuccessfully to work for the Office of Strategic Services, precursor to the CIA, where he was interviewed by his former college housemaster, who queried Burroughs dubiously about his Harvard "clubs." Burroughs of course, had no "clubs." He was a washout with his family, his class, and with himself.

In 1942, Burroughs went back to Chicago, where he rented a room at Mrs. Murphy's Boarding House on the near North Side. For eight months— the longest time that Burroughs would ever hold a job in his life—he was an exterminator, a bedbug specialist, going door to door with the line "Got any bugs, lady?" **He kept a gun in his closet and masterminded stickups in his dreams. He was an imaginary nihilist, which is the furthest thing from cool. All the time, though, Burroughs was sure there was something very wrong with him, some childhood trauma so deeply embedded in his subconscious that only a shrink could root it out.** He became certain he was possessed by what he called "the Ugly Spirit."

In the summer of 1943, an old friend of Burroughs's came to visit him in Chicago, a lanky, red-bearded thirty-one-year-old St. Louis pal named David Kammerer. With Klammerer was another St. Louisian from Burroughs's social orbit, Lucien Carr, fourteen years Kammerer's junior. The beautiful blond, green-eyed Carr and Kammerer had been carrying on a very Rimbaud and Verlaine–like friendship since Kammerer had been Carr's scoutmaster back when the latter was in junior high. Upon arrival, Carr and Kammerer tore up Burroughs's Gideon Bible and peed out of his window into the street, which was too much even for Mrs. Murphy. After this fresh eviction, Burroughs followed Kammerer, who was following Carr, to New York, where Carr planned to enroll at Columbia.

The beauty of Lucien Carr was the catalyst of the beat generation. At Columbia, Carr met sixteen-year-old Allen Ginsberg in a freshman dorm room. Carr met Edie Parker, a dark-haired Barbara Stanwyck type from Grosse Pointe, Michigan, at the West End Bar, the watering hole for several generations of Columbia and Barnard undergrads. Carr and Parker had a brief fling, then Parker introduced Carr to her boyfriend, Jack Kerouac, a former Columbia student and ex–football player who had just come home

Jack Kerouac
and Lucien Carr
at Columbia
University the
day before the
murder of David
Kammerer, 1944.

from the merchant marine. Carr, in turn, introduced Kerouac to Ginsberg.

Sometime around Christmas in 1943, Carr brought Ginsberg down to the Village to meet David Kammerer. When the freshmen arrived at Bedford Street, where Kammerer had taken up residence, a cadaverous figure in a three-piece suit greeted them: William Burroughs. Ginsberg was particularly impressed by Burroughs, thirteen years his elder—his erudition, his originality, his sardonic sense of humor. Burroughs lectured to the younger men about Korzybski. "This chair," he would quote the Count, slapping the back of the chair, "is not the word 'chair.'" That meeting was the beginning of a friendship between Ginsberg and Burroughs that would last for the rest of their lives.

Ginsberg brought Kerouac around to meet Burroughs. At the time, Kerouac was commuting between his parents' place in Ozone Park, Queens, where his father lay dying of stomach cancer, and an apartment on 118th Street that Edie Parker had begun sharing with another sometime Barnard College student named Joan Vollmer.

Edie Parker thought that Joan Vollmer was the smartest woman she'd ever met. The daughter of a prosperous factory manager, Joan had grown up in an affluent Albany suburb. The kind of world she wanted for herself, though, money couldn't buy. After she got out of high school, she took one of the few escape routes available to a young woman like her: she enrolled at Barnard College to study journalism. She soon married a law student named Paul Adams and dropped out of school. When Adams left for the war, Joan started going out with other men, and she became pregnant.

Joan Vollmer favored silky garments, bandannas, and peasant blouses worn casually off the shoulder. She subscribed to every newspaper in the city, and read them while receiving visitors, immersed in morning-long bubble baths. **She wanted to have the baby, so she concocted a scheme to fake madness and get herself admitted to Bellevue Hospital in order to lure her husband home, have sex with him, and then convince him that the baby was his.** She took to walking around Times Square in the rain with one foot in the gutter muttering to herself, and she was picked up and hospitalized. The rest of the plan went off without a hitch. Paul Adams went back to the war not much the wiser—they divorced after the war—and Joan went to stay with her parents. After her daughter, Julie, was born, mother and child returned to the city. She met

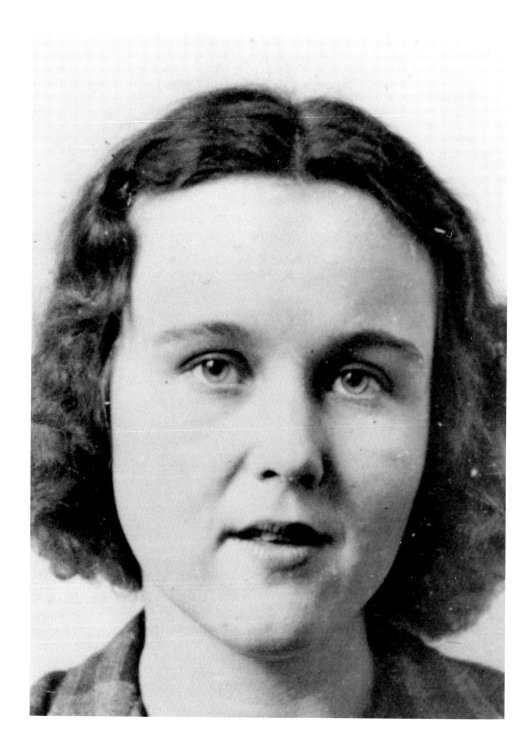

Edie Parker at the West End, and they decided to share a place. Not realizing that Burroughs was homosexual, Kerouac and Ginsberg thought that Joan Vollmer and Burroughs would be perfect for each other.

Burroughs, meanwhile, was living in a cheap furnished room on the edge of Hell's Kitchen, deep into what he tried to convince himself was an anthropological study of every bar on the West Side of Manhattan between Sixtieth Street and Times Square, "a seeker after cities and souls." Burroughs worked briefly as a bartender at the Angle Bar, a corner premise frequented by male hustlers, car thieves, second-story men, narcs, junkies, and others who from time to time availed themselves of the Angle's unique L-shape to duck pursuers by entering on the Eighth Avenue side and exiting onto Forty-third Street. He hung out at Bickford's, a cafeteria beneath the marquee of the Apollo Theater, which at the time was a "grinder" palace, continuously grinding out action twin bills twenty-four hours a day.

Times Square during those years must have seemed like it was under-sea, a multitiered labyrinth of subway platforms and elevated trains, arcades, shooting galleries, Pokerino palaces, cheap chop suey joints, and tropical fruit–drink stands decorated with artificial palms, an incandescent tumult of Mr. Peanut signs and neon Clydesdales and smoke rings blown from a billboard mouth eight feet wide. Every day the Times Square subway station disgorged 200,000 people into the square; elevated trains thundered up and down Eighth and Third Avenues. Trolleys rattled along Forty-second Street between the Hudson River ferry terminals and the East River bridges. There were three interstate bus terminals within walking distance. Journalist Jimmy Breslin once wrote that Times Square was actually *louder* than anyplace else, because when people stepped into the Square's bright, hot light, "they became excited and raised their voices."

For the sexual tourist, Times Square provided everything, especially the heady breath of anonymity. Young men in open shirts and dungarees loitered by "the hole," an IRT entrance in the Rialto Arcade known as a pickup point, waiting for the teenage servicemen who were flooding into the city. There were so many gay hustlers on Forty-second Street between Seventh and Eighth Avenues that the cops and the journalists referred to it as "Queens County." For the first time in his life, Burroughs must have felt at

Joan Vollmer in the only known photo of her when she was with Burroughs, probably late 1940s.

home. He was among Johnsons. No one would judge him here. He moved beside the bottom feeders, like a witness, pleased just to be able to watch.

Once a month, Burroughs showed up at the University Club to pick up the family check for two hundred dollars, a stipend contingent upon his continued visits to his new psychiatrist, Dr. Paul Federn, a seventy-two-year-old Viennese refugee who had been analyzed by Freud himself. Otherwise a loyalist to his mentor, Federn disagreed with Freud on one point: whereas Freud defined criminals as either sociopaths or psychopaths and inherently untreatable, Federn thought that psychopaths—by which he generally meant criminals—might be cured.

This thinking put Federn in step with his American colleagues. In those days, there was a sense of tremendous confidence in the American psychiatric community, a belief that the science of psychology could help overcome a wide range of social ills. Like prison psychologist (and later Norman Mailer's analyst) Robert Lindner, author of a popular 1944 report called *Rebel Without a Cause*, Federn believed that criminality could be successfully treated. Working with psychopaths in hospitals and jails, Federn felt he had achieved good preliminary results. He considered himself particularly attuned to what he surmised were Burroughs's problems.

Federn found Burroughs exceedingly difficult to analyze, though, because Burroughs's moral compass seemed so out of whack. **Burroughs told Federn that in America, crime is considered good and worthy of admiration; he also told Federn many dozens of dreams, most of which concerned lowlifes, gangsters, holdups, and muggings. From all of this, Federn concluded that Burroughs's homosexual and criminal tendencies were closely linked, that in his mind, Burroughs equated homosexual and criminal behavior.** In order to suppress the powerful sexual need that had gotten him in so much trouble with Jack Anderson, Federn reasoned, Burroughs wished that he were a gangster, but he wasn't. He was still too afraid, hiding behind his archness, his learning, and his irony. Burroughs was, in Federn's term, a "gangsterling"—a "gangster wanna-be." Federn finally gave up and handed Burroughs off to Dr. Louis Wolberg, an advocate of hypno- and narcotherapy, a technique that employed nitrous oxide to jog shell-shocked amnesiacs.

Burroughs's friend Kammerer, meanwhile, was going off the deep end. Lucien Carr's dad had died when he was a kid, and at one point Carr had needed and encouraged David Kammerer's attentions, which had always included a lot of wrestling and horseplay. Increasingly, though, Kammerer was demanding more overt affection from Carr. When Carr became involved with a woman named Celine Young, Kammerer started to lose it. He made drunken threats against Celine, and one night even appeared on the fire escape outside Carr's dorm-room window. Burroughs, alarmed for his friend, urged him to maintain his cool, but to no avail.

The night of August 13, 1944, Kammerer trailed Carr out of the West End, drunkenly begging Carr to let him blow him. When Carr refused, the larger Kammerer was all over him. Carr tried to fight Kammerer off, and finally, in the struggle, stabbed him to death with his Boy Scout pocketknife. Carr then threw Kammerer's body in the Hudson, weighting it down with stones. Then he went to tell Burroughs what he'd done, dramatically flinging a blood-stained pack of Lucky Strikes down in front of him with the words, "Have the last cigarette."

Burroughs tore up the cigarettes and flushed the pieces down the toilet, then loaned Lucien five dollars and suggested that he go ask his mother to find him a good lawyer. Lucien left and woke up Kerouac, who helped him drop the bloody murder weapon down a storm drain before Lucien turned himself in. Burroughs and Kerouac were arrested as material witnesses. For Burroughs, it was the closest he had ever come to being a real criminal. His parents made his five-thousand-dollar bail overnight and whisked him back to St. Louis. Kerouac's father was so disgusted with what was happening to his son, the first Kerouac ever to go to college, that he refused to bail him out. Kerouac and Edie Parker had to get married so she could use her family's money to get Kerouac out of jail. Charges were dropped against Burroughs and Kerouac. Carr pleaded guilty to killing Kammerer and was sentenced to prison for one to twenty years.

In St. Louis, Burroughs couldn't wait to return to New York and convinced his parents that he needed to put himself back in the hands of Dr. Wolberg. In the city again, he moved into a sunny three-bedroom apartment behind Barnard College with Joan Vollmer and her daughter, Edie Parker, Jack Kerouac, and a graduate student in anthropology from Denver named Hal Chase. Edie soon bailed and went home to Grosse Pointe, where she would eventually marry the local golf pro and forever ponder her what-ifs.

419 West 115th Street became the beat cradle, an urban cave where the beat generation founders pledged mutual allegiance, sharpened their intellects, and argued over the shape of the new culture.

And argue they did, for Kerouac and Ginsberg had their differences. Kerouac, the loner and watcher, the "spy in someone else's body," thirsted for personal salvation. Ginsberg, on the other hand, had dedicated himself to a kind of saintly, poetic communism. What they had in common was their feverish belief in their vision. In strikingly similar language, Kerouac and Ginsberg celebrated the fire. "The only people for me are the mad ones," Kerouac would write in perhaps the most famous passage in *On the Road*, "the ones who are mad to live, mad to talk, mad to be saved, desirous of everything at the same time, the ones who never yawn or say a commonplace thing, but burn, burn, burn, like fabulous yellow roman candles like spiders across the stars." In the great opening lines of his poem "Howl," Ginsberg describes, in strikingly similar language, "the best minds of my generation" as "angelheaded hipsters, burning for the ancient heavenly connection to the starry dynamo in the machinery of night." Maybe it was out of sheer madness, but Burroughs aspired to the rigorous analysis of logic, which is a product of cool.

Burroughs and Vollmer were into each other, united in their sardonicism and their attempts to dissect the earth's tortured soul in the last bloody year of the war. He introduced her to Benzedrine inhalers, which in those days could be had over the counter at the drugstore. By removing just one tube's accordion-folded paper strips and soaking them in a cup of coffee, one could get off for an entire day. Thus fueled, William and Joan spent hours sitting on Joan's bed, gobbling speed and talking. "We had all these really deep conversations about very fundamental things," Burroughs remembered. "Her intuition was amazing." And though Burroughs always considered himself to be homosexual, he claimed that Vollmer told him, "You're supposed to be a faggot, but you're as good as a pimp in bed." They never legally married, but by the end of 1946, Vollmer was referring to herself as Mrs. William S. Burroughs.

The apartment on 115th Street was Burroughs's first personal glimpse of a Johnson world. Everybody shared the eighty dollars' monthly rent and the food bills, Joan cooked, and Kerouac and Ginsberg studied at Burroughs's feet. He gave them reading lists that included Cocteau, Blake,

Allen Ginsberg in the merchant marine, New York harbor, 1947.

Kafka, and especially Spengler and Céline, admonishing them, "EEE-di-fy your mind, my boy, with the grand actuality of Fact."

Kerouac and Ginsberg even allowed Burroughs to psychoanalyze them, an incredible expression of trust considering their own fragile psychological situations. Ginsberg was living through the mental and emotional deterioration of his mother, which was exacting a terrible price, while Kerouac was only a couple of years removed from earning an honorable discharge "with indifferent character" from the navy after running naked across the parade ground at the Newport training station, screaming "Geronimo!" After months of saying little but taking copious notes, Burroughs suddenly warned Kerouac that he was going to strangle in his mother's apron strings. "That's your fate. That's your Faustian destiny."

Kerouac, aghast, went over to Ginsberg's dorm room to discuss Burroughs's prophecy. After talking all night, he fell into Ginsberg's willing arms. They were discovered the next morning by Kerouac's former freshman football coach. When as a result Ginsberg was suspended from school, he, too, moved in to 115th Street. Kerouac remembered this period of his life as his "Season in Hell," a "year of low, evil decadence" as he describes it in his novel *Vanity of Duluoz*, which ended with him in the hospital suffering from blood clots in his legs probably brought on by doing too much Benzedrine.

In the same book, Kerouac describes roaming Times Square with Burroughs on the night of August 14, 1945—V-J Day—celebrating Japan's unconditional surrender and the end of the war, eight days after the *Enola Gay* had dropped "Little Boy," the first atomic bomb, on Hiroshima. It was a night of drunken madness with thousands of uniformed servicemen roaming the Square kissing every woman they could get their hands on. In the fireworks' fierce apocalyptic glow, Kerouac says that Burroughs looked like "Lucifer's emissary," he who is the furthest thing from cool.

WHEN COOL AND BEAT WERE ONE

When you think about how much space a human being actually takes up in this world, Room 828 at the Chelsea Hotel isn't much—two steps from the bed to the old schoolroom map of the United States on the opposite wall, six or seven feet from the narrow window with its view across the midnight rooftops of Chelsea to the steel-clad door. Beyond the door are the Chelsea's dark, narrow, twisted halls. The radio plays softly: Cannonball Adderley with Brew Moore. Everything in the room seems like it came from the street—including Herbert Huncke, the man who lives here.

On top of a rickety dresser, a snapshot of a seedily attractive photographer named Louis Cartwright grins out from a cheap picture frame. Before Cartwright had become his lover, Huncke notes with a touch of pride, Cartwright had slept with William Burroughs and Jean Genet. In 1996 Cartwright was stabbed to death during a robbery outside the Kiev, a Russian restaurant on Second Avenue. From the way Huncke talks about him, it's plain that he really loved the guy.

When I phoned Huncke to ask for an interview, he quickly steered the conversation around to his fee. "At my age, do you expect me to go out and steal?" he snorted contemptuously into the horn. **At eighty-two, Huncke appears to be draped in shadow, as if he were hugging the darkness to keep him warm. When he shakes hands, his body is cool. When he speaks, his words are like flotsam drifting upward from a vanished hipster underworld. "We didn't become ace-boon-coons or anything like that," he says of someone who never became a close friend.**

Huncke is slight, even in his worn-out cowboy boots. His doelike eyes are liquid, ready to retreat, flatter, or con. In his autobiography, *Guilty of Everything,* Huncke writes, "Nobody deliberately sets out to be wrong. There may be some that do, perhaps, but basically, people are shooting to do whatever they think is the best thing they can do. They play it by ear." Whether in or out of jail, Huncke always tried to play it by ear, play it cool when "playing it cool" meant keeping out of the line of fire. **For Huncke, being cool was just a matter of survival, as it is for a raccoon or a coyote. Around the Sixteenth Precinct, Huncke was known as "the Creep," an individual so disgusting that the cops periodically ran him out of Times Square. Huncke was Ginsberg and Kerouac's guide to the underworld. Huncke turned Burroughs on to heroin; after that, Burroughs was cool. Herbert Huncke was cool when cool and beat were one.**

I hand Huncke his fee, five twenty-dollar bills from a cash machine. He

offers me a cigarette and a beer, then says he'll be right back. He stops at the door on his way out, turns back, and generously suggests that if I need to, I can pee in his sink. A lifetime of telling hard luck stories has made Huncke a brilliant storyteller. When he comes back a little while later, he's stoned, and the story of his life unfolds.

In 1934, at the age of twelve, Huncke ran away from his Chicago home for the first time. "I worked up a beef against my parents right away," he laughs. In *Guilty of Everything*, he tells what happened next. A hundred miles out of town, a guy gave him ten dollars for a blow job, and Huncke knew what to do. Later, he found himself standing beside an onion field near Geneva, New York, and he took a deep breath. "I thought 'this is the smell of real freedom.' I never dreamed it could smell so penetrating, so physical."

During the Depression, everything he owned fit in a cigar box, and he rode so many freight trains that the locomotive cinders turned his skin gray. "I had been aiming for New York since I was twelve years of age," he writes in his autobiography, and in 1940, he made it. "I was flat broke," he remembers with a dreamy smile. But "I'd learned a lot of little tricks along the way." When Huncke hit New York, he headed straight for Times Square—"where every young person ended up, because that was where the action was."

For Huncke, Times Square was home, a place where "you could hustle from one end of the street to the other." If he had the money, Huncke would "fall by" the local Horn and Hardart Automat, where he could get a little pot of baked beans with a strip of bacon draped across it for a nickel. He spent so much time over coffee at Bickford's that the help started calling him "the Mayor."

Huncke had a friend, a would-be hoodlum named Bob Brandenberg, who was temporarily employed as a soda jerk at a drugstore near Columbia University. One day in January 1946, a customer asked Brandenberg if he knew where he could unload a sawed-off shotgun and several boxes of stolen Syrettes—needle-tipped morphine tubes. The customer was William Burroughs, and Brandenberg invited him down to meet his friends on the Lower East Side: Vicki Russell, Phil White, and Herbert Huncke.

Burroughs and Huncke's relationship was symbiotic. Huncke introduced Burroughs to real criminals like Bill Garver, a spectral junkie whose specialty was stealing overcoats off of cafeteria coat racks. Burroughs and

Herbert Huncke, circa 1953.

Garver began pushing heroin around the Village in a small way, though they were mostly skeezing up the product. Forced to feed his first habit, Burroughs teamed with Phil White "working the hole," rolling lushes as a team in all-but-deserted subway cars. Burroughs would screen the victim from the prying eyes of other passengers holding up a newspaper as if reading, while the Sailor rummaged for the drunk's wallet.

For his part, Huncke, who'd always harbored a vague desire to be a writer, started coming around to 115th Street, intrigued by this new world of artists and intellectuals, some of whom seemed to have money. He brought his usual baggage of stolen property, unregistered weapons, and drug paraphernalia, as well as his usual crowd of mooches, grifters, drug addicts, and fuck-ups—who were soon followed by the police. Hal Chase, for one, sensed things spinning of control and bailed out of the beat generation entirely, not to resurface until the 1970s, when he popped up as the guru of a clan of hippie fishermen and boat builders along the Northwest Pacific coast.

Unlike Chase, Burroughs hung around, and in fact got drawn deeper into Huncke's world—one day, the Sailor went nuts and shot and killed a furrier using Burroughs's gun. MAD DOG NOONDAY KILLER blared the headline in the New York Journal-American. Huncke helped White dismantle the weapon and dispose of it in various places around Brooklyn. **Junk was eating all Burroughs's money now. His days of playing at cool, his time of studied detachments, had come to an end. Junk gave Burroughs a reason to get up in the morning and become a predator: he was cool at last.** "A junky does not want to be warm," Burroughs would later explain in Naked Lunch. "He wants to be cool-cooler-COLD. But he wants The Cold like he wants His Junk—NOT OUTSIDE where it does him no good but INSIDE so he can sit around with a spine like a frozen hypodermic." Burroughs was cool, but Burroughs was living in an uncool world, and he could feel the heat closing in.

In April 1946, somebody fingered Huncke and he got busted for possession of heroin in a fifteen dollar-a-month apartment Burroughs was renting on Henry Street. The next thing Burroughs knew, two cops were slapping cuffs on him and taking him downtown to the Tombs, where he was forced to kick his habit cold turkey. Joan, who was on Benzedrine and not making much sense, managed to bail him out. To do so, however, she had to ask Burroughs's psychiatrist, Dr. Wolberg, to sign Burroughs's surety bond. Wolberg, in turn, promptly notified Burroughs's parents that their son had been arrested for "hitting up croakers"—forging drug prescriptions. It was the first that Burroughs's family knew of their son using drugs.

As soon as his parents bailed him out, Burroughs started dealing. As a condition of his suspended sentence, Burroughs had to go back to St. Louis and live with his parents. There, Burroughs ran into his old friend Kells Elvins, just back from the war in the Pacific. Elvins had ten acres of citrus groves in the Rio Grande valley of Texas, and he and Burroughs hatched a plan to grow ruby-red grapefruit together. Burroughs persuaded his family, which was anxious to put some distance between their boy and his New York friends, to buy him fifty acres near Elvins. He and Elvins rented a house together near Pharr, Texas, and began farming.

With Burroughs gone and Huncke's crowd oozing into the 115th Street apartment, Joan Vollmer started to fall apart. Within a few months of Burroughs's departure, she suffered a breakdown and was taken to Bellevue after being found squatting on a Times Square sidewalk with her daughter Julie at her side. When Burroughs heard the news, he immediately drove to New York to rescue her.

On that trip in October 1946, William and Joan's son, William S. Burroughs, Jr., was conceived in a Times Square hotel. Burroughs brought Joan and her daughter back to the Rio Grande Valley, but the citrus ranch failed. By Christmas that year, with the help of his parents, they were combing the backroads and piney woods of East Texas for a quiet secluded place where people would leave them alone so that they could grow a marijuana crop.

VERY UNCOOL IN TEXAS

Texas never quite lived up to the Burroughses' expectations. In January 1947, they landed a broken-down ninety-nine-acre farm at the place where an old logging road dead-ended at a swamp. It was twelve miles outside of

New Waverly, Texas, not far from the State Penitentiary at Huntsville, where Kells Elvins had taken a job as a prison psychologist. There was no running water and no electricity, just a vine-covered barn that was about to cave in and plenty of tarantulas, centipedes, and scorpions—Burroughs would sometimes kill as many as ten scorpions a day. Burroughs decided to bring Huncke, fresh out of the Bronx jail, to Texas to be their farmhand.

As vultures circled over cypress stumps and black water, Joan, pregnant with William Jr., struggled with Benzedrine psychosis and let her daughter, Julie, run wild. Emerging from his room every morning in a coat and tie, Burroughs would drive into New Waverly to pick up the mail or dispatch Huncke to Houston to buy more drugs. In the evening's cool, they tended the marijuana. **At night, they all sat around on the front porch and got high by the light of a kerosene lamp, listening to Billie Holiday on a scratchy Victrola. Huncke remembers it as a good time. "I used to enjoy staying up nights, high on Benzedrine, just talking to Joan." On July 21, 1947, William S. Burroughs Jr. was born. With his heart-shaped face, "Billy" was a dead ringer for his mother. He was just as hooked on speed, too.**

Two weeks later, Allen Ginsberg showed up with a friend named Neal Cassady. A trim-hipped, muscular, semiliterate con man, Cassady had first hooked up with Ginsberg and Jack Kerouac the previous winter in New York, when he'd come to town on the Greyhound with his seventeen-year-old bride, LuAnn, to visit Hal Chase. When school was out the next spring, Ginsberg, dreaming of a romantic idyll, took off for Denver to visit Cassady, only to be caught up in Cassady's frenzied sexual drama, which also included LuAnn—Mrs. Cassady number one—and Carolyn Robinson, a college drama major who would soon become Mrs. Cassady number two. Cassady, who was primarily heterosexual, promised Ginsberg he'd sleep with him when they got to Burroughs's place.

When Cassady and Ginsberg arrived, Huncke built them a bed, which on their first night collapsed beneath them faster than Ginsberg's fervid dreams. Smarting, Ginsberg went to Houston and shipped out on a freighter for France. Burroughs decided that the family would depart immediately for New York, with Cassady at the wheel of Burroughs's old jeep and Huncke (who was suffering through Benzedrine withdrawal) in back alongside several duffel bags full of mason jars stuffed with pot.

The weed, as it turned out, was whack; and they ended up having to unload it in New York for a hundred dollars. Burroughs was soon strung out again. One winter midnight in Yonkers, he overdosed, and Vollmer had to walk him around all night, pouring coffee down his throat, to revive him. Burroughs checked himself into the federal narcotics farm in Lexington, Kentucky. While he was gone, Vollmer was picked up wandering around Grand Central Station and went back to Bellevue, where Burroughs had to rescue her again. Their search for visionary kicks had become a nightmare.

By February 1948, the Burroughses were back in New Waverly. Despite a welcome-home gift of two baby pigs from their nearest neighbor, the Burroughses wouldn't stay long. In May, William and Joan were arrested for having sex in their car outside of Beeville, Texas, and fined $173 for drunken driving and public indecency. **"Find things very uncool in Texas," William wrote to Kerouac and Ginsberg that June, announcing his family's imminent relocation to New Orleans, where he hoped to blend in, cool out, and feed the family habits in the French Quarter.**

With the money he got selling the New Waverly place, Burroughs bought a dilapidated house with a screened front porch at the foot of a levee in Algiers, a swampy suburb of New Orleans reachable only by ferry. On November 30, 1948, he wrote to Kerouac, declaring, "I am so disgusted with conditions I may leave the U.S.A. altogether." He was running out of places to hide.

COOL'S TRAGIC SHADOW

You can read about the year 1949 in *On the Road*: "The only thing to do was go." Just before Christmas 1948, Neal Cassady quit his job as a Southern Pacific switchman. Leaving his new wife, Carolyn, and their infant in California, he bundled his ex-wife LuAnn, fellow S.P. brakeman Al Hinkle, and Hinkle's wife Helen into a smoked-silver 1949 Hudson and blasted across the U.S. to pick up Kerouac and his mother in North Carolina, stopping on the way east to drop off Helen Hinckle at the Burroughses'. After

Overleaf: "Neal at the Wheel": Neal Cassady and Ann Murphy, 1950s.

depositing Kerouac's mother and her furniture in Ozone Park, New York, Cassady pointed the Hudson toward California.

William Burroughs was furious at Cassady for leaving Helen Hinckle, whom he'd never met before. "He is The Mover," he wrote Ginsberg, "compulsive, dedicated, ready to sacrifice family, friends, even his very car itself to the necessity of moving from one place to another." He was also angry at Kerouac for following Cassady around and giving him money.

When Cassady's now-battered Hudson steamed back into Algiers a few weeks later with Kerouac, Al Hinkle, and LuAnn, they found a dilapidated old house with sagging porches and weeping willows in the yard. **Joan was gobbling Benzedrine and scrubbing the floors with Lysol over and over again, while Julie, six, her hair matted with dirt, and Billy, one, ran around naked and filthy, shitting on the floors.** One night during her stay, Helen Hinkle woke to find Joan outside in the moonlight, trying to clean lizards out of a dead tree with a rake.

To Kerouac, Burroughs's flame seemed to be flickering out. The older man spent all day in a chair in the corner with the shades drawn, reading a book or a newspaper or nodding out. Sometimes, he'd take string and tie up the cats. He carried a gun everywhere, firing randomly into the swamp. In letters to Ginsberg, he fulminated against big-government liberals—"a cancerous element that will stifle every vestige of free life in the U.S."—and extolled the hard-right, anti-Semitic blatherings of Westbrook Pegler, "the only columnist, in my opinon," he informed Ginsberg, "who possesses a grain of integrity."

In April 1949, Burroughs took another fall. While cruising New Orleans's Lee Circle, Burroughs and a junkie friend were targeted by a patrol car. As it happened, Burroughs had an unregistered gun in the glove compartment, as well as a letter from Ginsberg referring to a marijuana sale, which made the police think that they'd just bagged a trophy dealer. They went back to Burroughs's place, found some smack, a jar of pot, and a half-dozen unregistered firearms, and arrested him. Now he was looking at a mandatory two to five years in the State Penitentiary at Angola, one of the most savage prisons in the South. A lawyer managed to get Burroughs out on bail so he could take a cure.

Nineteen forty-nine was a hard year for most of the 115th Street

"Johnsons." One bitter wintry dawn, Herbert Huncke arrived at Ginsberg's cold-water flat on York Avenue, just out of jail, starved, blood in his shoes, beaten by the cops, and warned never to come back to Times Square. Ginsberg took Huncke in. Vicki Russell and her current lover, an inept thief named Little Jack Melody, soon followed, taking over Ginsberg's bedroom. The apartment started filling up with stolen merchandise.

When a full-size cigarette machine wrapped in a blanket appeared in the kitchen, Ginsberg finally got up the nerve to tell them that they had to get rid of their swag. They acquiesced, but on their way to a fence on Long Island, they were spotted by a cruiser on Northern Boulevard in Queens. Little Jack panicked—he was out on parole and driving a stolen car—and took off. Attempting to negotiate a high-speed turn on Forty-third Avenue, the car overturned. Ginsberg tumbled out, and everyone was arrested.

Russell and Melody's families helped them get off with light slaps on the wrist, but Huncke ended up doing three years in Sing Sing. Since it was Ginsberg's first serious brush with the law, at the urging of his father and Ginsberg's eminent Columbia professor Mark Van Doren, he was remanded to the Columbia-Presbyterian Psychiatric Institute for seven months. Burroughs was furious with Ginsberg for letting himself be manipulated by "a lot of old women like Louis Ginsberg and Van Doren." He was even more angered at Huncke. "The more anyone has done to help him, the more certain he is to steal from or otherwise take advantage of his benefactor," he wrote to Ginsberg.

As Burroughs had predicted to Ginsberg, Cassady left Kerouac and LuAnn penniless in San Francisco and returned to his wife, Carolyn. But fortunately for Kerouac, Providence intervened in the form of a one-thousand-dollar advance from Harcourt, Brace for his first novel, *The Town and the City*. The money, and, as importantly, the acknowledgment of his ability, spurred a half-decade's writing that resulted in six of his greatest books.

Jack Kerouac wrote *On the Road* over three weeks in the spring of 1949 (it would take another eight and a half years to be published). One November evening in 1949, Kerouac was wandering up Lexington Avenue with a friend, the novelist John Clellon Holmes, speculating how their generation would be remembered. In his ruminations, Kerouac used the term "beat generation" for the first time, defining himself and his time for posterity as surely as F. Scott Fitzgerald did for his era when he called it "the Jazz Age."

Burroughs, meanwhile, was efficiently x-ing himself out of his friends' lives. Out on bail, he moved his family back to Texas, to the Rio Grande Valley, to plant a cotton crop and await trial. His new farm was close enough to Mexico that he could have fired his guns across the border, had the police not confiscated them, close enough to drive there, had the cops not impounded his car. Burroughs's cotton crop was a failure.

For Burroughs, no place in America was cool enough anymore. He was sick of being hounded by the law; to him, the civilized world seemed to be breaking up into the three warring camps led by Russia, China, and America described by George Orwell in his novel 1984, which was published in 1949. The Internal Security Act of 1950, too, which authorized detention centers for suspected American subversives, was just around the corner. "The U.S. drag closes around us," he would write a few years later in *Naked Lunch,* "like no other drag in the world."

He'd liked Mexico City the first time he'd seen it—as he recalled many years later in the introduction to a reissue of his very early novel *Queer*— with "its clear sparkling air, and the sky that special shade of blue that goes so well with circling vultures, blood and sand." The Distrito Federal, he reckoned, would be cool: drugs and boys would be easy to come by, and everybody—including the police—would leave you alone. "As authority figures," Burroughs wrote in the introduction to *Queer,* "Mexican cops ranked with streetcar conductors." In Mexico City, Burroughs could slip inside his cool and become the ultimate hipster, "El Hombre Invisible." Burroughs crossed the border in September 1949, inaugurating an exile that would last, with only a few brief, furtive interruptions, for the next twenty-four years.

Cool has a tragic shadow. When feelings are displaced by irony, cool can turn cold and hard. Later in his life, the cultural historian Ann Douglas writes, Burroughs came to feel that all his family relationships had been failures, and it would be hard to argue with his assessment. He couldn't respond to his father's sometimes abject pleas for love, and never visited his mother in a nursing home. His son committed suicide after writing that his father "had signed my death warrant." Burroughs's own shadow caught up with him on Thursday, September 6, 1951.

The Burroughses were in a sorry state. Joan had deteriorated badly since they'd come to Mexico. She'd caught polio in Texas, and it had withered her leg. Her teeth were turning black from the Benzedrine. William carried guns with him everywhere. Both were drinking heavily. Needing cash, Burroughs was looking for somebody to take a Star .380 automatic off his hands, because it shot low. On that September night, he had arranged to meet a potential buyer in an apartment above a bar called The Bounty.

The Bounty was a gathering spot for many of the Americans in Mexico City attending college on the G.I. Bill, several of whom had gathered in an upstairs apartment, drinking Oso Negro gin straight from the bottle when the Burroughses arrived for "the running party we always had," as one participant recalled later, on "the first of the month, when the checks came in." The conversation was desultory. William and Joan were sipping *limonada* and gin, when William, slouched about six feet across the room from Joan, suddenly pulled the .380 out of an overnight bag and said to Joan, "I guess it's time for our William Tell act." Joan, taking the cue, balanced her highball glass on her head, turned sideways and giggled, "I can't watch this. You know I can't stand the sight of blood." William shot once. Joan's head fell to her side, blood pouring from a hole in her temple as the glass, still intact, rolled around in a circle on the floor. All Burroughs's cool, his carefully calculated character, his ironic armor evaporated instantly. Moaning "Joan, Joan," he dropped to his dead wife's side, as the others ran for help.

THE
BODHISATTVAS
OF COOL

A COOL REVOLUTION

At midcentury, wrote poet and Trappist monk Thomas Merton, mankind was suffering "acute inner restlessness" and "threatened by the deepest alienation." North Korean troops were on the verge of driving the United States Eighth Army into the China Sea. The newly proclaimed People's Republic of China had just launched a full-scale invasion of Tibet. The U.S. government charged former Nazi scientist Edward Teller with developing a hydrogen bomb. The cold war had penetrated deep into the human psyche.

It's hard to remember how little people in the West knew about Zen—or any other kind of Buddhism—in 1950. Poet Gary Snyder says that when he wanted to learn how to do sitting meditation, he had to imitate a statue of the Buddha in the Japanese garden in San Francisco's Golden Gate Park. If people back then thought about Zen Buddhism at all, they probably connected it with Japanese militarism and World War II.

About 2,500 years ago Siddhartha—"He who accomplishes his goals"—Gautama, the thirty-five-year-old prince of a north Indian warrior clan, decided after years of spiritual struggle to plant himself beneath a tree near the town of Bodhgaya and not move until he achieved enlightenment. Seven days and seven nights later, Gautama had become the Buddha, "the Awakened." For the next forty-nine years, the Buddha walked around India with a community of people from all castes and walks of life, spreading the truth, the dharma, the method by which suffering is overcome and freedom is attained.

Zen Buddhism is an attempt to follow the Buddha's path. What is Zen? The word means "concentration" or "meditation." Zen arises out of "contradictoriness," Allen Ginsberg once explained to an interviewer from the Buddhist magazine *Tricycle*, "based on the fact that things both exist and don't exist at the same time." The aim of Zen is enlightenment, or satori—the absolute point where no dualism remains in any form.

D. T. Suzuki in New York, early 1950s. Zen teaches two basic routes to satori: zazen, long-term meditative sitting in the same posture the Buddha sat in, and koans, impossible riddles, brain-cracking conundrums like the famous "sound of one hand clapping"

that are passed from teacher to student. Both methods stress intuitive knowledge—wisdom transcending ordinary rationality. Solving a koan is impossible—yet all things are possible. Therefore, struggle with a koan is a strong spiritual preparation for a life of cool.

Teitaro Suzuki was born in 1870 into a family of physicians that for several generations had served a provincial samurai clan that had been impoverished almost overnight when the Meiji Emperor, Mutsuhito, abolished the feudal system. Suzuki's father died when the boy was six, leaving the family bereft of educational opportunities or a place in the world. At seventeen, Suzuki was forced to drop out of high school to support his mother. He used his rudimentary self-taught English to get a job teaching the language in a remote fishing village. "These misfortunes," he later wrote, "made me start thinking about my karma." Rinzai Zen, with its studied indifference to life and death, its austere and formal meditation practice, its Spartan monastery life, and its code of total obedience to a master, had long been associated with the samurai. Because of his samurai heritage, it was natural that Suzuki would turn to Zen. After his mother's death relieved Suzuki of financial responsibilities for anyone but himself, he entered the monastery at Engaku-ji in 1892.

The basic rule of conduct in Zen monasteries hasn't changed since the first century A.D.: "A day of no work is a day of no eating." As a novice monk Suzuki's life at Engaku-ji was rigorous and austere. He rose at 3:30 A.M. to meditate, sitting for extended periods in the cross-legged lotus position, encouraged to remain immobile by blows from a long wooden stick wielded by a senior monitor. Begging for their rice gruel, working at repetitive, menial tasks, the monks endured bitter winter cold with nothing but a tiny charcoal brazier for heat as they grappled with their koans.

In 1893, Suzuki's master, Shaku Soen, the abbot of Engaku-ji, received an invitation to a World Parliament of Religions scheduled to take place in Chicago. Soen asked Suzuki to write his acceptance letter, then accompany him and act as translator on the trip, the first known visit by a Zen Buddhist teacher to the United States. But Suzuki wouldn't be able to go until he solved the koan that Soen had given him: "Mu," meaning "nothing."

In Zen and Japanese Culture, Suzuki wrote, "No great work has ever been accomplished without going mad." Indeed, Buddhist literature is full of desperate monks on the verge of

suicide because they can't crack their koans. On the eve of his departure for the United States, Suzuki finally gave up on Mu and became the answer, and everything was cool.

As he remembered years later, the night after solving his koan, Suzuki was walking back to his quarters from the temple when he noticed "the trees in the moonlight. They looked transparent, and I was transparent too." Soen gave Suzuki a Buddhist name, Daisetz, which Suzuki told people meant "Great Stupidity." Others translated it as "Great Simplicity," implying a "skylike" mind emptied of all contradictions.

In Chicago, Suzuki met Dr. Paul Carus, the director of the Open Court Publishing Company in LaSalle, Illinois—a press primarily dedicated to reconciling science and religion. Suzuki's teacher went back to Japan, but Suzuki remained. He spent the next eleven years at Open Court translating some of the principal works of Buddhism into English, and working on the first of what would ultimately be an estimated 140 books on Buddhism in Japanese and English. On a lecture tour with his teacher, Suzuki met Beatrice Erskine Lane, a Radcliffe graduate and a Theosophist. Suzuki returned to Japan, with Lane, where they married in 1911, and lived in a small house at Engaku-ji. In 1919, they moved to Kyoto, where he became a professor at Otani University and taught courses on Zen and Western thought, while he and Lane published what was probably the world's first English-language Buddhist journal, *The Eastern Buddhist*. After Lane's death in 1939, Suzuki spent the war years in scholarly isolation at Engaku-ji.

In March 1947, two young Americans with an interest in Zen, Richard de Martino and Philip Kapleau, took a day off from their jobs with the International Military Tribunal helping to decide the fates of twenty-eight accused Japanese war criminals, and paid a call on Suzuki. After visiting with them for a while Suzuki knew it was time for him to return to the United States. In the winter of 1950–51, the seventy-seven-year-old scholar arrived in New York to lecture on Zen Buddhist philosophy at Columbia University.

The Department of Religion's new visiting professor's age, wit, buoyant spirit, and air of gentle, bemused detachment caught the public's fancy. Without any care or effort on his own part, Suzuki became an improbable celebrity. He was profiled in *The New Yorker*, interviewed in *Vogue*. Tiny, with, as *The New Yorker* put it, the "slim restless figure of a man a quarter of his age," impeccably dressed in the style of a Columbia undergraduate in a sport coat, khaki slacks and bow tie, Suzuki was, to the American mind, the very embodiment of Zen. "One cannot understand Buddhism," Thomas Merton said after meeting Suzuki, "until one meets it, in this existential manner, in a person in whom it is alive."

Suzuki wasn't a monk, as he was the first to acknowledge, and he practiced zazen only occasionally. He never pretended to be a roshi, a practicing Zen master, nor did he claim to have received the "dharma transmission," the wordless "mind-to-mind" transfer that is the master's seal of approval. Nevertheless, more than any other single person, Suzuki was responsible for what Robert Thurman, Columbia University Buddhist studies professor and the first Western-born Tibetan Buddhist monk, calls in his book *Inner Revolution* a "cool, inexorable, inner revolution," a social transformation based on individual transformation. Suzuki inspired an entire generation of "bodhisattvas of cool"—new, cool heroes indifferent to privilege, dogma, and attachment, in but not of the world.

"UNDERSTANDING CAME LATER —OR NOT AT ALL"

By 1952, John Cage was already on his way to becoming one of the most influential composers of the twentieth century. By the early 1940s, in compositions like the *Imaginary Landscapes* series, he was already incorporating many instruments and electronic sounds never heard before in Western music: tin cans and lead pipe, oscillators and buzzers, a piano "prepared" by attaching bolts and wood screws to the strings. Thanks to a widely publicized and well-reviewed 1943 Museum of Modern Art concert that had been featured in *Life* magazine, the then thirty-one-year-old composer was the best-known avant-garde musician of his time.

John Cage, 1940s.   Los Angeles–born (in 1912) and raised, Cage was the only child of an

inventor and the women's-page editor of the *Los Angeles Times*. After dropping out of Pomona College and wandering around Europe thinking that he might become an architect, Cage enrolled at the New School for Social Research in New York.

Founded by Columbia University history professor Charles Beard and other anti–World War I academics associated with the progressive *New Republic* magazine, the New School featured the first academic curriculum ever designed by artists, and it clearly emphasized the here and now. Poet Hart Crane's lover, Waldo Frank, gave the first college course on modern art. Composer Aaron Copland taught modern music. Dancer Doris Humphrey taught modern dance. Cage studied modern harmony and rhythm with Henry Cowell, "the open sesame," in Cage's words, "for new music in America."

In addition to composing pieces like 1925's *The Banshee*, which he played by moving a darning egg across piano strings, Cowell published experimental music, presented avant-garde concerts, and imported music from all over the globe (Cowell, in fact, coined the phrase "world music") In 1938, Cowell sent Cage to meet Lou Harrison, a composer, percussion-instrument collector, and student of Balinese and Javanese gamelan. Harrison catalyzed Cage's interest in Asian culture and musical ideas.

Before leaving for New York, Cage was working in a Los Angeles arts-and-crafts shop when he met Xenia Kashevaroff, one of six tall, striking, talented, and volatile daughters of a Juneau, Alaska, Russian-Orthodox priest. For Cage it was love at first sight. A few weeks later he took her out to dinner for the first time and asked her to marry him. In 1935, after he returned to L.A. from the New School, she said yes.

In 1938, Cage was working as the composer-in-residence at the Cornish School, a progressive arts academy in Seattle. Playing piano for a dance class, he saw Mercier Cunningham, a nineteen-year-old Cornish dance student from Centralia, Washington, for the first time. Cage and Kashevaroff asked Cunningham to join their percussion ensemble.

Cage had been sexually involved with men since his trip to Europe, when he hooked up with an aspiring artist named Don Sample. Cage and Sample were living together in Los Angeles, in Viennese architect Rudolph Schindler's King's Road house, a center for political, artistic, and sexual experimentation in the 1920s and '30s, when Cage met Xenia. Cage insisted in later years he was open with his bride-to-be about his attraction to men. "I didn't conceal anything," he avowed. The three of them began a love affair that was cut short when Martha Graham came through town and asked Cunningham to join her dance company in New York.

For their part, Cage and Xenia made it to New York in 1942. Cage had been exempted from the wartime draft because his father was working on a top-secret device to help airplane pilots navigate through fog. In the four years since they'd been together in Seattle, Merce Cunningham had become one of Martha Graham's principal male soloists. He'd even partnered with Graham in the popular triumph of *Appalachian Spring*, but Cunningham never allowed himself to be drawn into Graham's powerful orbit. Cage and Cunningham rekindled their collaboration in April 1944, with a joint recital, inaugurating a personal and professional relationship that would last for the rest of Cage's long and productive life.

In 1945, Cage and Xenia separated, and Cage moved to the top floor of a tenement building at Monroe and Grand Streets on the Lower East Side. There, Cage created a whitewashed aerie with views stretching from the Queensborough Bridge to the Statue of Liberty. He kept it empty but for a long marble table and a grand piano.

Over the previous few years, Cage had become increasingly frustrated with his inability to communicate his feelings through his music. He poured all of his "loneliness and terror that comes to one when love becomes unhappy" into *The Perilous Night*, a six-movement suite for prepared piano, for example, only to have one critic bark that it sounded like "a woodpecker in a church belfry." Cage was "confused," he said, "both in my personal life, and in my understanding of what the function of art in society could be." Friends suggested psychoanalysis, and he tried it. A Jungian analyst whom he consulted predicted that after Cage was cured, he'd write more music. "Goodness," Cage thought, put off, "I already write too much music, it seems to me."

In 1950, Cage was teaching at the New School when a sixteen-year-old pupil named Christian Wolff brought him a copy of the I *Ching*, the Chinese Book of Changes, which had just been published in English for the first time. The four thousand-year-old I *Ching* is a set of oracular images, sixty-four

Overleaf: Merce Cunningham rehearsing his company, circa 1957.

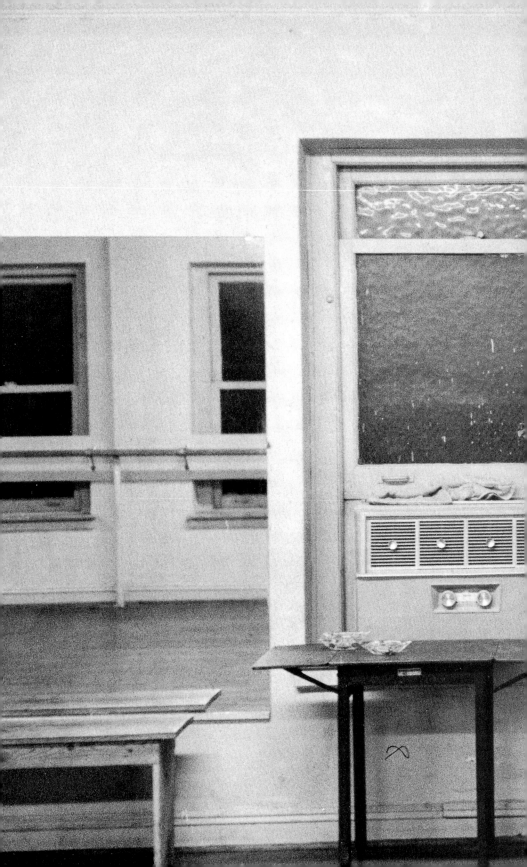

hexagrams composed of six straight or broken lines, that express archetypal human situations, such as "Conflict" (hexagram 6) or "Youthful Folly" (hexagram 4). Using a set of fifty yarrow stalks or three coins, a questioner may be able to divine the future; but **Cage says he was drawn less by the wisdom of the I Ching than by its ability to help him compose music. Cage used the I Ching system of broken and unbroken lines as if it were a computer. By manipulating the yarrow stalks or by flipping the three coins again and again. Cage realized the opportunity to "liberate [his] music from every kind of like and dislike."** With the I Ching, Cage later wrote, "It was immediately apparent to me that I could devise a means of composing by using these operations."

In 1952, a wealthy young architect named Paul Williams bought one of the first commercial tape recorders so that Cage could produce one of the very first pieces of electronic music. Cage tossed I Ching coins thousands of times to decide every aspect of what would become known as the Williams Mix. It was four minutes long, composed of sixteen layers of sound, hand-spliced onto eight tape tracks, and every decision regarding the frequency and amplitude of five or six hundred different sounds was generated by the I Ching.

Normally, Cage and his editing assistants—a young composer named Earl Brown; Brown's wife, Carolyn, a dancer who'd later become a star with Merce Cunningham's dance company; and David Tudor, a pianist who came to specialize in the recital of Cage's piano works—spliced twelve hours a day. Every Friday afternoon, at a little before two o'clock in the afternoon, they put down the razor blades, talcum powder, and sticky tape—which were then the tools of the editor's trade—pushed back from the glass-topped table in a studio at 9 West Eighth Street, and took the subway uptown to Columbia University to listen to D. T. Suzuki.

Precisely at 4:00 P.M., Suzuki, accompanied by Mihoko Okamura, his very pretty, very young, very devoted secretary and companion, would enter a lecture room in the northwest corner of Philosophy Hall. Stroking and caressing his books—which he often referred to as his "sins" because, as he frequently acknowledged, writing about Zen was an impossibility—Suzuki began to discourse very quietly and at great length on the philosophy of Zen.

Though Suzuki was formally appointed a visiting professor in the Department of Religion, his class was unusual for Columbia because it straddled the religion and philosophy departments. It was also unusual because, at the insistence of Suzuki's sponsor, plumbing fixtures mogul Philip Crane, nonstudents were allowed to take it, and many did. Few did so for credit, yet the chairs were always filled. In addition to Cage and his friends, the auditorial overflow spilling out the door represented a cross-section of the New York avant-garde. Frequently, it included Eighth Street Artist's Club members like Ad Reinhardt and Philip Guston. Betty Parsons, Jackson Pollock's dealer, attended the class. After their love affair fizzled, Karen Horney, the first important woman psychiatrist in the United States, and Erich Fromm, the radical psychoanalyst and social philosopher, found themselves taking Suzuki's class.

As Suzuki crisscrossed the blackboard with his notes, illustrating his points with a bewildering maze of diagrams and catchwords, speaking in a kind of analog English-Tibetan-Sanskrit-Sino-Japanese, his eyebrows flaring upward like the wings of a gull, it was not uncommon for many of his bewildered students to nod off. Occasionally, even he himself would "do a Suzuki," as his students started calling it, closing his eyes for long minutes until no one could tell whether he was meditating, entering samadhi, or simply fast asleep. No one ever found out: maybe the students were too polite, or too bewildered or too cool to ask.

"Suzuki never spoke loudly," Cage later recalled. "When the weather was good, the windows were open, and the airplanes leaving La Guardia flew directly overhead from time to time, drowning out whatever he had to say. He never repeated what had been said during the passage of the airplane. In Suzuki's class, you could easily ask yourself whether you had learned anything or understood anything. Understanding came later—or not at all."

Suzuki never argued. He had a genius for deflating windy argument or academic pedantry without giving offense. "He had a certain comfortable quality," one student remembered, "which immediately set me deeply at ease in body and mind." Suzuki liked to talk about satori, the "turning over of the mind," which he called the essence of Zen, the fundamental experience of awakening from dualism. "When you have enough faith," Suzuki would explain, "then you have enough doubt. And when you have enough doubt, you have enough satori."

Suzuki's Buddhism was optimistic. It could be summed in a single *mudra*, the Buddha's stylized hand gestures. The Buddhists say the *abhaya mudra* originated when an angry elephant charged the Buddha. The Buddha raised his right hand in the universal, open-handed gesture of friendly greeting, and the elephant stopped dead in its tracks. Henceforth, that gesture became known as the *abhaya*, or "fear not," *mudra*. "Peace," Suzuki reassured his students, be cool. In the end we will all become Buddhas. Suzuki took it further, though. Once we become Buddhas, he taught, we have to come back to the world, cool as a bodhisattva, and assist all sentient beings to become Buddhas, too.

As one of the best known Buddhists in Japan during the 1930s, Suzuki was inevitably tainted by the Japanese Buddhist establishment's eager embrace of Japanese militarism, though his age and his venerable reputation allowed him to stay aloof from direct involvement. General Hideki Tojo, widely regarded as the architect of the sneak attack on Pearl Harbor and the creator of the notorious Unit 731, which conducted biological experiments on Chinese captives, who later was hanged as a war criminal, had been one of Suzuki's students. When asked by his class what he thought of Tojo as a student, Suzuki replied, "Not much."

In his class, Suzuki excoriated the Buddhist religious establishment for its lack of education, its failure to take a worldview that stretched beyond the islands of Japan, its simple ass-kissing of those in power—Buddhism might be better off, he suggested, if all the Buddhist monasteries were burned to the ground—and its overemphasis on satori. Just being enlightened wasn't good enough. There had to be some sense of social responsibility. John Cage took from Suzuki's class that it's not enough just to be cool. You have to teach cool to the world

SILENCE

In its twenty-five years of hardscrabble existence, Black Mountain College never had more than 125 students. The school had been founded in 1933 by dissident academics led by John Andrew Rice, who'd been driven out of Rollins College in Florida in a dispute over academic freedom, and decided to start their own college. They located a YMCA conference center in the Blue Ridge Mountains, eighteen miles east of Asheville, North Carolina, and booked it for the winter. Their guiding principles were vague. "If there was any general statement of the college's educational aims and ideal," Rice remembered, "it was certainly nothing more definite than 'we shall see what we shall see.'"

The faculty at Black Mountain received little more than room and board in return for their teaching. In an effort to create a more democratic learning community, everyone worked on the school farm, which produced much of the meat and vegetables consumed on campus. Everybody, male and female, wore blue jeans, overalls, slacks, or shorts during the day, and dressed for dinner. **Regulations that normally guided students through the academic year during that era did not exist. There were no required courses, and so few people ever graduated that every diploma was handmade. The students had only one rule: "Be intelligent."** To the surrounding communities, the college's lifestyle and its large number of Germans, Jews, and Yankees made it seem like a hotbed of radicalism. To the students, it was something more. Many books have been written about Black Mountain College, but only one by an actual student there. Writer and artist Fielding Dawson arrived at Black Mountain during the summer of 1949. In *The Black Mountain Book*, he recalled what attracted him in the first place. "Black Mountain *was* freedom. . . . It had an organic understanding of itself being transient. . . . It was not uncommon for people to drift in off the highway, strangers who were not strangers at all, but kindred souls."

Dawson arrived at Black Mountain at the end of an era that had been shaped by intellectual exiles from Nazism, many of whom were associated with the Bauhaus. Josef Albers, the rector of Black Mountain until 1949, had been in the experimental German school's first graduating class, and the head of its furniture studio. His wife, Anni, a brilliant weaver, had been his student. History has come to regard the essence of Bauhaus style as pared down and without ornament; but during its brief existence, the school was notorious in Germany for its flamboyant lifestyles, its long-haired boys and short-haired girls. One of the Bauhaus's most famous professors was

Johannes Itten, who advocated Mazdaznan, a macrobiotic regimen that alternated fasts with a garlic-flavored mush that turned its devotees' skins green. The Nazis shuttered the Bauhaus as soon as they came to power. When asked on his arrival what he hoped to achieve at Black Mountain, Albers answered simply, "To open eyes."

In the late 1930s, as Albers's English improved, he began making a concerted effort to attract young, practicing American artists and innovative thinkers to Black Mountain, organizing a series of summer institutes that combined work camp with an informal academic program aimed at breaking down the barriers between artists and students. By the late 1940s, the summer programs were attracting so many New Yorkers that painter Franz Kline called Black Mountain "Downtown Manhattan."

The summer institute of 1948 looms large in Black Mountain lore as the season that saw a generation of American artists come into their own. Merce Cunningham taught technique of dance and produced an evening of new pieces. Willem de Kooning designed the sets for Erik Satie's lyric comedy *The Ruse of Medusa*, which starred Buckminster Fuller. **That summer's student body included future California arts educator Ruth Asawa, future fluxus artist Ray Johnson, future painter Kenneth Noland, future director Arthur Penn (*Bonnie and Clyde*) and Robert Rauschenberg, who'd enrolled because he felt he needed discipline and he'd read that Josef Albers "was the greatest disciplinarian in the United States."** The main project for the summer was the attempted erection of Buckminster Fuller's first geodesic dome using venetian blinds, which collapsed, leaving Fuller to shrug cheerfully that the freedom to experiment was what college was for.

Cage enthralled the community with a series of after-dinner concerts, playing the then almost completely unknown piano music of Erik Satie through a window for an audience reclining on the lawn in the long summer twilight. In a lecture before the first recital, however, Cage scandalized his mostly Eurocentric listeners by stating "immediately and unequivocally that Beethoven was in error" in defining harmony as the basic structural element of composition; Beethoven's influence was "deadening to the art of music." Cage played his *Sonatas and Interludes* for prepared piano while Cunningham danced. The students and faculty were so delighted

Josef and Anni Albers arriving in New York from Nazi Germany on their way to Black Mountain College, 1933.

with the performance that they loaded Cage and Cunningham's car with gifts of art and food when the pair departed.

When Cage and Cunningham returned to Black Mountain College during the summer of 1952, much had changed. The buildings were falling apart, the grounds were overgrown and cluttered with trash. The teachers weren't much older than the students, and everybody was living on peanut-butter-and-jelly sandwiches. Though Cage's benefactor, Paul Williams, was doing what he could to help out financially, Black Mountain was so strapped that it had to sell off pieces of the property to pay taxes before finally shutting its doors permanently in 1956.

In photographs taken during the 1930s and '40s, Black Mountain students look like kibbutzniks, busting sod behind a horse-drawn plow, or earnestly pounding nails. **Black Mountain students of that era were marked by their sense of optimism, their belief in their ability to bring about social change, and their faith in the goodness of the earth and its bounty. By the early 1950s, however, students had begun to chill, to distance themselves from the values of the dominant culture and withdraw from public and political life.** In a 1951 photo, the eyes of three of the last twenty or so Black Mountain students, Joan Heller, Ed Dorn, and Dan Rice, hunkering down on the steps of a school building, all show a furtive, hipster quality. Black Mountain had become a community of aliens almost cut off from the outside world, a tiny band of Johnsons led by its rector, the Brobdingnagian, iconoclastic poet-scholar Charles Olson.

To experience Charles Olson in 1952, when he was forty-three, leaning in, eyes glittering with challenge, mouth filled with food or sucking down smoke from a cigarette or reefer, mind moving from idea to idea like a Pleistocene hunter, must have been overwhelming. "He is six feet eight or nine," "Fie" Dawson wrote his sister and brother-in-law from Black Mountain, "and has shoulders like an ox. He must weigh about two hundred and sixty or seventy." In class, "when he hit something funny, he would begin to wheeze, then out he would come with this great torrent of laughter, mounting higher and higher and louder and louder till crescendo."

The spirit of the French poet-actor-madman-writer-director Antonin Artaud was very much in the air at Black Mountain during the summer of 1952. Four years earlier, Cage had brought a copy of Artaud's manifesto col-

Charles Olson in Gloucester, Massachusetts, 1963. Photo by Gerard Malanga.
© *Gerard Malanga.*

lection *The Theatre and Its Double*, home from France. Teacher Mary Catherine Richards, shocked to discover a French writer she'd never heard of, started translating it immediately, reading portions of it aloud to Cage, Cunningham, and David Tudor as she worked. Artaud's essays, especially "No More Masterpieces," sounded a visionary wake-up call to destroy, in the name of a "Theatre of Cruelty," all forms of language and all social proprieties in an effort to "overturn" the Western mind.

All this set the stage for a performance that many have come to view as one of the most influential of the twentieth century.

This first "happening"—to use a term that would be invented a half-decade later in Cage's Composition of Experimental Music class at the New School—was created one day after lunch and presented the same evening. Nobody wore costumes; everybody played themselves. Cage had an idea of what each performer had decided to do. He never made specific assignments because he didn't want to be a traditional Western composer, "someone who tells other people what to do." **He used *I Ching* coin tosses to determine when each person would perform, and how long they would do it. He was trying, he later explained, to find a way "to let sounds be themselves rather than vehicles for man-made theories or expressions of human sentiments."** Merce Cunningham explains further:

> "Nothing was intended to be other than what it was, a complexity of events that the spectators could deal with as each chose."

Because Black Mountain had never been able to afford to build its own theater, the performance, like all performances at the school, took place in the dining hall. The audience seats were arranged in concentric circles divided into quadrants by four aisles, and the action occurred in the middle of the circle, outside it, and in the aisles, so that the performance had no real center—the center was everywhere. "Everyone," Cage wrote of the arrangement, "is in the best seat." He based this seating on a Buddhist idea: "Every sentient and non-sentient being," said Cage, "is the Buddha. These Buddhas are all, every single one of them, at the center of the Universe."

The piece was cool enough to be nameless; though it eventually acquired—nobody knows how—the title *Theatre Piece #1*. Few among the faculty, students, and Black Mountain community people who were there that evening agree on what happened, exactly how long it lasted, or even the date or time of day on which it occurred. David Tudor, most believe, performed throughout the entire performance, which lasted about forty-five minutes, but nobody remembers what he played. Cage himself stood on a stepladder reading—though reading what, no one, including Cage himself, could recall; possibilities include the fourteenth-century mystic Meister Eckhart, Huang Po's *Doctrine of the Universal Mind*, a Suzuki lecture that included the line "a piece of string, a sunset, each acts," to the United States Constitution's Bill of Rights or the Declaration of Independence. M. C. Richards, who would go on to become an eminent potter, educator, and philosophical essayist (*Centering: In Pottery, Poetry, and the Person*), and Charles Olson read from other stepladders. One chronicler states that Olson gave his students fragments of a poem, which they stood up and recited in sequence. Robert Rauschenberg played scratchy Edith Piaf records at double speed on an ancient wind-up phonograph with a horn loudspeaker, while another student, Nick Cernovich, projected handpainted slides and movies of the school cook and mountain sunsets on the walls and on four of Rauschenberg's "White Paintings," which were hung from the rafters in the shape of a cross. A dog chased Cunningham around the room as he danced.

M.C. Richards remembers that most people liked the performance. Lou Harrison, then teaching music at Black Mountain on the recommendation of Cage (Harrison was recovering from a nervous breakdown, an incident his résumé refers to as simply "lost mind"), thought it boring. Composer Stefan Wolpe, a onetime theatrical collaborator of Bertolt Brecht, stomped out in disgust. The widow of Viennese conductor Heinrich Jalowetz, who'd been at Black Mountain almost from its inception, muttered, "This is the Dark Ages." Cage himself saw in the piece the potential of the composer as an instigator. *Theater Piece #1* was a mighty trumpet blast, a fanfare for the demise of the rational, but it nevertheless wasn't cool—it was too frantic. Cool for John Cage would come later, with silence.

John Cage's interest in silence dated back at least to his student days at Los Angeles High School. In 1927, he won first place in the Southern California Oratorical Contest at the Hollywood Bowl, with a declamation suggesting that the United States lead the world by dedicating an hour a week to be being "hushed and silent," in order that the nation experience

Overleaf: Antonin Artaud (right) as a priest in Carl Dreyer's The Passion of Joan of Arc, *1928.*

the heart of that undisturbed calm "most conducive to the birth of a Pan-American conscience."

Cage may have been further intrigued by silence and its uses when in 1946 he learned that in Indian philosophy, all nine permanent emotions are eventually swallowed up by silence. He first mentioned using silence in a composition in a lecture that he gave at Vassar College in 1948. Then, in 1949, *Time* magazine quoted him saying that he wanted to compose a piece of music that used silence and offer it to Muzak, whose peppy, soothing, piped-in "functional music" had spread rapidly through postwar America's factories and offices in an attempt to alleviate boredom in the workplace. Well before newly elected President Dwight D. Eisenhower had it installed in the White House in 1953, Muzak had become, amongst hipsters, a metaphor for mind control.

At the same time, however, Cage had come to question whether silence even existed. In 1951, he'd gone into an anechoic chamber in the physics laboratory at Harvard University, but instead of hearing nothing, he heard the high-pitched sound of his nervous system and the low-pitched rush of his blood circulating. For Cage this was a confirmation of what D. T. Suzuki had taught him about the void—that it is "filled with possibilities."

Cage envisioned a piece of silent music as the ultimate in nonduality, the vanishing point between life and art—an exercise in meditation, a way to quiet the mind. He hesitated before actually pursuing such an idea, fearing that it would be taken as a joke. Eventually, convinced that "if it was done it would be the highest form of work," Cage decided to make music composed of "sounds not intended," with no sound intentionally produced. After settling on three silent movements, Cage used a set of homemade tarot cards to determine their duration. The piece's name was the time it would take to play: 4'33".

The world premiere of 4'33" was scheduled for August 29, 1952, at the Maverick Concert Hall in Woodstock, New York, where it would be part of a program of avant-garde music. Because the event benefited the Artists' Benevolent Fund, many members of the New York Philharmonic were in the audience. The back of the concert hall was wide open to the fields and woods.

Robert Rauschenberg, 1968.

When the moment came, David Tudor began 4'33" by opening the key-

board cover, starting a stopwatch, and depressing a piano pedal. For the rest of the first movement, his hands were folded in his lap. His back was erect, his expression serious and concentrated. At the end of the movement, he closed the keyboard cover. He reopened it to signify when the next movement had begun, then closed and opened it again for the final movement.

Though seemingly bereft of content, 4'33" is, like the void, rich with possibilities. At Maverick, during the first movement, listeners heard the sound of wind in the woods. During the second movement, there were raindrops on the roof. In the final movement, the audience added its own baffled murmurs and perplexed mutterings. "It is one of the most intense listening experiences you can have," David Tudor later reported. "You really listen. You hear everything there is. It is cathartic: four minutes and thirty-three seconds of meditation." Not all shared Tudor's assessment: according to Earl Brown, who was also on the program, most of the audience left "infuriated."

Cage often cited 4'33" as his all-time favorite piece and regarded it as his most important work. "I use it constantly in my life experience," he said. "No day goes by without my making use of that piece in my life and in my work. I listen to it every day." For Cage, 4'33" was the answer to the riddle of cool, it was the sound of one hand clapping, the sound of one hand, the sound of one. 4'33" is the simplest gesture, the barest hint, a finger pointing at the cool new moon.

THE YEN FOR ZEN

At the end of 1953, Jack Kerouac was staying at Neal and Carolyn Cassady's house in Los Gatos, California, near San Jose, just coming off the most sustained period of creation he would ever experience. In the previous two years, he'd written the original three-week teletype-roll version of *On the Road*, a vast meditation on America called *October in the Railroad Earth*, and four novels: *Visions of Cody, Doctor Sax, Maggie Cassidy,* and *The Subterraneans*. Though he knew himself to be a great writer, he was still unpublished. His emotional life was in turmoil. He was thirty-one years old, drinking hard, and hiding from Joan Haverty, the pretty model with whom he'd lived while he was writing *On the Road*, and her insistence that he pay child support for Jan, their baby daughter. Meanwhile, he had become involved with Carolyn—with Cassady's apparent blessing. As Carolyn Cassady recounts in the movie *What Happened to Kerouac?*, her husband encouraged her and Kerouac to have an affair. On his way out the door one day in his Southern Pacific brakeman's uniform, Cassady suddenly turned to Jack and Carolyn and grinned "my best gal, my best pal . . ." at which Carolyn laughs. "After that it was not hard to arrange." **For Kerouac, the affair had to have been bittersweet. He knew that Carolyn wasn't going to leave Neal. And while he loved to play daddy with the Cassadys' small children while Neal was working on the railroad, he knew he could never take care of them—he wouldn't even acknowledge the daughter he already had.**

Yet although Cassady gave Kerouac asylum—and Carolyn—by 1953, the blood-brother bond that the two had shared and which Kerouac celebrated in *On the Road* was beginning to fray. Sick of listening to Neal and Carolyn rattle on about Edgar Cayce's theories of reincarnation—a popular subject at that time in an America grappling with the specter of a thermonuclear war—Kerouac began hanging out at the San Jose Public Library reading room, where he happened on Dwight Goddard's *A Buddhist Bible* (dedicated to D. T. Suzuki), the first popular collection of Buddhist writings published in America. The book launched Kerouac into a three-year period of concentrated Buddhist study and sitting meditation, even as he crisscrossed the continent.

March 1954 found Kerouac living in a skid-row hotel in San Francisco near the railroad station at Third and Townsend, working as a brakeman on the Southern Pacific. A month later, he was back with his mother in Richmond Hills, New York, working on a railroad at the Brooklyn docks. In the winter and spring of 1955, he was at his sister and her husband's place in Rocky Mount, North Carolina. In the early part of summer he was in Greenwich Village, sleeping on the couch at Lucien Carr's—Carr was on parole and working at United Press International—then he hitchhiked to Mexico.

That fall, after riding buses, hopping freights, and hitchiking from Mexico City, Kerouac showed up at Allen Ginsberg's rose-trellised backyard cottage in Berkeley with a backpack full of new manuscripts, including

Tristessa, a novel about his friendship with a Mexico City junkie whore, and *Mexico City Blues*, 242 choruses of meditative Buddhist jazz poetry: "I have no plans/no dates/no appointments with anybody/so I leisurely explore/souls and cities." Ginsberg lost no time introducing Kerouac to his neighbor, Gary Snyder, then twenty-five, whom he'd met the year before though Kenneth Rexroth, a poet, anarchist, and leading figure of San Francisco bohemia. Snyder was living in a tiny, sparsely furnished Berkeley cottage of his own while studying classical Chinese and contemporary Japanese at the University of California.

He had grown up in the state of Washington, on a dairy farm that his grandfather homesteaded not far from Puget Sound. On a visit to the Seattle Art Museum when he was eleven or twelve, he saw Chinese landscape paintings for the first time. He was struck, he remembers, by how much the landscapes reminded him of the Cascades, the mountains he'd been exploring since he was a kid, and he felt "an instantaneous, deep respect for something in Chinese culture that always stuck in my mind." From the paintings and the interest that they sparked, Snyder moved on to the T'ang dynasty poets and to Zen.

The first time he read D. T. Suzuki, Snyder was twenty-one years old and on his way to grad school in anthropology at the University of Indiana. **As he recalls, "It was September of 1951, and I was standing by the roadside in eastern Nevada hitchhiking the old Route 40,"** when he fished a copy of *Essays in Zen Buddhism* out of his rucksack. **"I didn't know it at the moment, but that was the end of my career as an anthropologist."** The next year, he hitchhiked back to the Bay Area and enrolled at Berkeley.

Snyder and Kerouac became fast friends. For the next year, until Snyder left for a Japanese monastery and they never met again, they shared a burlap-lined cabin with no utilities at the top of a hillside horse pasture above Mill Valley, California. They rolled Bull Durham, slugged wine from a jug, and debated Buddhism deep into the night. Kerouac's Buddhism focused on the first Noble Truth, that suffering is the basis of existence and man's only reason for being on earth is to practice kindness. He claimed not to be interested in Zen, terming it "mean," on account of "All those silly Zen masters throwing young kids in the mud" just because they couldn't unravel the meaning of their koans. Snyder responded with big friendly grins and a twinkle in his eye; and the next morning Kerouac would roll out of his sleeping bag with a hangover to find Snyder hours-deep into sitting meditation.

Politically, Kerouac and Snyder couldn't have been further apart: Kerouac was a rabid defender of Senator Joe McCarthy's anticommunist witch hunt, while Snyder reflected his anarchist–left-wing roots in the Pacific Northwest. Nevertheless, Kerouac saw the flinty Snyder as the real deal, a new kind of American hero, the first of what Kerouac named "dharma bums": a "great rucksack revolution thousands or even millions of young Americans wandering around with rucksacks, going up to mountains to pray, making children laugh and old men glad, making young girls happy and old girls happier, all of 'em Zen lunatics . . ."

In April 1956, just before departing for Daitoku-ji monastery, Snyder threw a big going-away party for himself at the Mill Valley cabin. As immortalized in *The Dharma Bums*, it was a sprawling, seventy-two-hour hoot: people got drunk, played guitars, sang, and danced naked around a bonfire. Among the guests was the prodigiously gifted writer and self-described "religious entertainer" Alan Watts.

In the late fifties, according to Philip Kapleau, one of the first American-born Zen teachers, "hardly a cocktail party was given at which some Zen aficionado did not spout his latest self-devised koan." If anybody was responsible for this "yen for Zen" (a phrase coined by another American-born Roshi, Robert Aitken)—part of a late fifties enthusiasm for all things Japanese, which Gary Snyder says included "*Sunset* magazine garden books, the game of go, Samurai movies, and a single flower in a bottle, sitting on the floor"—it was the erudite, raffish Watts, who was already becoming famous in the Bay Area for his Buddhist seminars and radio rambles. In his aptly titled autobiography, *In My Own Way*, Watts credits his own "easy and free-floating attitude to Zen" for the "notorious 'Zen boom' . . . which flourished among artists and 'pseudointellectuals' " in the era.

Born in 1915, Alan Watts grew up in Chislehurst, Kent, England, in a house full of Korean celadon vases, Japanese embroidered cushions, chinoiserie, and Indian curios—gifts his mother received from her boarding-school students, the daughters of Protestant missionaries serving in the far-flung reaches of the British Empire. When he was sixteen, he dropped out of

Overleaf: Gary Snyder on the Sea of Japan, 1959.

King's School, Canterbury, the incubator for the Anglican church, without graduating and turned his back on Oxford in favor of London's Buddhist Lodge where, amidst Persian rugs, wafting incense, and golden Buddhas, a mystical barrister named Christmas "Toby" Humphreys introduced him to D. T. Suzuki's *Essays in Zen Buddhism*. Watts's first book, *The Spirit of Zen*, a highly precocious attempt to explain Suzuki's concepts to the masses, was published when Watts was eighteen.

In 1936, the year he turned twenty-one, Watts met Suzuki for the first time when the scholar arrived in London for the World Congress of Faiths. "Suzuki fascinated me," Watts says in *In My Own Way*. He found Suzuki "wisely foolish, gently disciplined, and simply profound . . . at once the subtlest and simplest person I have known." **His previous elucidation notwithstanding, to Watts, the meaning of Suzuki's Zen proved elusive. "The moment you thought you had finally grasped his point, he would slip from your grasp like wet soap, thereby showing that Zen was neither a formulable idea or concept, but something like dancing or the movement of a ball on a mountain stream."**

That same year, Watts found his first willing girlfriend, sixteen-year-old Eleanor Everett, whose mother, the redoubtable Ruth Everett—ex-wife of a Chicago industrialist, friend and student of Suzuki, and probably the first Western woman ever to study in a Japanese monastery—had come to London to lecture at the Buddhist Lodge. In 1938, with war clouds looming, Eleanor Everett found herself pregnant. The two young Buddhists (she was eighteen, he was twenty-three) were married with Anglican pomp, exiting the church to a theme from the last movement of Beethoven's Ninth Symphony, then sailed for New York.

When they arrived, the newlyweds found Ruth Everett dedicating her energies to the Buddhist Society of America, an organization built around the Zen missionary Sasaki Sokei-An, her second husband. She secured the newlyweds an apartment next to hers at Eighty-seventh and Riverside, where Eleanor gave birth to their first daughter, Joan. While Eleanor stayed home with their daughters (a second was born in 1942), Watts plunged into his mother-in-law's Bohemian social whirl. He was soon giving seminars on Oriental philosophy, incorporating elements of Zen, yoga, Christianity, and psychotherapy. The religious editor at Harper & Bros. heard Watts talk

Alan Watts, 1950s.

one night and asked him to write a book, and in 1940, Watts published *The Meaning of Happiness*. Meanwhile, Eleanor was falling into a deep depression and drinking too much. She developed eczema, and grew enormously fat. One day, stopping to catch her breath at St. Patrick's Cathedral, she experienced a vivid vision of a silent Jesus, which must have been unnerving for someone who considered herself a Buddhist. She began to long for the Chicago suburbs and the peaceful, conventional childhood she had never known.

With the Selective Service breathing down his neck, Watts decided to become a minister. But what kind? According to Monica Furlong's biography of Watts, *Zen Effects*, memories of the Anglican hymns and rituals drew him back to the religion of his youth, Episcopalianism. But even as he donned the cloth, Watts told himself he wouldn't be abandoning Buddhism. By celebrating the Mass he'd be conveying the mystery inherent in all religions. Through friends of Eleanor's family, he was appointed to the chaplaincy at Northwestern University in Evanston, Illinois. On Ascension Day, 1944, Watts assumed the clerical collar he would wear for the next six years.

Father Watts was the kind of priest of whom it is said that "he had everything but faith." He loved conducting the religious ceremonies and candlelit processions redolent with swinging bowls of incense, punctuating them with Gregorian chants and Renaissance polyphonies. On campus, Watts's services were a big hit. In 1947, *Time* magazine dubbed him one of the new enfants terribles bringing the church in line with modern life. His and Eleanor's living arrangements, however, were about to land him in big trouble: each of them had taken student lovers and moved them into the parsonage. Eleanor had a son by her student lover, and his parents threatened to bring charges. In 1950, Eleanor wrote to the bishop, telling him why she wanted her marriage annulled. Watts was forced to resign his priesthood.

Eleanor's departure and Watts's sudden fall from grace released him forever from the need to be a respectable person. "I am a mystic in spite of myself," he declared in his autobiography, "remaining as much of an irreducible rascal as I am, as a standing example of God's continuing compassion for sinners, or, if you will, of Buddha-nature in a dog, or light shining in darkness. Come to think of it, in what else could it shine?" He married his lover, Dorothy De Witt, which got him excommunicated from the Episcopal

Church, as he was still married to Eleanor. To escape it all, he holed up in Millbrook, New York, writing *The Wisdom of Insecurity*. When he finished, he and Dorothy and his two kids headed for San Francisco.

Watts was lecturing at the American Academy of Asian Studies, then located in a rambling old mansion in Pacific Heights, when he and Snyder met. Snyder and poet Philip Whalen, who had been a roommate of Snyder's at Reed College in Oregon, were studying basic Buddhist philosophy at a Berkeley Buddhist church when Watts came to give a lecture. Still "very straight, very British, short hair, necktie," in Snyder's words, Watts, then forty-one, had not yet taken to the "Japanese gentleman's kimono with cigarette ashes down the front" that Whalen describes Watts in later. Watts and Snyder found they shared interests in classical Chinese, calligraphy, translation, and the writings of D. T. Suzuki.

According to Whalen, Watts thought that Zen's discipline and rituals were "all right if you were a fifteen-year-old plow jockey coming to the temple, but not necessary for anybody beyond the age of reason." Nevertheless, Watts so admired Snyder's desire to take on the cold, sleeplessness, and deprivation that Japanese Zen monks have to endure, to take "tough discipline with a light heart," that he convinced his ex-mother-in-law, Ruth Everett, to arrange a travel grant to get Snyder to Japan. "When I am dead," Watts wrote of Snyder in his autobiography, "I would like to be able to say that he is carrying on everything I hold most dearly." He kept his word: at his death in 1973, Watts bequeathed Gary Snyder his lacquered Japanese longbow, a boxed set of nineteenth-century armor-piercing battle arrows fletched with eagle feathers, and his traditional Buddhist staff with bronze rings.

Watts and Kerouac, however, didn't get along. For a working-class novelist like Kerouac, Watts's high-church mannerisms must have screamed for parody, Snyder speculates. In Watts's eyes, Snyder presumes, Kerouac was devoid of "grace or polish." Watts may have been jealous of Snyder and Kerouac's friendship as well. In *The Dharma Bums*, Kerouac mockingly records his first meeting with Watts, who he renamed Arthur Whane in the book: "Whane stands there in the firelight, smartly dressed in suit and necktie, having a perfectly serious discussion about world affairs with two naked men." When someone asks him to define Buddhism, Whane responds, "Buddhism is getting to know as many people as possible." In his autobiography, Watts retaliated, condescendingly referring to Kerouac as "a warm and affectionate dog."

In 1959, in a dollar pamphlet published by City Lights Books called *Beat Zen, Square Zen, and Zen*, Watts acknowledged that the American "hullabaloo about Zen" had reached a point where it required more clarification. "Square Zen," he explained, was formal Japanese Zen, the Zen of established tradition and defined hierarchy. "Beat Zen" was a rubric for a spectrum of anti-establishment attitudes and pursuits. "The 'Beat' mentality," Watts stated, "is a younger generation's nonparticipation in the 'American Way of Life' . . . a revolt which does not seek to change the existing order but simply turn away from it."

Certain artists, Watts sniffed, were using "Beat Zen" to justify their caprice. Robert Rauschenberg's "blank canvases" and John Cage's "silent music," for instance, were "therapy . . . not yet art." Jack Kerouac's writing in particular "is always a shade too self-conscious, too subjective and too strident to have the flavor of Zen." **True Zen, Watts believed, "can never be accurately and fully formulated, being an experience and not a set of ideas." After experiencing Zen, Watts asserted, one "continues to play his social role without being taken in by it. He does not precipitately adopt a new role or play the role of having no role at all. He plays it cool."**

Watts went on to become a revered personage in the sixties counterculture, one of the central figures in the Human Be-In in Golden Gate Park in January 1967, the high-water mark of Haight-Ashbury hippie culture. Yet, "strictly speaking," Gary Snyder would observe many years later, "Alan was not cool in our ongoing in-house sense of detached, ironic, fellaheen hip, with an outlaw/anarchist edge. He was cool in relation to the people around him, who were more middle class, needy, and graduating toward hippie looseness in the mid-sixties, but never actually cool. You *know* what I *mean*, as the Big Bopper says."

In September 1957, *On the Road* was published, and, as Kerouac wrote to Cassady soon thereafter, "everything exploded." Gilbert Milstein of the *New York Times* described the publication of the book as a "historic occasion . . . the most important utterance yet made by the generation Kerouac himself named years ago as 'beat.' " The beats became a worldwide social phenomenon, greeted as liberators and reviled as primitives, the shock troops in a cultural war that would continue for decades. In October 1958, in an attempt to capitalize on his sudden notoriety, Kerouac published what he later disparaged as a "potboiler," *The Dharma Bums*. Written in ten Benzedrine-fueled fifteen- to twenty-thousand-word writing sessions, *The Dharma Bums* made Gary Snyder a hero and teacher to a generation, and it proved to be one of Kerouac's most popular and lasting novels.

On October 15, 1958, the day *The Dharma Bums* was published, Kerouac, Ginsberg, and his lover Peter Orlovsky were on their way to the book party when Kerouac jumped into a phone booth and called D. T. Suzuki, who by now had retired from Columbia but was still living near the campus with Mihoko Okamura's family, to see if they could stop by. When, Suzuki wanted to know. "RIGHT NOW!" Kerouac shouted into the phone, knowing that Suzuki was going deaf. Suzuki graciously acquiesced.

When they arrived on West Ninety-fourth Street, as Kerouac told a Berkeley Buddhist magazine interviewer two years later, Suzuki served them thick, soupy, green Japanese tea in cracked soup bowls, and studied his visitors silently. "Why did Bodhidharma come from the West?" Kerouac suddenly shouted. Suzuki made no reply. "When we left," Kerouac remembered, "he pushed us out the door, but once we were out on the sidewalk he began giggling at us and pointing his finger and saying, 'Don't forget the tea!'" In other words, "Be real." As they were walking away, Kerouac turned and called out "I would like to spend the rest of my life with you." The eighty-eight-year-old Suzuki held up his finger and answered, "Sometime."

SIGNALING
THROUGH
THE
FLAMES

GROWING UP ABSURD

Nineteen fifty-five was the apex of the Age of Ike, the year that President Dwight Eisenhower, in golfing togs, climbed into an electric cart with the presidents of General Electric and General Motors and rolled down the fairway. Business was good and the country was easy, and the French surrender to the Vietnamese army at Dien Bien Phu was happening half a world away. A retired general was running the country, and that was good, because the United States and the Soviet Union were in the middle of an arms buildup, and the Soviets had just raised the ante by developing their own hydrogen bomb—very likely employing secrets stolen from the U.S.

The dizzying inconsistencies of prosperity and the Cold War made 1955 the nadir of American paranoia. The breathless staccato of the young Baptist evangelist Billy Graham erupted from the airwaves; "Repent!" he urged "time is desperately short. These are the Final Days." UFO sightings in the United States spiked to an all-time high. On each succeeding cover of the *Bulletin of the Atomic Scientists*, the doomsday clock hands inched ever closer to midnight. Hipsters put on dark sunglasses to protect their eyes from the nuclear flash. In the movies, these almost incomprehensible fears were embodied by fantastic monsters: In 1954, Godzilla was born in a low-budget Japanese sci-fi flick, summoned from a vanished age by a nuclear explosion. The same year, mutant killer ants the size of school buses crawled out of a hole beneath the Nevada Test Site and invaded the Los Angeles River in the Hollywood low-budget sci-fi flick *Them*.

Convinced that the gravest threat to national security came not from the enemy's nuclear weapons but from Americans' irrational fear of those weapons, the United States Atomic Energy Commission launched an effort aimed at reassurance, invoking the peaceful atom's limitless potential— "the sunny side of the atom," as a CBS-TV documentary of the time dubbed it—promising a day when "an aspirinlike tablet of U-235" would power supersonic airplanes and high-speed trains and provide "atomic medicine to all who need it."

At the same time, though, the Civil Defense Administration undertook

Judith Malina and Julian Beck as Antigone and Creon in the Living Theatre production of Antigone, 1968.

a campaign to prepare Americans for nuclear war, distributing 16 million copies of *Survival Under Atomic Attack*, a pamphlet that depicted a well-adjusted nuclear family huddled cheerfully in their fallout shelter awaiting the all-clear. The California Federation of Republican Women produced *Grandma's Pantry*, a how-to manual for stocking the family bomb shelter's larder. In 1951, the New York City Board of Education issued dog tags to every school kid so that their bodies could be identified after a nuclear holocaust. In 1954, President Eisenhower authorized Operation Alert, a simulated Russian nuclear attack on the United States. Everyone in the entire country was required to take cover for fifteen minutes. New York State made noncompliance with the exercise punishable by a year in prison.

Early on the morning of June 15, 1955, hypothetical wave after hypothetical wave of Russian Tupolev bombers appeared over the North Pole, launching nuclear attacks on sixty major American cities. As the invaders penetrated the Distant Early Warning System (DEW) line, Judith Malina, twenty-six, a fiery, black-eyed beauty in a white lace dress, crossed New York's City Hall Park looking for one of her actors, Jackson Mac Low. Mac Low was part of an anarchist group called Resistance that was planning a protest against Operation Alert, and he had called the night before to warn her that he might have to miss a rehearsal because he thought he might get arrested.

Malina, cofounder of the Living Theatre with her husband, Julian Beck, was raised in politics. Her Polish rabbi father had dedicated his life to saving European Jews from the Nazis. As a kid, she'd helped him stuff leaflets asking "Do you know what has happened to your Jewish neighbors?" into thousands of shampoo packets being shipped to Germany. Though she'd never been to a demonstration before, she'd subscribed to *Resistance*, the magazine edited by Mac Low's political collective, for years. Today, she took action. Leaving her six-year-old son, Garrick, at home with her husband, Malina went downtown to join the demonstration at City Hall .

As President Eisenhower and his top aides were being helicoptered from the White House lawn to a top-secret underground command center in Maryland, Mac Low spotted Malina, "her black hair streaming like a Southern belle," as he remembered in 1999. Looking back, Malina evokes

Mac Low's "disciple's beard" and his "thin hands" holding a ski pole with a large hand-printed sign as he walked around the edge of the park so that the workers in City Hall and at police headquarters—the very loci of civil authority—could read his warning against the dangers of atmospheric nuclear testing.

Mac Low introduced Malina to Ammon Hennacy, a lean conscientious objector with a snaggletooth grin and a thick crop of wavy gray hair. Hennacy had spent most of World War II in solitary confinement in a federal prison for refusing to register for the draft. Every year on the anniversary of Hiroshima, he went to the New York office of the Internal Revenue Service to repeat his vow to never pay taxes to support the U.S. war machine and fasted in penance for being a citizen of the country that dropped the first atomic bomb. Hennacy handed Malina a bundle of *Catholic Worker* newspapers to sell and introduced her to Dorothy Day.

Until her death in 1980, Brooklyn-born Dorothy Day was the guiding light of the Catholic Workers, a Depression-born, grassroots network of some forty "hospitality houses" and communal farms across the United States. Fifty-eight years old at the time of Operation Alert, she wore her thick white hair in tightly wound braids. A Hopi cross hung at her throat. **She lived on Chrystie Street on the Lower East Side, at a Catholic Worker Hospitality House that served eight hundred free meals a day, slept fifty homeless people a night, and supplied several hundred people a week with donated clothes. She shrugged off widespread calls for her beatification with a cool "Don't dismiss me so easily."**

Now, in the mid-fifties, as publisher, editor, and writer for *The Catholic Worker*, the movement's eight-page tabloid, Day reached nearly forty thousand people a month with arguments and beliefs that repeatedly put her at odds with the Catholic Church hierarchy—though "not in a spirit of defiance and rebellion," as she always insisted, but in an effort "to obey God rather than man." Just as World War II was threatening to draw in the United States, Day had journeyed to Washington to testify against the reinstatement of the draft. Under Day's aegis, The Catholic Worker may have been the only organization to actively defy the wartime law that made it illegal to encourage potential draftees not to register. Now, in the depths of the Cold War, Day and Hennacy were at it again—as Day wrote in the War Resister's

League magazine, Liberation—"setting our faces against the world."

At 1:45 P.M., Eastern standard time, Civil Defense sirens rent the city air. Traffic inching past City Hall Park on Broadway ground to a halt. Passengers piled out of buses and taxis, and men in white CD helmets herded them past newly minted black-and-yellow "fallout shelter" signs into the bowels of Manhattan. When all the subway platforms were full, stragglers jammed into vestibules and doorways—anywhere to get out of the sun.

At 1:50 P.M., a hypothetical hydrogen bomb exploded with the force of 5 million tons of TNT above the intersection of Kent Avenue and North Seventh Street in Brooklyn. At the moment that 4.5 million New Yorkers were being hypothetically incinerated, Malina, Mac Low, Hennacy, and Day, along with about twenty other religious pacifists, moved quietly to park benches underneath the park's leafy canopy of London plane trees. **To make it more difficult for any newspaper photographers to distort their message, they held up signs protesting atomic testing and Operation Alert. They also apologized for Hiroshima and Nagasaki to the only reporter present, who happened to be Japanese.**

Within seconds, Civil Defense wardens swooped in, handcuffed the unresisting protesters together, and threw them into a paddy wagon. In addition to Mac Low, Hennacy, Day, and Malina, the prisoners included the venerable Dutch Reformed minister A. J. Muste, who'd scandalized Christian America on the eve of World War II by announcing that as a Christian pacifist, "If I can't love Hitler, I can't love at all"; and the gay African-American Quaker political organizer Bayard Rustin, who only days later would journey to Montgomery, Alabama, to help Martin Luther King Jr. organize the bus boycott that sparked the civil rights movement.

At their arraignment, the magistrate totally lost it, screaming at the prisoners that they were murderers responsible for millions of hypothetical deaths.

When he mispronounced Ammon Hennacy's name, Malina tittered. He snapped at her: "Have you ever been committed to a mental institution?" "No, have you?" she shot back. The judge exploded. "That's enough! You are hereby committed to Bellevue for psychiatric observation." A scuffle broke out in the court; roaring "No! You have no right, no legal, no moral right to do this!" Malina's husband, Julian Beck, lunged at the judge. In the ensuing

Dorothy Day in jail after an anti–Civil Defense protest in New York, July 1954.

Marlon Brando, turmoil, Beck somehow made his escape, but Malina was carted off to the
circa 1954. criminal psychiatric observation ward at Bellevue Hospital.

Beck immediately contacted Malina's psychiatrist, the poet, playwright, and anarchist social theorist Paul Goodman. Goodman is probably best known today for writing Growing Up Absurd, a collection of essays that helped to define the fifties, and for inventing the "encounter group." In 1955 much of his reputation was based on Gestalt Therapy, a 1951 collaboration with Frederick Perls and Paul Hefferline that helped launch the human potential movement. Goodman was able to muster up enough juice to get Malina sprung from Bellevue.

Very thin, with golden hair curling down to his shoulders, Julian Beck was no stranger to drama. Born into a prosperous Upper West Side household, to a father who distributed German motorcyle parts and a mother who taught in the New York public schools, Beck was in the same sped-up, pre-war prep-school class at Horace Mann as Jack Kerouac. His brief Yale career ended in 1943 in the middle of a freshman geology final, when he decided that, as an artist, he could no longer "serve the system." Unlike most men his age, he did not have to worry about the draft: he'd already been classified 4-F by his draft board after declaring that he considered sex between men a revolutionary act, and that he was a revolutionary.

Malina and Beck were still teenagers when a mutual friend introduced them at Genius Inc, a bar off Times Square that catered to the acting crowd. **Although Beck originally thought of himself as a painter, almost from the moment they met, Malina and Beck knew that they wanted to create a theater that would explore the most important social, political, and sexual issues of their time.** They enrolled together in Erwin Piscator's Dramatic Workshop at the New School.

A short man with a flowing mane of silver hair, Piscator was best known for producing "epic theater": working-class political street-theater events in Berlin and Moscow that pioneered the use of projected movie images to create a "living wall." His attempt to build a professional theater and an allied dramatic academy at the New School attracted teachers like Harold Clurman and Stella Adler, and a brilliant crop of theatrical hopefuls that included—in addition to Malina and Beck—such future luminaries as Mel Brooks, Harry Belafonte, Rod Steiger, Bernie Schwartz (before he became

Tony Curtis), Ben Gazzara, Shelley Winters, and Walter Matthau. Marlon Brando too attended the workshop and became one of Adler's "protégés," though he repeatedly clashed with Piscator. In just one such incident only a few months before scoring his first Broadway part in I Remember Mama in 1944, Brando was expelled from the Dramatic Workshop's Sayville, Long Island, summer session when Piscator discovered him A.W.O.L. from the director's class, having sex with an actress friend in the hayloft of a campus barn. Before a 1951 Senate Un-American Activities Committee subpoena sent him fleeing to East Berlin to avoid answering questions about his connections in the Communist Party, Piscator instilled in Beck and Malina a deep commitment to political theater.

In 1948, Malina found out she was pregnant with the first of her and Beck's two kids, and the pair married at City Hall. They incorporated the Living Theatre, "the most important work of my life," as Malina wrote in her diary, the same year. It was an uphill battle.

When their first attempt to open a theater space in a Wooster Street basement in the Village in 1949 fell through, they were forced to put on the first staged readings in their living room. Then, in 1951, Beck poured his entire six thousand dollar inheritance into bankrolling the Theatre's first real home at the Cherry Lane Theater, where members of the company binged on work, slept where they fell, analyzed each other endlessly, and carried on intense love affairs. They managed to put on plays by Paul Goodman and San Francisco poet Kenneth Rexroth before a fire inspector shut them down for breaking what even Beck admitted was "every law there is to break." But they persevered.

At the end of 1953, Malina and Beck built a second theater in a defunct beauty parlor on the third floor of an old wooden building at Broadway and 100th Street. They scavenged lumber from abandoned buildings and seats from a movie theater that was being demolished, transporting it all through the streets on their shoulders. Before the building inspectors shut them down for code violations in 1955, the Living Theatre began to hit its stride with a production of Tonight We Improvise, Pirandello's "absurd" comedy in which actors take over the plot of a play. Its theme—the effort to obliterate the difference between life and art— would characterize most of the Living Theatre's greatest work.

COOLER WITH A SAINT

June 15, 1955, was not the last of Operation Alert: it was an ongoing exercise to ready Americans for a nuclear conflict that might erupt at any time. The protests also continued. In July 1956, there was a second protest against Operation Alert. Dorothy Day called Judith Malina from a pay phone in Washington Square Park and urged her to join the pacifists and anarchists who were again refusing to take shelter. Malina couldn't because she was taking care of her mother, who was dying of breast cancer. As she hung up the phone, Malina could hear from her house window the air raid siren at the top of the telephone poll at the end of her block screaming "like the world in pain," as she put it in her diary that day. Hennacy and Day and a few others were arrested. The first year the peaceniks did five days. The second year they did ten.

One spring day in 1957, Malina and Beck were bouncing around Greenwich Village with Merce Cunningham and John Cage, two of the many artists who were being drawn into the Living Theatre's ever-expanding orbit, in a Volkswagen Microbus (which Cage had recently won on an Italian television quiz show answering questions about mushrooms). At the corner of Fourteenth Street and Sixth Avenue, they spotted an empty two-story building, the former Hecht's department store. They brought Cage's patron Paul Williams to look at it, and he agreed to design and underwrite a dance rehearsal and recital space for Cage and Cunningham, and a new home for the Living Theatre, in the building.

Underwriting and design was the easy part: it took another massive communal effort to build the new theater, a task that included knocking down sixteen-inch-thick brick walls from ten in the morning until the communal meal at eleven at night. One broiling July day, Malina and Beck and their friends formed a chain gang and passed 225 ninety-pound sacks of cement into the building and 3,400 bricks out. The work paid off. The Living Theatre's first production in the new space was William Carlos Williams's *Many Loves*, a play—three seemingly unrelated love stories based on cases Williams witnessed as an intern at the old French Hospital in Manhattan—

that Beck and Malina had wanted to stage since the Living Theatre began. On opening night, *Many Loves* got eleven curtain calls.

In August, Beck and Malina both joined another Operation Alert protest. As the air raid sirens whined the signal to take cover, the protesters marched out the front door of the Catholic Worker hospitality house on Chrystie Street and, holding up their signs, walked toward Sarah Delano Roosevelt Park on the Lower East Side. For the first time a TV news crew was present and immediately started trying to stage-manage the event, unsuccessfully urging the protesters to come out of the hospitality house a second time so they could get it on film. As the demonstrators entered the park, a Civil Defense colonel in full uniform asked Malina, Beck, Day, Hennacy, and four others if they would take shelter. When they all answered no, they were placed under arrest.

At the arraignment, Ammon Hennacy tried to explain that the protesters were doing penance for America's nuclear attacks on Hiroshima and Nagasaki. The judge cut him off: "You are a bunch of heartless individuals who breathe contempt of the law. I have no sympathy for you or for your cause." The peace demonstrators' lawyer tried to get them to plead not guilty, but they refused. Led by Dorothy Day, they all pleaded guilty, guilty, in their own eyes of breaking an unjust law. They were given thirty days.

Julian Beck and the rest of the men were sent to the Tombs, Manhattan's decrepit, overcrowded downtown prison. The "air raid ladies," as they became known to their sister prisoners, were locked up in the old Women's House of Detention—now a garden!—which for nearly half a century blighted the corner of Tenth Street and Greenwich Avenue in the West Village.

Dorothy Day later wrote an article for the liberal Catholic magazine *Commonweal* describing "Judith Malina Beck" entering prison. "Young and beautiful, she is an actress, which means that she carries herself consciously, alert to the gazes of others. Her black hair hung down around her shoulders, her face was very pale, but she had managed to get some lipstick on before the officers took all her things away from her." According to Day, a prisoner "with short hair and a leather wristband" spotted Malina and barked out to a guard, "Put her in my cell!" Up to that point, Dorothy Day had borne everything, including a vaginal search which had left her bleeding and in pain, quietly. Now she spoke out, calling out to the guard with implacable authority. "She [Malina] is to be put in my cell." Malina and Day became "cellies," sharing a dark, airless, cockroach-infested six-by-nine foot cement room. That first night, Malina cried herself to sleep.

Dorothy Day was nobody to mess with, as anyone who came into contact with her would attest. In her autobiography, *The Long Loneliness*, Day writes easily about her upbringing, the only girl in a family of hard-drinking Irish Catholic New York City newspapermen. Unlike her brothers, Dorothy loved to read, and she was religious enough in high school to make a study of the early Christian saints. In college at the University of Illinois, she organized the socialist club's women's section. She dropped out of school when she was nineteen and returned to New York, where she wrote for the Socialist Party's daily newspaper, *The Call*. She interviewed Trotsky when he was living on St. Marks Place. She stood guard at an abortion clinic.

Day is much less forthcoming, however, about her Greenwich Village years. In her sixties, she was not amused when Malcom Cowley wrote in a *New Yorker* profile that when Day was in her twenties, "gangsters admired her because she could drink them under the table." Back then, Day had an affair with Mike Gold, who would go on to edit the Communist *Daily Worker* and pen the classic American proletarian novel *Jews Without Money*. She married a man twenty years her senior, and divorced him within a year. She had an abortion. She lived upstairs from the Provincetown Players on MacDougal Street and drank rye whiskey with Eugene O'Neill at the Golden Swan, a radical hangout at Sixth Avenue and Fourth Street, where he was mooning over journalist Louise Bryant.

In 1923, she published a thinly disguised autobiographical novel, *The 11th Virgin*, sold it to Hollywood for $5,000, and bought a fisherman's shack on Staten Island, where she gave birth to her daughter, Tamar, whose father was an English anarchist and atheist named Forster Batterham. Throughout her pregnancy she had been praying every day. Now she insisted that Tamar be baptized, and the couple quarreled bitterly. The day of the baptism, Batterham prepared a feast from his lobster traps, then moved out. When he returned a few weeks later to attempt a reconciliation, Dorothy Day sent him away. She was baptized and took communion for the first time as an adult the next day. In 1929, she did a brief stint as a screenwriter at Pathé Motion

Picture Company in Hollywood, than traveled with her daughter in Mexico. She writes that she was on the verge of losing her faith when she met Peter Maurin, an itinerant mystic from the French Pyrenees in a single ill-fitting suit bulging with pamphlets and books. Sharing a determination to do something to ease human suffering; they cofounded the Catholic Worker. For Day and Maurin and the thousands who've joined the Catholic Workers since, faith and action are one. Their Christ is the revolutionary Christ, their model the communitarian life shared by Christ and his disciples. The life of a Catholic Worker, as conceived by Day and Maurin, was a life motivated by profound faith and intellectual rigor, a life of compassion and cool.

Everyone at the Women's House of Detention was awed by Dorothy Day, Malina reports. "No one sassed her." Though she felt guilty about not being able to help her daughter Tamar, who by now was expecting her eighth child, Day welcomed the opportunity to spend time in jail. "We visited prisoners by becoming prisoners ourselves," she later wrote in *The Catholic Worker*. Most of the guards were Catholic, too, and many of them brought around their daily missals for Day to autograph.

By day, the seventh floor of the prison reverberated with the clanging metal of keys and cell doors, and rec-room television blare punctuated by the shouts and jeers and taunts of nine hundred prisoners. "I think eight hundred were prostitutes," Malina later told an interviewer, "and about seven hundred of them were drug addicts." Malina mopped floors and Day ironed in the prison laundry. Every evening, women would stop by Cell 13, Corridor A to drink Kool-Aid, eat Ritz crackers, and shoot the breeze. Dorothy Day had been around, and it showed in the nonjudgmental, open-hearted manner with which she received these guests. Though Malina had spent most of her young life in radical politics and on the experimental edge of the theater world, this was the first time that she'd been immersed in a world of cool in its slavery-born sense, where attitude and stance is the only self-defense against overwhelming rage. "I like you," Malina says one prisoner told her, "but let's face it. You're a square."

Every night after their visitors left, Dorothy Day would read to Malina from the lives of the saints. Then, following lights out, Malina would lie awake in her bunk listening to a junkie named Thelma Gadsden rock the cell block with her raucous bedtime routines, which transformed the sad fact of the prisoners' lives into high comedy, transmuting powerlessness into cool, making a dollar out of fifteen cents.

THE WHITE NEGROES

The San Remo, or the "Sans Remorse," as Judith Malina sometimes refers to it in her diaries, had been a bar at the corner of Bleecker and MacDougal for almost as long as there had been a Little Italy in New York. After World War II, the "Remo's" atmosphere, its pressed-tin ceiling, black-and-white floor tiles, and dollar salads with all the bread and butter you could eat started attracting a more Bohemian crowd. "Professor Seagull," gray-bearded Joe Gould, a madman and a sweet, pathetic old goof, was a San Remo icon— standing in the middle of the room with a cardboard sign over his shoulders selling his nonexistent "Oral History of The World," flapping his arms and squawking like a gull. On his maiden visit to the San Remo in 1950, future writer Ron Sukenick, straight out of Midwood High in Brooklyn, saw a woman wearing blue jeans for the first time.

In *The Subterraneans*, Jack Kerouac has his Allen Ginsberg character, Adam Moorad, describe the denizens of the San Remo (which Kerouac transposed to San Francisco's North Beach and renamed the Mask) as "hip without being slick . . . intelligent without being corny, they are intellectual as hell and know all about Pound without being pretentious or talking too much about it, they are very quiet, they are very Christlike."

The San Remo crowd fascinated LeRoi Jones, who arrived in the Village in 1957 after getting kicked out of the air force as a security risk. (One of his offenses was subscribing to the then–left-wing *Partisan Review*.) Raised middle-class, he was anxious to jump into the growing bohemian scene. He was taken by "not just the wild-looking women in black stockings," as he writes in *The Autobiography of LeRoi Jones/Amiri Baraka*, "but the whole scene . . . This was the Village. Weird! Something else was happening other than what I knew about. Wild stuff. Free open shit. Look at that weird-looking woman. I bet she'd fuck. I bet she knows about all kinds of heavy shit. And I bet she'd

fuck." **At a time when thirty states still had laws banning miscegenation, the San Remo was one of the places in the United States where interracial couples knew they would be cool.**

In the early fifties Judith Malina went to the San Remo nearly every night. There, she met the beat daddies: William S. Burroughs, Allen Ginsberg, Jack Kerouac, and Gregory Corso, who was born practically across the street in an apartment above the funeral parlor at 190 Bleecker. The Remo was where she got to know Maya Deren, the first important female independent filmmaker, who roamed the Village with her cats; it was where she met Miles Davis and Tennessee Williams and Gore Vidal. Introduced to Malina and Beck at the San Remo, the street photographer Weegee asked them to pose nude for his book *The Village* (they passed). John Cage taught Malina to throw the *I Ching* at one of the Remo's scarred wooden booths.

Throughout the fall of 1953, Malina met James Agee at the San Remo, where he was drinking himself to death while writing his novel *A Death in the Family*, which would receive a posthumous Pulitzer Prize; they would retreat to his candlelit room in a backyard house on Cornelia Street and make love.

Malina was being torn in many different directions: between family and theater, her husband, and her many lovers.

After passing out one night in the San Remo, she started seeing her shrink, Paul Goodman, three times a week. The flamboyantly bisexual Goodman, who had been refused a permanent teaching position at Black Mountain by Olson after he spent the 1950 summer session cruising the male students, caused Malina and Beck all sorts of problems. He encouraged Beck to take male lovers. He hustled them both mercilessly to produce his talky, stilted verse dramas. But he instilled in them the necessity of "drawing a line" between themselves and the mainstream culture. Increasingly the Living Theatre would confront the mainstream with its bohemian values. Cool was coming out of the shadows.

Already famous for his critically acclaimed and hugely popular World War II novel *The Naked and the Dead*, Norman Mailer took it upon himself to define the hipster phenomenon, first in his column, "Advertisements for Myself," which appeared in the earliest issues of *The Village Voice*, and then, in September 1957, in an essay called "The White Negro: Superficial Reflections on the Hipster" published in the magazine *Dissent*. At the time,

Gregory Corso at the "Beat Hotel," 9 rue Git-Le-Coeur, Paris, 1957.

Norman Mailer,
early 1950s.

most hipsters dismissed Mailer's efforts as the work of a hopeless square, a mainstream mind trying to annex the avant-garde. But Mailer was in a genuine state of crisis. His second novel, *The Deer Park*, had tanked. His second marriage was falling apart. And despite the fact that he was an original investor in the *Voice*, he'd resigned his column after less than four months, claiming to be fed up with the typos that kept appearing in it. For the only time in his life, Mailer was smoking a lot of pot and gobbling diet pills. Surrounded by hipsters, yet not one of them, Mailer was smart enough to recognize that the subterraneans were no longer restricted to the San Remo. They were part of a phenomenon spreading across the land. For the sake of his own sanity, Mailer had to understand cool.

The world is a "giant jungle," Mailer stated in "The White Negro," and cool a survival tool. According to Mailer, a "cool cat" said " 'I dig' because neither knowledge or imagination comes easily" and "one must occasionally exhaust oneself by digging into the self in order to perceive. It is essential to dig the most," Mailer went on, "for if you do not dig you lose your superiority over the Square, and so you are less likely to be cool (to be in control of a situation because you have swung where the Square has not, or because you have allowed to come to consciousness a pain, a guilt, a shame, or a desire which the other has not had the courage to face)." **If one were not cool, as Mailer well knew, one was in danger of being put down, "and of course one can hardly afford to be put down too often, or one is beat, one has lost one's confidence, one has lost one's will, one is impotent in the world of action."**

According to "The White Negro," the source of all cool "is the Negro, for he has been living on the margin between totalitarianism and democracy for two centuries." To Mailer, cool was sexual, or more accurately, postcoital, the result of a "ménage à trois" involving the bohemian, the juvenile delinquent, and the Negro. To "be considered a white Negro," a "wise primitive," or a "psychic outlaw," to absorb "the existentialist synapses of the Negro," Mailer wrote, it took good sex. In other words, cool was capable of being seduced.

IS THIS THE WAY COOL PASSES FROM BLACK TO WHITE? IS THIS HOW COOL ENTERS THE MAINSTREAM?

"At lilac evening I walked with every muscle aching among the lights of 27th and Welton in the Denver colored section, wishing I were a Negro, feeling that the best the white world had offered was not enough ecstasy for me, not enough life, joy, kicks, darkness, music. Not enough night."

—Jack Kerouac, *On the Road*

Jack Gelber remembers being fifteen or sixteen the first time he heard the word "cool." "If you were a black musician, wore a certain kind of clothes, had a certain kind of attitude," he explained, "you were cool." The good-looking blond son of an alcoholic Jewish tinsmith, a hipster from the South Side of Chicago who'd been listening to jazz since he was a kid, Gelber put himself through the University of Illinois, then moved to San Francisco in 1953. He worked on the docks when he needed money and hung out at Jimbo's Bop City, in the Fillmore, cool ground zero, listening to tenor players like Dexter Gordon and Wardell Gray. If there were a cool hall of fame, Jack Gelber would already be in it for painting the gold inside the lettering of the original City Lights Bookstore sign.

After drifting to New York in the mid-fifties, as he reminisced nearly a half-century later while relaxing on a couch in his comfortable West Eighteenth Street loft, Gelber "got involved with a group of junkies" on the Lower East Side, and one day the cops kicked down his door. Though he claims to have been just making cocoa, they busted him for possession of heroin, and he spent the next several weeks in the Tombs. When he got out, his pregnant wife supported the family by working as a secretary while he wrote *The Connection*, a play he says is based on people he met hanging out in a "shooting gallery" over a Chinese laundry in North Beach.

In April 1958, Gelber, then twenty-five, ran into a friend on the street who'd just seen a Living Theatre production. "He told me they ought to do my play," Gelber remembers, so Gelber dropped off a script at Judith Malina and Julian Beck's apartment. Within hours, the way Malina remembers it, Beck burst into their bedroom, waving Gelber's script and screaming "We've got to do this play!"

The Connection is about eight sick junkies in a dingy downtown Manhattan loft, waiting for a dealer named Cowboy to come back with the "horse." Featuring nearly identical casts, both the Living Theatre production and the 1961 movie version directed by Shirley Clarke (who in 1964 would make a documentary-style feature about Harlem street kids called *The Cool World*) open with Sol (Jerome Raphael)—who looks like a kind of ragged, scholarly bum, wearing a ripped sweatshirt and in need of a shave—squinting into a pair of binoculars at a day-world filled with squares, far, far away on the other side of a grime-streaked window. A second white guy, Ernie (Garry Goodrow), wears white sneakers and a trench coat and is passed out, face down on the only table in the raw loft, much to the disgust of his host, Leach, played by a third white guy, Warren Finnerty, with an extremely cool walk that has him bobbing on the balls of his feet, shoulders hunched like a boxer's, as he scurries around tidying up the pad.

Sam (Jimmy Anderson), junkie number four, pads around the loft in a grimy T-shirt and torn flip-flops. In contrast to Sol, who can read Greek and Hebrew, Sam probably can't even read and write English. Still, Sol, who is white, and Sam, who is black, are two of a kind: they live to get high, rubbed by the awful simplicity of their lives down to a nub of pure yen. A quartet of real-life bop musicians enter, hauling their instruments up the loft stairs, led by pianist Freddie Redd and alto saxophonist Jackie McLean. All-too-real drug problems had cost all the band members their cabaret cards, which is why they became very available to work at the Living Theatre for thirty-five dollars per week. They too have come to Leach's to score, and they utilize the waiting to rehearse some of Redd's tunes.

As the most down junkie in the room, the man with the least, the closest to the street, Sam is the ultimate arbiter of cool. He can't stand Leach, who gets his dope free in return for letting the other junkies use his place. When Leach produces a pineapple out of his old wood-burning stove, then

Carl Lee as Cowboy in The Connection *with Ira Lewis as Jaybird in the background, 1959.*

only offers slices of it to the musicians, Sam comments that Leach is "queer without being queer. He thinks like a chick."

Sam doesn't like Ernie, either, because Ernie once threw a junkie who'd overdosed out a fifth-story window without even making sure the guy was dead. But Sam admires Sol. "He breaks me up," he chuckles appreciatively. "A stand-up cat. Solly was born hip." Sol winks at the audience. "I'm the only white man the natives trust." Ernie says that Sam and Sol connect with each other through the music: "Both of them dig music. I mean they *dig* it. I mean they have an emotional digging."

The figure of Charlie Parker looms large above *The Connection*. In the late Fifties, Jackie McLean was widely considered to be Charlie Parker's most brilliant protégé. The only photo on the wall of Leach's loft is of Parker. And the band just hangs around scratching themselves and muttering until a mysterious tramp comes in, silently plugs a portable 78 RPM Victrola into a light socket, and plays a piece of a Charlie Parker solo, which goads them into rehearsal. By 1959, though, Charlie Parker had already been dead for four years, and cool meant Miles Davis. When the dealer, Cowboy (Carl Lee, son of Canada Lee, the first black Broadway musical star), finally arrives with a doddering Salvation Army volunteer (Sister Salvation, played by Barbara Winchester) leaning on his arm, he is dressed all in white—"immaculately sharp," in the words of Jackie McLean—with impenetrable shades and a red bandanna knotted at his neck like a noose. Like Cowboy, Carl Lee worked hard at the part, at his cool. **Jack Gelber remembers Lee as "the epitome of cool"; Garry Goodrow says that Lee once dragged a big-time heroin dealer down from Harlem to critique his performance. Lee worked as the maître d' at the Café Bohemia, a Village jazz club, where he'd become friendly with Miles Davis, who played there all the time.** Goodrow says that Cowboy was Carl Lee's conscious attempt to emulate Miles's style.

In *The Connection*, everybody wants to be cooler. The white junkies want to be as cool as the black junkies, and all the junkies want to be as cool as the musicians, who never seem to lose their cool. Freddie Redd is so cool, so completely unadorned and understatedly dressed as he plays his chunky chords, a cigarette dangling out of one corner of his mouth, that he could pass by on the street like a phantom, like an old-time paradigm of cool, flying beneath the radar. The one person who never loses his cool, even

when he's so stoned that he falls off his stool, is Jackie McLean—the only person in the movie version who actually says, "It's cool."

Of all the white junkies yearning to be cool—to get their cool fix—Ernie, toting around a trumpet mouthpiece that he pretends to play, complaining all the while that he's been forced to hock his horn to buy junk, is the most pathetic. Claiming that he needs to make a gig, Ernie begs Jackie McLean to lend him his horn. Many in *The Connection*'s audience would have been familiar with the story of Charlie Parker borrowing McLean's horn outside the Open Door on the pretext of needing it to play a gig and then pawning it. In *The Connection*, McLean doesn't even dignify Ernie's plea with a reply.

Soon after the musicians arrive, Jim Dunn (William Redfield), a white documentary filmmaker, bursts in, his black cameraman in tow. It quickly becomes apparent that the heroin deal is being financed by the overbearing filmmaker, who wants to make a documentary about junkies, even though he'd never actually met one until his cameraman introduced him to Cowboy, a childhood friend. "I'm not interested in making a Hollywood movie," Dunn tells anyone who'll listen. "I'm trying to make an honest human document."

Bustling about nervously, shoving a light meter in the junkies' faces, assaulting their dilated pupils with his camera lights, the director does his best to bring everybody down, then acts wounded when his subjects get pissed off. "Hey," he warns, "let's not get hostile." Tension mounts as the director's crudeness forces even Cowboy to momentarily lose his cool. He removes his shades—drops his cool—and reveals the weariness beneath his hip, reptilian veneer. "I'm followed every night. I'm tired, man," he almost pleads to Dunn. Then, recovering his swagger, he sneers, "Is that what you want, *mannn*?"

One by one, the junkies retreat to Leach's toilet to get off, as Sister Salvation, the old white lady, gazes on serenely, completely oblivious to what is going on right under her nose in the cool world. When they're all high, they offer the director a taste, almost as a joke. To their surprise, he jumps at the chance. When he comes out of the bathroom, he's talking hip for the first time. "Don't be a drag, man," he giggles to J. J. Burden (Roscoe Lee Browne), his cameraman, scratching himself as he slips into a nod. Seduced by the dope, Dunn tells Burden to finish the film himself, but when he comes down, he doesn't act like he thinks his decision was worth it. "Is this all?" he asks everybody. "Is this all?" The junkies shrug impatiently: Dunn can't expect to become cool in a day.

As soon as Leach shoots up, he starts to whine. "I'm not high, Cowboy. I didn't get a flash." "Oh cool it, man," Cowboy replies. "You just got a higher tolerance, dig? It's been ten years since I had a flash." Leach pleads for another hit. Cowboy finally relents, palming him a glassine envelope with a shrug. "It's your life." Leach hits himself up and immediately collapses to the floor with an o.d.

Proffering a lame excuse, Ernie bugs out immediately. The musicians suddenly remember that they have someplace else to be. Cowboy, Sam, and Sol are left to save Leach's life. They lay him face down on the bed, and Cowboy squats down and pounds Leach's back to keep his heart beating, trying to sustain a pulse. *The Connection* ends with the return of the silent tramp, who plugs in his portable record player once again and spins the same Charlie Parker solo as Cowboy rides Leach like a horse, humping him from behind, seduced. Is this the way cool passes from black to white? Is this how cool enters the mainstream?

The Connection was savaged by the mainstream press; the Times, for example, sent a second-string reviewer who called the play "nothing more than a farrago of dirt, small-time philosophy, empty talk and extended runs of 'cool' music." Lame reviews from the mainstream press couldn't kill The Connection, though; Bohemia had grown too powerful. 1959 was the year that off-Broadway theater came into its own. In 1959, for the first time, more plays were produced off Broadway than on. There was an audience for these shows, and it was growing and getting its information from people like *The Village Voice*'s theater critic, Jerry Tallmer, who leapt to *The Connection*'s defense, and Norman Mailer and Allen Ginsberg, who also chimed in favorably. Bad-boy British critic Kenneth Tynan called *The Connection* the most exciting American drama since the war.

Every night, the 160 people packed into the theater leaned out of their seats with their eyes glued to Warren Finnerty as he knotted a belt just above his elbow and stuck a spike into his vein. "Is it real?" audiences whispered to each other, as he slumped to the floor unconscious. In his "unauthorized autobiography" *What Did I Do?*, painter Larry Rivers says Garry Goodrow told him that "there was real heroin in the capsules handed out to

Overleaf:

Warren Finnerty as

Leach in The

Connection, 1959.

the anxious actors waiting onstage, some of whom shot up in front of the audience." "*The Connection*," Julian Beck wrote later in his life, "depicts the confessions of the dregs of society as so pitiably human that they become all of us." During intermission, the cast members convincingly hustled people in the lobby for dope money.

Malina and Beck dedicated the production to the memory of Thelma Gadsden "and all the other junkies dead or alive in the Women's House of D." A few months after she got out of prison, Thelma Gadsden died going cold turkey in a Salvation Army shelter, Malina explained. In the program, Malina and Beck reprinted Antonin Artaud's essay "The Theater and Culture," which equates participants in theater with victims of the Inquisition who while being "burnt at the stake" were so intent on delivering their apocalyptic message that they were "signaling through the flames."

When I told Jack Gelber I was writing about Judith Malina for *Birth of the Cool*, he snapped, "I can't imagine anybody less cool than Judith Malina," citing hassles he blamed on Malina and her husband's overblown emotions during *The Connection*'s New York run that still rankled forty years later. But it was very cool to have produced *The Connection* and to have succeeded in flinging it into the face of the mass culture. Beck and Malina *were* cool, as consumed by their vision as the junkies were by their heroin, as the victims of the Inquisition were by the flames.

"A COOL PLAY"

"I'm not a Catholic," Judith Malina shrugged, "so I don't know about saints. But as far as human sanctity goes, Dorothy went as far as one could go. She was good as one can be." It was 1997, and we were seated on a couch in the Upper West Side apartment that once belonged to Julian Beck's parents and now doubles as the Living Theatre's office and Malina's stateside residence. The Living Theatre now spends half the year in Europe, but when Malina's in New York, she shares this place with her lover, Hanon Reznikov, her and

Beck's daughter Isha, and Isha's son. Though Julian Beck's been dead for ten years, the room is still dominated by racks of his canvases. There are suitcases everywhere. Most of the furniture is covered with sheets. It feels like everybody is about to hit the road.

At seventy, tiny and energetic, sporting big Mexican silver earrings and a peace sign on a chain around her neck, Malina tried to articulate what Dorothy Day meant to her. "People make her out now to be very somber and strict, but she was a woman of enormous humor and charm. Most of our conversations were either practical or long, narrative chapters out of our life stories," Malina reflected. **"It was by her actions and her restraints that she showed me what to do. I felt myself to be in the presence of someone in whom I could have complete faith, someone who does the right thing, even the holy thing, at every moment."**

Malina says that whatever she knows about "the theatricalization of politics," she learned from Dorothy Day. "Whenever you organize mass demonstrations, whenever you have a public protest, it is likely to take its natural form, which is to end up in riot and battle. But the leap from confrontation to violence is cooled out by theatricalization." Every time the Living Theatre is in Times Square giving the performance they stage whenever one of the three thousand men and women currently on a death row in America is executed, Malina says she thinks about Dorothy Day.

As part of the play, she and the other actors confront total strangers and try to get them to promise not to kill anybody. Malina says she starts by trying to persuade the cornered passerby to promise at least not to kill her. If they're willing to go that far, she explains, the actor tries to get the pedestrian to promise he or she will never bomb a city, never shoot into a crowd. "If you confront someone," she explains, "the problem becomes immediately to make it a loving relationship." Suddenly Malina the actress is in the middle of a tense Times Square confrontation, rapping with an angry cop, cajoling him, seducing him with her voice and eyes, trying to cool him out. "Like, if he's your arresting officer, how do you soften this guy up?" she asks. "How do you let him know it's cool to be in my play?" She smiles at me as if I were a policeman and she were Dorothy Day. "It's a cool play."

THE AGE
OF COOL

"COOL ON EVERYTHING"

By the end of the 1950s, cool was getting hot. With the explosion of television and independent cinema and American teens' embrace of cool rebels, cool was becoming a commodity.

In 1944, in the mainstream media, there was still something slimy about cool. In Robert Siodmak's *Phantom Lady*, one of the most expressionistic and psychologically charged of all film noirs, the jazz drummer, Cliff, played by the pint-sized Elisha Cook Jr., is a leering grotesque in a zoot suit. "You like jazz?" he asks Ella Raines, the girl he's just picked up, who is masquerading as a band groupie in an attempt to discover who really murdered her boss's wife. "I'm a hip kitten," she winks. "Ooh, baby," Cliff grins in anticipation, leading her down the steps into a Manhattan basement for a whiskey-fueled jam session.

By the mid-fifties, cool had come up from the underground in a slew of mainstream movies aimed at teenagers. Cliff's swaggering, aggressive, hot sexuality had evolved into a potent, laid-back cool. In Laslo Benedek's *The Wild One* (1954), Marlon Brando, sporting sunglasses and a leather cap in his role as the leader of one of the two outlaw motorcycle packs that's taken over a little town, deliberately set out, he told biographer Bob Thomas, "to do something worthwhile, to explain the psychology of the hipster." To Brando, a hipster was somebody brave enough to stand against the whole world, yet cool enough not to make a big thing out of it. "Hey, Johnny," the local coffee shop waitress calls out to him, "what are you rebelling against?" Brando's shrugged comeback came to symbolize cool in the fifties: "Whaddya got?"

As the troubled teen trying to make sense out of his life, James Dean in Nicholas Ray's *Rebel Without a Cause* (1954) showed every high school outsider coping with the world's hypocrisies that he or she could be cool. "Mom, Dad, this is Judy," Dean mumbles shyly, introducing Natalie Wood to his parents at the end of *Rebel*. "She's my friend." With the right attitude, the right stance, even a loser can get the girl. When Bill Haley and the Comets sang "Rock Around the Clock" as the credits rolled over a New York cityscape of finger-popping, head-bobbing, tousle-headed hip urban teens in

James Dean in Nicholas Ray's Rebel Without a Cause, 1955.

Blackboard Jungle (1955), cool exploded from movie screens across America. *Glenn Ford and* Movie cool was no longer the province of gangsters like Paul Muni and *Sidney Poitier* George Raft, but of the *misunderstood*. *(back center) in*

In "The Philosophy of the Beat Generation," an article he wrote for *Richard Brooks's* *Esquire* magazine in March 1958, Jack Kerouac tried vainly to explain that all *Blackboard* of this furor had nothing to do with what he'd meant by cool. Post–Korean *Jungle, 1955.* War teenagers had "picked up the gestures and the style"—Elvis Presley's sideburns, Marlon Brando's white T-shirt, James Dean's "'twisted,' slouchy look" were the examples he used—but they missed the passion and yea-saying exuberance included in his own conception of cool. His heroes were "hot," he insisted, not "cool and beat." But nobody was listening: Kerouac was like a man screaming into a cold wind.

By the end of the fifties a spate of articles simultaneously celebrating and deploring beatniks in *Life*, *Time*, and *Newsweek* had inextricably linked beat and cool in the public mind to the point of both intentional and unintentional parodies.

In 1959, schlockmeister Albert G. Zugsmith produced *The Beat Generation*, starring Mamie Van Doren. That same year, Maynard G. Krebs, played by Bob Denver, became the world's best-known beatnik via the television series *The Many Loves of Dobie Gillis*. To confirm Kerouac's very worst fears, in 1960 a ludicrous film version of *The Subterraneans* (still the only one of Kerouac's books made into a movie or TV show), starred the very white Leslie Caron in pedal pushers and a striped sweater snapping her fingers as Mardou Fox.

Thomas Frank points out in his highly influential study of hip consumerism, *The Conquest of Cool*, that by the beginning of the sixties the "counter-cultural style" had become a permanent fixture on the American scene. For the first time, Frank maintains, Americans were buying things not simply because they needed them, or to try to fit in or to keep up with the Joneses, but to demonstrate that they were wise (in Dizzy Gillespie's sense of the word "hip") to the ways of American culture.

Advertisers were quick to take note. Ads like Volkswagen's ostensibly low-budget black-and-white Beetle ads actually made fun of Madison Avenue's traditional sunny, family, full-color approach to selling automobiles. By playing to the perennial adolescent need to rebel against whatever is established or received, sixties advertising, climaxing with Columbia Records' notorious 1968 advertising campaign, "The Man Can't Bust Our Music," encouraged Americans to critique the world by buying different things. In Frank's sense, even Miles Davis's *Birth of the Cool* was an attempt to turn cool into a commodity. To Thomas Frank, cool was "just a stage in the development of the values of the American middle class."

Cool had moved so far toward the mainstream consciousness that there was a hipster backlash. By 1959, comedian Lenny Bruce was doing a send-up of the kind of "like, dig man" coffee house poetry: "Psychopathia sexualis / I'm in love with a horse / That comes from Dallas." Vampira, star of *Plan 9 From Outer Space*, often considered the worst movie ever made, recites poetry in *The Beat Generation*. In 1961, Chicago's improvisational comedy troupe The Committee put out an LP, *How to Speak Hip*, making fun of cool. On it, John Brent tries to explain to Del Close the difference between cool and uncool: "It's uncool to claim you used to room with Bird, or to claim you have his ax. Or to ask, 'Who's Bird?'"

In his autobiography, the socialist writer and organizer Michael Harrington, himself a San Remo and Catholic Worker alum, says that in the late fifties and early sixties, hip was a victim of its own success. "Bohemia," he states, "could not survive the passing of its polar opposite and precondition, middle-class morality . . . deprived of the stifling atmosphere without which it could not breathe."

In 1964, Marshall McLuhan, the director of the Center for Culture and Technology at the University of Toronto, published *Understanding Media,* the first effort to describe the psychic and social consequences of TV. Television, he posited, was a cool medium, as opposed to hot media like radio and newspapers, which were data-rich. A "cool medium" like television, with its relatively meager amount of information, "leaves much more for the listener or user to do," is more involving, in the same way that dark glasses create an "inscrutable and inaccessible image that invites a great deal of participation." Dark glasses encourage us to complete a face's physical features, says McLuhan, as TV leaves it to the viewer to resolve the mosaic beamed from its screen. "The hot form excludes," McLuhan pronounced, "and the cool one includes."

Lenny Bruce,
1959.

In media terms, the age of cool began at precisely 10:00 P.M. Eastern Standard Time on February 14, 1962, when CBS-TV News preempted its dra-

matic series *Circle Theater* for "A Tour of the White House with Mrs. John F. Kennedy." Kennedy's was the first presidency to understand TV, a fact that had been made clear by the first-ever televised presidential debate in the summer of 1960, also on CBS, when a suntanned JFK, fresh from a California motorcade, soundly defeated a drained, cadaverous, and demoralized Richard Nixon and assured himself the presidency.

Upon the Kennedys' arrival in Washington, Jacqueline Kennedy set out to transform the dowdy executive mansion room by room. She started by persuading Congress to place the White House under National Park Service jurisdiction, which made donations to restore the building tax-deductible. Then she created the position of White House curator and established a fine arts committee to advise her on restoration. She published a White House guidebook, restocked the White House library, and restored the Rose Garden. To let people know about her campaign, she invited a CBS camera crew to view the early results—hence the Valentine's Day, 1962, broadcast.

With her breathy yet cultured whisper, in those flat pumps she wore so she wouldn't be so much taller than everybody else, and her triple strand of pearls, Jackie led distinguished senior correspondent Charles Collingwood on a White House tour that included stops in the freshly restored State Dining Room, the Red Room, and the lavish East Room, where just a few nights earlier Pablo Casals had serenaded a dinner honoring American Nobel Prize winners. Along the way, she discussed each room's history.

These, however, were only the White House's public rooms. From the days of Andrew Jackson until the early twentieth century, every New Year's Day the White House doors were flung open and anybody could come in and shake the president's hand. Neither the press nor the general public, however, were customarily permitted upstairs into the family quarters. **At Mrs. Kennedy's invitation, for the first time ever, the public and press were ushered via the CBS camera crew up the stairs and into the Lincoln bedroom, then into the Madison family's sitting room, where they were joined by the president,** fresh from a top-secret wrangle over whether to commit the first American helicopters and "advisors" to prop up the government of South Vietnam. Now, with the first "television war" only months away, television had penetrated the "New Frontier." Cool had entered the White House.

STRUGGLING TO REMAIN COOL

In 1957, the actor John Cassavetes, twenty-seven, went on Jean Shepherd's
Night People on WOR, the hippest radio show in Manhattan, to publicize his
new movie, a pedestrian Martin Ritt *policier* called *Edge of the City*. The New
York–born son of a Greek immigrant importer-exporter, the handsome,
dark-eyed Cassavetes was already making a name for himself playing edgy
misfits and tightly torqued tough guys in low-budget double-feature fodder
like *The Killers* and *Crime in the Streets*. Shepherd, a wildly improvisational
radio monologist, was then at the top of his game and he boasted a large
and dedicated audience. Shepherd's flock responded enthusiastically when
Cassavetes claimed that he could make a better movie than Martin Ritt, and
if they wanted to see an alternative to the Hollywood mindset, they should
send in money to fund a project Cassavetes was creating in collaboration
with his drama workshop. Over the next few days, two thousand dollars in
bills and coins poured in.

A week later, Cassavetes started his film, shooting with the then-
revolutionary hand-held sixteen-millimeter black-and-white camera, rented lights, a volunteer crew, and a cast composed of members of his acting
workshop. Every take of the movie—which took two years to complete—was
improvised, and shot in Cassavetes's apartment, his friends' apartments, or
on streets and in alleyways in a semidocumentary style using real names.
Bass player Charles Mingus did the score. The final product was titled
Shadows.

"We were an intentional collection of people who decided to make a
movie," Maurice (Moe) McKendree, who helped produce and edit the film,
told me, "and we did." They felt like they were on a mission to, as *Shadows*
star Lelia Goldoni puts it forty years later, "break the forms of the past."
They were so poor that the first few scenes of *Shadows* were lit by a floor
lamp using a two-hundred-watt bulb that they carried around the streets
and plugged in wherever they could find an outlet. "Whatever it was we
were doing," says Moe McKendree, "at least we were doing *something*!"

The focus of *Shadows* is two weeks in the lives of a trio of African-

American siblings living together in a Greenwich Village pad crowded with rickety bookshelves full of paperback books. Hugh (Hugh Hurd), the older brother, is a button-downed Ivy League alumnus in clothes worn so tight that he looks like his head is going to explode. He is a singer—hard-working and dedicated, but amazingly untalented—who accepts a horrible job as an emcee at a strip club so that he can help support his younger brother and sister, who are too immature and self-centered to show any gratitude.

His younger brother, Ben (Ben Carruthers), is a skinny hipster with a sallow, subterranean pallor. With his gravelly Miles Davis mumble and his impenetrable wraparound shades, Ben is a trumpet player without a trumpet. Like Garry Goodrow's Ernie in *The Connection*, he's hiding emotional vulnerablility behind his hipness. Hugh and Ben's little sister, Lelia (Goldoni), is just nineteen, recently back in New York from Los Angeles, all fluttery, nail-bitten intelligence and raw nerve—aware that she is beautiful but trying to figure out who she is.

Bored with the belabored come-ons of a stuffy white intellectual who's just published a novel about the beat generation (a character likely based on Chandler Brossard, the *New Yorker* "Talk of the Town" contributor whose novel of the San Remo set, *Who Walk in Darkness*, had just been published), Lelia loses her virginity to Tony (Tony Ray, son of Nick Ray, director of *Rebel Without a Cause*), a handsome white boy who moves in on her with a macho cool. When Tony meet's Lelia's much darker-skinned brother Hugh, Tony realizes that Lelia is black and dumps her—not that she seems to care too much. But Tony can't stay away. When he tries to see her again, though, Lelia's two older brothers threaten to kick his ass for being such a racist.

The coolest thing about *Shadows* is that, without preaching, it turns the concept of race upside down. Lelia Goldoni's parents were Sicilian; Ben Carruthers was only about one-sixteenth African-American. (In the year after the making of *Shadows*, the two got married and divorced.) In the racially charged American atmosphere of 1957—at the same time they were shooting the film, President Eisenhower was sending federal troops to desegregate Little Rock Central High School—they were sexual outsiders. In *Shadows*, Cassavetes represents race as a total illusion. In Greenwich Village, race has been subsumed in the desire to be cool.

John Cassavetes.

When they started shooting *Shadows*, none of the participants knew

what they were doing. Actors improvised, and the story evolved as the shooting progressed intermittently over the next two years. As a result, the scenes were wildly uneven in tone, jittery with hesitation and false starts. There is little physical action, and everybody appears hemmed in and ready to explode, struggling to remain cool.

Lelia Goldoni in John Cassavetes's Shadows, 1960.

Their coolness, then, is almost a defense mechanism; as Ray Carney, probably Cassavetes's most astute critic, writes, cool "was a symptom, not of not caring, but of caring too much. Given such an emotionally exposed and vulnerable position" as that which *Shadows* required, "it was necessary to maintain one's cool as much as possible." But Cassavetes was never a hipster, says Moe McKendree, "and wouldn't have considered himself so." He didn't want his characters to act cool: he wanted them to explore their feelings and share them with each other. The tension between the director and his cool actors is at the core of *Shadows*'s emotional resonance.

Cassavetes premiered *Shadows* around Christmastime, 1958, at the Paris Theater in Greenwich Village, where there was an audience waiting for a movie that told the story of their lives. More than 2,000 people showed up for three midnight screenings. Among the throng was Jonas Mekas.

At the time he saw *Shadows*, Jonas Mekas was emerging as the voice of the New American cinema. Just nine years earlier, in 1949, he had been a nineteen-year-old poet newly arrived in New York with his brother Adolfas after surviving both the Russian and Nazi occupations of his native Lithuania, followed by five years in a displaced-persons camp. On his second night in the city, living in Brooklyn, he writes in his autobiography *I Had Nowhere to Go*, he saw *The Cabinet of Dr. Caligari* at a Times Square theater. **Growing up in a village of a hundred people, he'd never even seen a movie camera, but a few days later he borrowed three hundred dollars, bought a 16-millimeter movie camera, and started shooting footage that would eventually be edited into his bleak and fleeting diary-like films such as *Guns of the Trees*.** In 1955, he and his brother founded the quarterly *Film Culture*, "America's Independent Motion Picture Magazine." Jonas served as publisher and editor-in-chief while Adolfas was one of the editors. In November 1958, while still editing *Film Culture*, he became *The Village Voice*'s first film columnist.

Sitting in the Paris, Mekas was looking for something special. By 1958,

France's Nouvelle Vague had washed across the Atlantic, with Jean-Luc Godard's *Breathless*, François Truffaut's *The 400 Blows*, and Alain Resnais's *Hiroshima, Mon Amour* becoming U.S. underground hits. *Breathless*, with Jean-Paul Belmondo as the young thief and flaxen-haired Jean Seberg as his American dream girl selling the *New York Herald-Tribune* on the Champs-Elysées, had already entered the pantheon of cool. **Unlike American movies, which were primarily the product of movie factories, or studios, the French "New Wave" reflected the outsider sensibilities of the films' directors.** Now Jonas Mekas was looking for an American new wave to ride. He had became aware of *Shadows* while it was in production, and says that he even shot a small part of it. After the Paris Theater screening, he wrote in his "Movie Journal" in *The Village Voice* that *Shadows* was "the most frontier-breaking American feature film in at least a decade"—the first time the story of cool had been told from the inside.

Mekas became the film's champion, arranging for a second series of screenings at the YMHA on Ninety-second Street. In 1960, calling Cassavetes's film a masterpiece, *Film Culture* gave *Shadows* the journal's first annual Independent Film award. *Shadows*, Mekas wrote, "breaks with the official staged cinema, with made-up faces, with written scripts, with plot continuities. The tones and rhythms of a new America are caught in *Shadows* for the very first time." To Mekas's astonishment and chagrin, however, Cassavetes repudiated *Shadows* soon after receiving the award.

Mekas blamed the director's about-face on Nico Papatakis, a Parisian entrepreneur who had managed La Rose Rouge, the left-bank night club where Juliette Greco sang to the existentialists, and had produced Jean Genet's long-banned 1950 homoerotic short film *Un Chant D'Amour (A Song of Love)*. Perhaps because of his own mixed parentage (an Ethiopian mother and a Greek father) he was drawn to *Shadows*. Papatakis saw *Shadows*'s commercial potential, Mekas says, and offered to bankroll a new version. "Cassavetes fell for it."

Contrary to Mekas's opinion, Cassavetes critic Ray Carney writes that Cassavetes was embarrassed by *Shadows* from the very first screening, not only on account of its sound and lighting problems, but also, as Moe McKendree admits, because the story didn't make sense. Still, this couldn't

Jonas Mekas, 1959.
Overleaf: Jean–Paul
Belmondo and
Jean Seberg in
Jean–Luc Godard's
Breathless
(A Bout de
Souffle), 1959.

have mattered less to Mekas, who two years later would be one of the cameramen on Andy Warhol's landmark film *Empire*, an eight-hour, motionless camera portrait of the Empire State Building. Mekas reveled in *Shadows*'s rawness and celebrated the communal spirit of the production.

Whatever his real feelings about the way *Shadows* turned out, Cassavetes didn't know what to do about it. "The final months of editing and trying to make sense of inadequate sound and ill-lighted scenes had drained him," Moe McKendree explained, and Cassavetes knew that any reedit for Papatakis was going to be a nightmare. There was no written script, and no one had thought to keep a record of what the improvising actors had said in different takes. The reason Cassavetes finally decided to remake his movie, McKendree says, was "to justify the efforts of the actors whose careers could benefit." (His actors shared the sentiment: "The actors undertook the second version," actor Ben Carruthers later explained, "in the hope that the sale of the film would result in exposure for us.") Cassavetes borrowed thirteen thousand dollars from Nico Papatakis and went to work.

The only way to salvage the film, Cassavetes decided, was to write a series of new scenes to cut into the original sixty-minute version. According to Ray Carney, the second, ninety-minute *Shadows* contains less than thirty minutes of the original footage, most of it transitions and establishing and action shots. Most of the important dramatic interactions were now scripted, and the film was resequenced. There were new scenes, including one set in the sculpture garden of the Museum of Modern Art.

Almost exactly a year after its original version premiered, the new *Shadows* appeared at the Paris Theater double-billed with the first screening of Robert Frank and Al Leslie's beat generation classic, *Pull My Daisy*. Based on Kerouac's play *The Beat Generation* (they couldn't use the original title because it had been taken by Albert G. Zugsmith) *Pull My Daisy* stars Allen Ginsberg, Peter Orlovsky, Gregory Corso, musician-composer David Amram, and painter Larry Rivers playing Neal Cassady as a freight train conductor, and features an inspired, semi-improvised voice-over narration by Jack Kerouac.

Writing in his January 17, 1960, *Voice* "Movie Journal," Jonas Mekas reacted to the new version of *Shadows* as if he'd been rapped in the mouth.

The "second and commercialized version," Mekas wrote, "is just another Hollywood film." He felt "ruthlessly betrayed" by the "'improved version' with the same title but different footage, different cutting, story, attitude, character, style, with everything I was praising completely destroyed."

From Pacific Palisades, California, where he had gone to live with his wife, the actress Gena Rowlands, and their son, Nick, Cassavetes roared back that he remade his movie because, no matter what the audience or a few supportive critics thought, the original version was no good. **In his own words, the realization that** *Shadows* **suffered from "the thinness of the characters, the lack of all-around design in the storytelling, and inconsistencies with the character development . . . came as a shock, a shattering admission of our own ineptitude."** Both versions of *Shadows*, he added, were made "with unbending honesty, care, and disregard for critics."

The second version of *Shadows* took the Critics' Prize at the 1960 Venice Film Festival and became the first American film to take the festival route to success. Finally released in 1961 by British Lion, it was perhaps the first American film to move from the underground and college circuits into commercial distribution. *Shadows, Pull My Daisy,* and Shirley Clarke's film of *The Connection* eventually came to constitute an American New Wave.

In 1962, Mekas started the Film-Makers' Cooperative, a profit-sharing film-distribution system which even into the new century continues to accept any filmmaker looking for an outlet for his or her films. For years at the Cooperative, he says, "I slept under the table. Every waking moment was consumed with making, promoting, and distributing underground films." In 1970, he founded the Anthology Film Archives, now located in a century-old New York City courthouse and jail at the corner of Second Avenue and Second Street in the East Village, where he still works. The walls of his basement office are papered with posters for underground classics like Jack Smith's *Flaming Creatures* and Stan Brakhage's *Dog Star Man.*

When I visited him in the spring of 1999, he was in the center of a whirlwind of activity, a flurry of ringing phones and whirring copy machines. Before heading out the door to meet a trio of French women filmmakers for a *vin rouge* at a nearby café, Mekas handed me a poster-sized copy of his "Anti-100 Years of Cinema" manifesto. In blown-up typewritten

Overleaf: Larry Rivers, Jack Kerouac, Gregory Corso (with his back to the camera), David Amram, and Allen Ginsberg take a break from filming Robert Frank and Al Leslie's Pull My Daisy, 1959.

script broken by the occasional hand edit, he wrote, "In the times of bigness, spectaculars, one hundred million movie productions, I want to speak for the small, invisible acts of human spirit, so subtle, so small that they die when brought out under the Kleegue [sic] lights."

Soon after he hit L.A., John Cassavetes got the title role and even directed a few episodes of *Johnny Staccato*, a 1960 NBC-TV series about a hip private eye who moonlights as a jazz pianist, jamming at the imaginary Waldo's nightclub in the Village on his nights off. For the next thirty years until he died in 1989, Cassavetes fashioned a career that most actors only dream of; with the money earned from Academy Award–nominated acting jobs in commercial hits like Roman Polanski's *Rosemary's Baby* and Robert Aldrich's *The Dirty Dozen*, Cassavetes assured himself complete artistic control over a string of self-produced and -directed films, from his first black-and-white L.A. independent feature like *Faces* to Hollywood studio–distributed films like *A Woman Under the Influence* and *Love Streams*. Cassavetes' vision may have been, as Lelia Goldoni insists, larger and more encompassing than the cool world, but Cassavetes rode cool into Hollywood. The original version of *Shadows* no longer exists.

AMERICAN COOL

Less than a week after a train from Pittsburgh deposited him in Penn Station in the summer of 1949, Andy Warhola, twenty-one, was working. His first shoe drawings, signed—for the first time—"Andy Warhol," appeared in the September 1949 issue of *Glamour* magazine. Assignments from *Charm* and *Mademoiselle* quickly followed. That he found work so quickly, and in a field involving art, should have surprised no one. Andy Warhol had worked hard all his life. His dad, a Czech immigrant coal miner and construction worker, died when Andy was a kid, leaving three young sons for his wife, Julia, to raise in a house in the shadow of Pittsburgh's steel mills. And wherever young Andy worked growing up—selling vegetables off the back of a truck, delivering milk, clerking at a five-and-ten—he carried a sketch pad. At the end of each school year at Pittsburgh's Carnegie Tech, he sold his class projects to the other students. "He had the working-class attitude about money," notes poet and *New Yorker* magazine art critic Peter Schjeldahl, who knew Warhol: "GIMMEE!"

His first year in New York, Warhol shared a place on Manhattan Avenue and 103rd Street with some dancers, but as soon as he could afford it—1950 or '51—he got his own place and brought his mother out from Pittsburgh to keep house. **The source of much amusement and speculation among his friends, Mrs. Warhola lived in the back room of her son's incredibly cluttered floor-through apartment at 242 Lexington, directly above a bar called Florence's Pinup. She knitted, went to a Czech church, watched *I Love Lucy*, and took great pride in her son, with whom she shared eight cats, all named Sam.**

In those early years, Warhol started publishing titles like *A Is an Alphabet* and *Love Is a Pink Cake*, little picture books and portfolios of his own trademark blotted-ink drawings that he gave away as presents to friends and people who could help him. He also built a reputation for doing whatever art directors asked, making changes without sacrificing his own "look." In the mid-fifties, Warhol's fancifully drawn, full-page shoe ads in the Sunday *New York Times* for I. Miller, an established shoe manufacturer that had lost its sense of style, revitalized the company. Though he never seemed to be working hard, he was extremely productive, enlisting friends to help when he got too busy, and earning better than $60,000 a year.

Andy Warhol's central creation was himself. When he was growing up, Warhol had scarlet fever and St. Vitus' dance, the combination of which caused a loss of skin pigmentation and made his eyes so light-sensitive that he had to wear shades. He started wearing wigs while still in his early twenties, and had his first plastic surgery around 1956, a moderately successful attempt to correct a congenitally bulbous nose. He dressed in Brooks Brothers chinos, untied shoes, or paint-spattered loafers with mashed-down heels. And even though he was shy, he went to parties every night, sometimes three in an evening, combining business and pleasure, and making himself well-known. **"He would try to appear artless and naïve," a close friend of Warhol's from the mid-fifties tells Patrick Smith in his *Andy Warhol: Conversations About the Artist*, "but he really knew the effect he was having. Always. Always."**

From the day it opened in 1953, he hung out at Serendipity 3, a chic restaurant-boutique in the cellar of an Upper East Side brownstone, attracted at least partially by the hot fudge sundaes. Back then, when most people still considered Tiffany lamps junk, Serendipity pioneered mix-and-match Americana—it was perhaps the first store to publicly cater to a camp sensibility. In *Warhol: Conversations About the Artist*, those who knew him say there was nothing bohemian about Warhol. He and his mother went to St. Thomas More's, a Catholic church around the corner from where they lived, every Sunday. Once he started making money, he loved treating his friends to lavish dinners, operas, and Broadway shows. "Buying is much more American than thinking," he would later say, "and I'm as American as they come."

In the mid-1950s, Gene Moore, the head of display at both Tiffany and Bonwit Teller's New York store, began commissioning then-unknown young artists like James Rosenquist, Roy Lichtenstein, Robert Rauschenberg, Jasper Johns, and Warhol to trim his windows. For probably the first time, Warhol had a chance to observe the great young artists of his generation close-up, and it was a disturbing revelation: Warhol had earned a lot more money and recognition than they had, he'd received the Art Direction Club's highest awards, and the Museum of Modern Art shop carried his ink-blot cherub-drawing Christmas cards. Yet he completely lacked their authority in the art world. Rauschenberg and Johns would soon join the then up-and-coming Leo Castelli Gallery and make big splashes in MOMA's 1959 "Sixteen Americans" show, which signaled the emergence of a post–abstract-expressionist American art. Warhol, meanwhile, was still showing at the Bodley, a little-known art gallery for the Serendipity set. Ted Carey, a fabric and textile designer who met Warhol at Serendipity and often accompanied him on shopping sprees, says that Warhol was very affected by Rauschenberg and Johns, "not so much by their produced work but by their personality and their success and their glamour."

One Saturday afternoon in the late fifties, Warhol and Carey dropped into the Museum of Modern Art's Art Lending Service, where they came across a small Robert Rauschenberg collage that contained a cut-off portion of a man's shirt sleeve. "Oh, that is fabulous," Carey exclaimed. "I think that's awful," Warhol responded cattily. "Anyone can do that. I can do that."

"So," Carey challenged his friend, "why don't you?"

Warhol did. By the beginning of the sixties, Warhol was doing well enough to afford a four-story, thirteen-room townhouse on the Upper East Side, at 1342 Lexington Avenue near the southwest corner of Eighty-ninth Street, which he began to fill with his growing holdings—cabinets full of Fiestaware, hundreds of cookie jars, grocery bags full of unmounted semi-precious stones, and piles of Navajo rugs and Kwakiutl masks, to name just a few of the objects he collected. While a trusted assistant, Nathan Gluck, fulfilled Warhol's obligations to I. Miller, Warhol concentrated—for the only time in his life—on drawing and painting, turning for inspiration to the things that were most familiar and comforting to him as a child: comic books and food.

Warhol used an opaque projector to superimpose and enlarge cartoon characters like Superman, Popeye, the Little King, Nancy, and Dick Tracy on canvases. He then he traced in their outlines, covering sections of the images with paint. He gave much the same treatment to comfort foods, employing magazine and newspaper display ads for Del Monte peach halves, Kellogg's corn flakes, and Coca-Cola (which Warhol would later praise as America's most "democratic" product because everybody, rich and poor, buys the same drink at the same price), and Campbell's soup.

An English art critic who later became a Guggenheim Museum curator, Lawrence Alloway, coined the term "pop art" in the mid-fifties to describe what he saw as paintings' increasing use of "popular art sources" like "movie stills, science fiction, advertisements, game boards, [and] heroes of the mass media," but pop as art or sensibility didn't begin to reach the general public until 1962. That year, in conjunction with the Sidney Janis Gallery's "New Realists" show, which featured work by Claes Oldenburg, Wayne Thiebaud, Roy Lichtenstein, James Rosenquist, and Tom Wesselmann alongside Warhol's *200 Campbell Soup Cans*, the Museum of Modern Art held the first Symposium on Pop Art. Inspired by Thiebaud's yummy-looking painting *Bakery Counter*, *Time* magazine dubbed Janis's "New Realists" as the "Slice-of-Cake School," but the only painter pictured in the article was Warhol, pretending to eat out of an open Campbell's soup can.

Warhol had his first pop art show that same summer, with a wall of lit-tle canvases with Campbell's soup cans painted on each of them at the

Ferus Gallery on La Cienega Boulevard in Los Angeles. The show caused a ruckus among L.A.'s tiny gallery-going public when an art space up the street started selling genuine Campbell's soup for 99 cents. The Ferus's young director, Irving Blum, sold a few of the soup canvases for a hundred bucks each, but ultimately he withdrew the sales and hung on to the pieces, a wise aesthetic and economic decision, as things turned out. The art world had only recently accepted action painting's aesthetic—that the canvas held the evidence of an almost holy struggle. It wasn't ready for Warhol's view of art as a commodity; but time has proven him correct. "Warhol understood that America meant mass culture," as Peter Schjeldahl observes. "If fine art was going to exist in America, it would exist as mass culture."

As a good capitalist, Warhol was eager to find ways to produce more art faster. Initially, he produced serial images on a single canvas, using, for example, ink and carved gum erasers to produce a set of larger-than-life-size seven-cent U.S. airmail stamps. Quickly, however, he turned to silk-screening, a technique borrowed from advertising in which paint is squeegeed through a screen onto a canvas. In *Warhol*, David Bourdon, an art critic and long-time friend of the artist, says that Warhol was well-known for asking people what kind of art he should do next. In 1962, Ted Carey introduced Warhol to a gallery owner named Muriel Latow, hoping that she would give Warhol a show. According to Carey, Latow told Warhol that she knew what he ought to paint next, but it would cost him fifty dollars to find out. Warhol ran for his checkbook. What means more to you than anything else in the world, she wanted to know. "Money!" Warhol replied instantly. "Money!"

"It wasn't that he was greedy," explains poet and photographer Gerard Malanga, who went to work making silkscreen frames for Warhol in June 1963 and stayed for seven years. "The dollar bill was a symbol of his dream"—of becoming *somebody*, like the people in *Variety Photoplay*, and the other movie magazines he loved to pore over before he was even in his teens. Warhol started drawing money as an act of mimetic magic, first a dollar at a time, then a wad of cash stuffed into an empty Campbell's can. But he needed more. He silkscreened *80 Two-Dollar Bills*, then *200 One-Dollar Bills*. For Warhol, Malanga says, money and fame "went hand in hand."

"Even when he was already becoming media famous, *celebrity*-famous, he was like, 'Oh! Here comes Elizabeth Taylor! There goes Liza Minnelli!'—like he couldn't believe it." Warhol's friend and biographer David Bourdon agrees: **Warhol, he says, "loved nothing better than being recognized and asked for his autograph." Warhol had always worshipped fame, but Truman Capote—a gay outsider from the provinces only two years older than himself who'd become a celebrity overnight with the 1949 publication of his book *Other Voices, Other Rooms*—was the first celebrity with whom Warhol could truly identify.** Warhol kept a framed copy of *Other Voices's* famous back cover photo, featuring its author stretched languorously across a divan, in his bedroom. In the early fifties, Warhol wrote Capote letters every day for a year, and, when he got no response, took to loitering outside Capote's apartment building. In 1969 when Warhol started *Interview* magazine, the first journal dedicated to the study of fame, Capote was one of the first people he brought on board.

Marilyn Monroe died on the same day Warhol's Ferus Gallery show closed—August 5, 1962—and a few days later, in New York, Warhol produced his first garish silkscreened portrait of her by enlarging a 1950s publicity still and tarting it up with off-register acrylic red lips, yellow hair, blue eye shadow, and pink-purple skin. With the help of Gerard Malanga, working in a decommissioned fire station on Eighty-seventh Street that the city was selling off, without electricity or running water, lit only by daylight, they turned out a steady stream of large-scale silkscreened movie-star portraits—gun-toting Elvises from the western *Flaming Star*, blue Elizabeth Taylors from *Cleopatra*, silver Marlon Brandos from *The Wild One*.

The fire station was sold at the end of 1963. In February of the following year, Warhol took over the premises of a shuttered hat factory in a commercial building at 231 East Forty-seventh Street. **"The Factory," as people almost immediately began calling the fifty-by-one-hundred-foot-fourth floor loft, soon became the epicenter of pop culture. "It was seductive," remembers one visitor fondly of the Factory era. "It was that feeling of being *really* where the action was."** The windows were painted black so no light could get in or out, and everything else—the walls, the pipes, the fixtures—Billy Name, a reclusive photographer who lived in a Factory closet and functioned as its majordomo, and his crew of amphetamine heads either spray-painted metallic silver or covered with tinfoil. The creaking freight elevator disgorged visitors from all classes and social milieus—some famous, some not, some invited, most not—at all hours of the day and night.

"The point was to be fabulous," remembers Danny Fields, a long-time New York music industry entrepreneur and Factory regular who now works for the Rock 'n' Roll Hall of Fame. "If you were an outsider and weren't sure what was going on," Fields says, it was critical to be cool, "to behave minimally," to "let people wonder what was on your mind." As psychodramas raged all around him, Warhol, fueled by diet pills and the sinuous rhythms of the Jaynettes' hit 45 "Sally Go 'Round the Roses" playing over and over again at maximum volume, worked with Malanga on his *Disaster* silkscreens—lavender electric chairs and orange car crashes and black-and-white images of Jackie Kennedy in her widow's weeds at the funeral of her husband. He aspired to become an emotionlessly efficient machine: "Machines have less problems." He signed his art with a rubber stamp; he sent Alan Midgette, a tanned, dark-haired, part–Cherokee Indian actor who looked nothing like him to colleges and art museum to screen Warhol films and lecture as Andy Warhol. He suggested that an interviewer "just tell me the words he wants me to say and I'll repeat them after him." **He encouraged the already overwrought personalities of the Factory regulars because they allowed Warhol to put aside any personality of his own and coolly drain his life of all emotions. "I like being a vacuum," he told one reporter, because "it leaves me alone to work."**

Andy Warhol at the Factory, 1964. Photo by Lorenz Gude. Courtesy of the Gerard Malanga Collection.

Danny Fields says it was Malanga who introduced Andy Warhol to the Velvet Underground—Sterling Morrison, bass; Lou Reed, guitar; John Cale, guitar and electric viola; Maureen Tucker, drums—at the Café Bizarre in the Village. "The first thing that I liked about Andy," Lou Reed says in Malanga and Victor Bockris's *Up-Tight: The Velvet Underground Story*, "was that he was very real." In the backseat of a limousine on their way uptown to the Apollo Theater to see James Brown on New Year's Eve, 1965, Warhol and the Velvets sealed their deal. Warhol bought the Velvet Underground new amplifiers and let them rehearse at the Factory. He also introduced them to Nico, a German (though everyone thought she was Yugoslavian-Spanish) ice goddess who sang in a velvety monotone, a beautiful heroin addict who'd made her first splash at fifteen in Federico Fellini's film *La Dolce Vita*. The Velvets became the house band at the Exploding Plastic Inevitable.

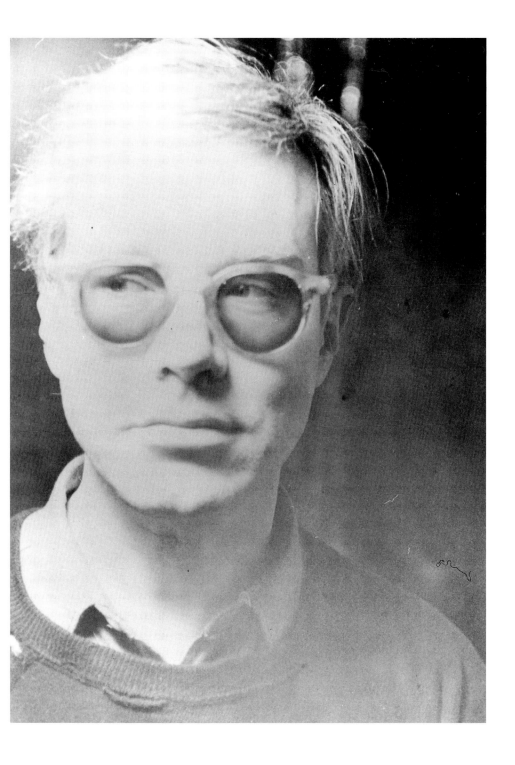

For a month in the spring of 1966 at the Dom, a Polish dance hall on St. Marks Place on the Lower East Side, Warhol produced a multimedia psychedelic extravaganza originally billed as *Andy Warhol, Up-Tight* and then renamed *The Exploding Plastic Inevitable*. "It was very exciting," remembers one frequent visitor. "It was the kind of place where your blood pressure jumped thirty points when you entered the door." Warhol projected his movies on the floors, ceilings, and walls as strobe lights flashed and Mary Woronov, a statuesque Cornell University girl with a taste for sadomasochism, and Gerard Malanga danced with bullwhips and giant flashlights. Amidst ear-splitting feedback, the Velvets in their insect-eye shades, tight black jeans, and stiletto heels screamed through "Venus in Furs" and "Waiting for the Man" and backed up Nico on "Femme Fatale" and "I'll Be Your Mirror." For Warhol, the Dom was the ultimate canvas. He was no longer just a painter, he was a conductor, a conduit for people's emotions and ideas.

The Velvets' first album, *The Velvet Underground and Nico*, produced by Andy Warhol, came out in March 1967 with Warhol's silkscreened image of a banana peel on the cover; its centerpiece was Lou Reed's towering "Heroin," probably the most powerful and moving drug song ever written. Ubiquitous today on lists of greatest rock albums, *The Velvet Underground and Nico* came out at the wrong time. Nineteen sixty-seven was the year for San Francisco and tie-dyes and bell bottoms and flowers in your hair. Accordingly, the V.U.'s West Coast tour was an unmitigated disaster. The volatile San Francisco promoter Bill Graham hated them; a review of their Los Angeles show at the Trip on the Sunset Strip predicted, "They will replace nothing except maybe suicide." Undeterred, that summer they were back in the studio in New York recording the feedback and fuzz-drenched *White Light/White Heat*, a steel-toed bike boot in the teeth of the "Summer of Love."

The Factory era coincided with the blossoming American independent-film movement. For the first time, portable 8- and 16-millimeter movie cameras were available to artists everywhere. Inspired by the hand-held aesthetic of Jack Smith's transvestite extravaganza *Flaming Creatures*, which had just been confiscated by the New York City police, and supported by the enthusiasm and practical distribution know-how of Jonas Mekas, Warhol made more than sixty movies over five years, starting in the summer of

1963 with *Sleep*, a six-hour portrait of the handsome young stockbroker-turning-poet John Giorno sleeping naked on a bed in his Upper East Side apartment, his torso wrapped in a sheet. Warhol's second film, *Eat*, featured artist Robert Indiana in his studio taking forty minutes to eat a mushroom.

Feeding reel after reel of silent film into a stationary camera mounted on a tripod, then splicing the reels together end to end, Warhol could not have made movie-making more simple. **Warhol grasped the essence of his new medium immediately: "The lighting is bad, the camera work is bad, the projection is bad, but the people are beautiful."** In 1963 and '64, he worked primarily with Malanga on silent films, a series of three-minute-long portraits called *Screen Tests*; on *Blow Job*, a half-hour close-up of an anonymous Factory visitor's face as he is supposedly being brought to ecstasy just beneath the frame; and on *The Couch*, a sex flick starring one of the Factory's only pieces of furniture.

After he bought his first sound camera at the end of 1964, Warhol coined the term "superstar" to describe the people in his movies. A few of them, like Mario (Maria) Montez, the thrift-shop, drag-queen star of Warhol's first sound film, *Harlot*, were underground-movie veterans, but most had never acted before. The women tended to be beautiful, slightly twisted offspring of the ruling classes like Edie Sedgwick, the tragic blond daughter of a wealthy Santa Barbara family with a history of mental illnesses; or Viva, a Catholic schoolgirl rebel with a skinny body and a nasty mind. The men tended to be desperate and uninhibited street boys like Candy Darling, who died of cancer in 1974 brought on, many felt, by the female hormones he was injecting, and Eric Emerson, who died two years later.

During the summer of 1966, Warhol was shooting as many as three movies a week. Many of them were scripted by Ronald Tavel, an avant-garde novelist and playwright from Brooklyn who had worked with Jack Smith. Tavel's fruitless attempts to convince the casts to memorize their lines often turned into part of the film. At the time, three of Warhol's reigning female superstars—Nico; Brigid Polk, the zany, kindhearted daughter of Richard Berlin, president of the Hearst Corporation, who'd assumed her surname in honor of her favorite way of ingesting speed; and Susan Bottomly, a vain young model from Boston who performed under the name International Velvet—were all living at the Chelsea Hotel on West Twenty-third Street.

Though many of his reels were actually shot at the Factory or in a West Village apartment, Warhol decided to set all of his films at the Chelsea.

Chelsea Girls, Andy Warhol's greatest film, is a cold shot. Its three and a half hours actually contain seven hours of color and black-and-white film simultaneously projected on side-by-side screens, giving the viewer a sense that all of these vignettes (which can be screened in any sequence) are occurring simultaneously. Not that anything actually happens in *Chelsea Girls*: Nico lethargically brushes her hair. Brigid talks speed with a caller who has no idea that their conversation is being filmed. An earthy New Jerseyan, Ingrid Superstar, frequent butt of Factory jokes, discusses her sex life. Brigid gives Ingrid a poke. Mary Woronov tortures her female costars in "Hanoi Hannah, Radio Star," a Ronnie Tavel scenario loosely based on the story of Tokyo Rose. Eric Emerson, tripping on acid, slowly takes off his clothes, his beautiful body awash in colored spotlights.

Chelsea Girls's most chilling moment occurs in a scene starring Ondine, a brilliantly demented urchin usually dressed in leather and rags, described by Warhol biographer David Bourdon as "the most flamboyant and mercurial of the Factory's speed freaks." After shooting up on camera, Ondine perches on the Factory couch and announces that he is the pope—"My flock consists of homosexuals, perverts of any kind, queens, thieves, criminals of any sort, the rejected of society"—and is ready to hear confessions.

A woman named Rona wanders in as if entering an old-time stag film. She and Ondine ruminate on eternal bliss, but Ondine is impatient for her confession. Rona says that she can't confess to him, because he's a phony. Ondine explodes, genuinely enraged. "I'm a phony, am I?" he screams, slapping her hard in the face. Stunned, she demands Ondine stop it, but he hits her again. She runs off camera and he follows her. Warhol's camera continues to focus on the empty sofa as we hear Ondine scream at her off-camera, calling her "a dumb bitch" and "a filthy whore" for questioning his veracity.

Eventually Ondine walks back into frame, exhausted, and throws himself down on the couch. Warhol, however, insists that he keep talking because there's still several minutes of film left. Off-camera, Rona continues to sob. Running out of things to say, but unable to leave, Ondine, like all the other characters in *Chelsea Girls*, appears genuinely trapped in a hell of his

Nico at The Factory, 1966. Photo by Gerard Malanga.
© Gerard Malanga.

own invention, with Warhol's motionless camera emphasizing a sense of implacability. Many years later, Ondine, his body finally giving out after a lifetime of dissipation, admitted as much to interviewer Patrick S. Smith. "There's no way out of that film [*Chelsea Girls*]," he said, because Warhol got "from everybody involved . . . everything that they could do."

The film was released only weeks after Warhol finished shooting. Writing in *The Village Voice*, Jonas Mekas compared it to D. W. Griffith's *The Birth of a Nation*. Record crowds at the first screenings of *Chelsea Girls* at the two-hundred-seat Filmmaker's Cinemathèque led to the most successful commercial release of any underground film ever. In the summer of 1967, *Chelsea Girls* played to sold-out art houses in big cities across the United States.

In a piece called "American Cool" in the January 1999 *Art Issues*, Las Vegas–based culture analyst Dave Hickey writes that for the first decade of Andy Warhol's career, his work was usually described by critics as "ironic and cool." Both irony and cool, Hickey contends, are "modes of deniable disclosure"—but that's where the similarities fade. To Hickey, there is something craven about irony; it "is a way of eluding the wrath of your superiors . . . when we use irony, we suppress the sense of what we mean." Cool, on the other hand, "is a mode of democratic politesse . . . a way of not imposing on your peers." From Hickey's point of view, irony is an acknowledgment of servitude, cool a way of leading by example.

Hickey compares Andy Warhol with George Washington, Gertrude Stein, and Henry James. They were all cool, he says, because "presuming to embody their beliefs, they decline to plead them." To be cool, one does not have to "assert anything. One simply declares some truth to be self-evident on one's own embodied authority as a citizen without deigning to invest it with fancy justifications, personal explanations, or expressive urgency." For Hickey, the ultimate "figure of cool" is George Washington at the Second Continental Congress, sitting with his legs crossed and his hands in his lap, saying little or nothing. When the debate grew especially heated or wandered from its purpose, according to Hickey, Washington would redirect discussion by simply shifting his weight in his chair. "That, my friends, is cool."

In late 1965, Max's Kansas City opened on Union Square. Its proprietor, Mickey Ruskin, started letting artists run a tab in exchange for artworks, which quickly helped establish Max's as the preeminent artist hangout of its time in New York. And whereas fifteen years earlier the Cedar Tavern had been barely big enough for Jackson Pollock, Franz Kline, Willem de Kooning, and their friends and lovers, Max's was big enough to accommodate the wider worlds of film, theater, literature, and, later, rock 'n' roll.

One of the artists that Ruskin's arrangement attracted was Andy Warhol. By 1967, he was having trouble feeding his entourage and had become notorious for showing up at dinner parties with seven or eight hungry and uninvited associates. Ruskin allowed Warhol and his entourage to run a tab in exchange for the occasional painting, and the Factory crowd took over Max's back room.

People who were there reminisce about "Andy's booth," or "Andy's round table," but Gerard Malanga says that there really wasn't a particular place: wherever Warhol sat was the center of the room. Eerily illuminated by Dan Flavin's red fluorescent tubes cantilevered out from the wall to lend the room the flavor of a supermarket rotisserie, the habitués orbited, angling for Warhol's attention with outrageous acts; studying him out of the corners of their eyes, transfixed. Meanwhile, Danny Fields says, Warhol was like a white hole sucking everything in, giving everybody something to do, something to be.

In hindsight, the summer of 1967 was the end of the Warhol era. A year later, Warhol would be shot by a factory hanger-on named Valerie Solanas, and he never really recovered, psychically or physically, from his wounds. Both his health and his art would decline. The summer of 1967 was the crest of a wave. Paul Morrissey, who was about to take over the actual making of Warhol's films, was a regular in the backroom at Max's that summer, usually sticking the velvet knife into the back of Ondine, whom he looked on as a talentless fuck-up. Billy Name and Ingrid Superstar were still around. The dapper Fred Hughes, who would soon take over Warhol's business enterprises and move the Factory to much more respectable quarters, had started to come by. Nico and the Velvet Underground were going their separate ways by then, but she still showed up. Even if they were too cool to show it, everybody in the room was focused on Warhol—wondering what he was thinking, speculating about what he would do next, trying to understand his meaning, and—though this nearly always went unspoken—gauging where they stood in his world. In my mind's eye, it was like watching the Last Supper.

The summer of 1967 was a stormy one for me. I was living on St. Marks Place, working at a bookstore, and selling a little pot on the side while my wife modeled at the New School. I got stuck up at knifepoint on Eighth Street that summer, and spent every night I could drinking at Max's, and though I didn't know anybody there, I sometimes wandered into the back room. One night, in response to something someone in his inner circle had just murmured to him behind the back of her hand, I caught Warhol mouthing a nearly silent "Oh, wow," a phrase that Warhol's old friend Ivan Karp says Warhol often used to express his "perpetual state of amazement, his constant surprise; his admiration." To me, the silent circle of his mouth, the eyebrow arched in slight surprise represented cool—a universe of emotions from total acceptance to cynical dismissal to utter passivity to final judgment. I saw his ability to take the precise temperature of the room and alter it with a flicker of a smile, and at that moment I experienced a shiver of cool—simply by being there and understanding what I saw.

COOL ON EVERYTHING

Bobby Zimmerman was born to be cool, but his was a particularly American cool, less influenced by French surrealism than by rhythm and blues. Late at night with the lights off, mother, father, and younger brother sleeping, the nine-year-old future Bob Dylan would lie in bed in his solid two-story house in a middle-class neighborhood of Hibbing, Minnesota, underneath the covers with his ear up against the speaker of his old Zenith radio, sucking in the sounds of Howlin' Wolf, B. B. King, Johnny Ace, Chuck Berry, and Jimmy Reed.

For most of us, age fourteen is critical in the birth of a cool. Bobby Zimmerman was fourteen in 1955, the year that James Dean died in his white Porsche Spyder on the way to a sports-car race in Salinas, California. *Rebel Without a Cause* and *Blackboard Jungle* hit Hibbing's Lybba Theater in 1955. In 1955, Bobby was listening to Elvis Presley, Little Richard, and Buddy Holly and started his first band, the Golden Chords. Even when he was play-

Bob Dylan in New York, 1965.

© Daniel Kramer.

ing the Hibbing High Jacket Jamboree Talent Festival, he was telling people he was going to be a rock 'n' roll star.

In the fall of 1959, Zimmerman enrolled briefly at the University of Minnesota in Minneapolis. He lived in a Jewish frat house, Sigma Alpha Mu, for a few months, but gravitated toward Dinkytown, a bohemian neighborhood between the campus and the Mississippi River. Like many a member of Minneapolis's mini-Bohemia, he made his way to the Ten O'Clock Scholar, a coffeehouse with a four-inch elevated platform in the front window from which performers entertained the customers and passed the hat. **When Zimmerman asked if he could play, the manager asked him his name. He blurted out "Bob Dylan," and from then on, that's who he became. "I needed a name in a hurry and I picked that one," Dylan told Anthony Scaduto, his first serious biographer. "It just came to me as I was standing there in 'The Scholar.'"** In Robert Shelton's biography *No Direction Home*, Echo Helstrom, Dylan's Hibbing girlfriend, says that Dylan had already come up with the name by the time he was a junior in high school. "I know what I'm going to call myself," he told her one day in 1958. "I've got this great name—Bob Dillon."

Dylan hooked up with a local folksinger, "Spider" John Koerner, who owned a trove of rare folk-music recordings from the Library of Congress and Folkways, Moe Asch's stubborn little record label with the thick cardboard sleeves that introduced the world to Leadbelly (né Huddie Ledbetter), Big Bill Broonzy, Doc Watson, Sonny Terry, Brownie McGhee, the Reverend Gary Davis, and Woody Guthrie.

In the fall of 1960, a Dinkytown connection turned Dylan on to *Bound for Glory*, Woody Guthrie's 1943 autobiography. Woodrow Wilson Guthrie hailed from Okemah, Oklahoma, a farm town on the Colorado River made up of equal parts Cherokee, Anglo, and black, the son of a land speculator well acquainted with the frontier cycle of boom and bust and a mother who slowly lost her life to Huntington's chorea. Around the time Woody's father died in a hotel-room fire in Oklahoma City, Woody hit the road.

When he was seventeen, in Pampa, Texas, the vortex of the Dust Bowl, his square-dance fiddler uncle Jeff taught him how to play the guitar. During the Depression, Guthrie hitchhiked and hoboed around the United States, marrying three women and siring five kids along the way while writing "This Land Is Your Land," "Roll On, Columbia," "Dust Bowl Refugee,"

"Pretty Boy Floyd," "So Long, It's Been Good to Know You," and more than a thousand other songs that continue to echo in the American spirit. "I hate a song that makes you think you're not any good," Guthrie wrote in *Bound for Glory.* "I hate a song that makes you think you're born to lose . . . I am out to sing the songs that make you take pride in yourself and your work. . . . I am out to sing songs that will prove to you that this is your world."

Two days after reading *Bound for Glory*, recalls fellow guitarslinger and Minneapolis buddy Tony Glover, Dylan seemed to turn into Guthrie, complete with Okemah twang. He taught himself every Guthrie song he could get his hands on, at one point singing nothing but Guthrie songs for six months. Every time Bob got drunk during the fall of 1960, he tried to call Guthrie in Greystone Park Hospital in New Jersey, where Guthrie was suffering the same rare degenerative nerve disorder that killed his mother. Guthrie hadn't been able to sing since 1952; now he could barely move or talk. In December 1960, Dylan dropped out of school and hitchhiked to New York to meet his hero.

Bob Dylan landed in Greenwich Village on a wintry January day in the middle of the folk boom, a scrawny figure in a sheepskin jacket with an unruly hair mop stuffed into a black corduroy cap, and no place to stay. At the Fat Black Pussycat, the Fifth Peg, the Café Wha?, and a half-dozen other "basket houses" clustered near the intersection of Bleecker and MacDougal Streets, young folk musicians including Dave Van Ronk, Phil Ochs, Maria Muldaur, Richie Havens, and Fred Neil eked out a living passing a wicker basket around to the clusters of beatnik-seeking tourists. Dylan talked his way in to see the manager of the Café Wha? His first night in the city, still in his traveling clothes, Dylan made his New York debut at an open-mike.

The next day, Dylan hitched to East Orange, New Jersey, to meet Woody Guthrie. Guthrie often spent the weekend with longtime fans and friends Bob and Sid Gleason, who on Sundays would host an open house that had become a gathering place for the time's best folksingers, who stopped by to play music for Woody and for each other. Over the next few months, Dylan would meet them all, from Guthrie's long-time sidekick Cisco Houston, who was on his last legs—nearly dead of cancer himself at forty-two—to Ramblin' Jack Elliott, Josh White, and Odetta. None was more important,

though, than Pete Seeger, the guiding spirit of the folk explosion, who would soon take Bob Dylan under his wing.

Woody Guthrie, 1943.

Pete Seeger came from a long line of principled rejecters. One came over on the *Mayflower*, another fought at the Battle of Bunker Hill. "These ancestors of mine," Seeger pointed out in his autobiographical *The Incompleat Folksinger*, "were all subversives in the eyes of their governments."

A dropout from the Harvard class of 1940—John F. Kennedy was a classmate—Pete Seeger was collecting field recordings for the Library of Congress when he met Woody Guthrie at a benefit for migrant farmworkers in March 1940. Alan Lomax, Seeger's boss at the Archive of American Folk Song, has said that the American folk music renaissance could be dated from that night. At twenty-seven, Seeger was ten years Guthrie's junior and far less experienced in the world. **As Seeger recounts in *The Incompleat Folksinger*, Guthrie suggested that they head out west. Seeger, in turn, asked Guthrie how they were going to see the country if they didn't have any money. "We'll use the rule of thumb," Woody drawled, "and if you can't hitchhike, ride a freight train."** On that trip—a swing through West Texas to see one of Guthrie's families on the way to visit the great dam-building projects of the Northwest, of which Guthrie was the bard—Seeger became Guthrie's avatar.

Seeger and Guthrie formed half of the Almanac Singers, who had a huge radio hit in 1942 with "Ruben James," a ballad about the ninety-five American merchant marines who'd been drowned in 1941 when their ship was torpedoed by a German U-boat before the United States entered World War II. The Almanac's brief run of commercial respectability ended abruptly, though, when it became known that some of them were communists. ("I'm not a communist," Woody Guthrie protested, "but I've been in the red my whole life.") During the thirties, Seeger had in fact been a member of the Party. In response to the revelation, Decca canceled the Almanacs' record deal, and their agent, William Morris, dumped them. In order to pay the rent on their Thirteenth Street commune in New York, they threw rent parties, which they called hootenannies, a term they had picked up in Seattle the year before to describe a group sing.

By the late forties, Guthrie's health had begun to fail, and Seeger had become a member of the Weavers, a quartet of singer-songwriters who helped spark an interest in folk music during the winter of 1949–50 with an improbable hit version of "Goodnight, Irene," in which they sanitized Leadbelly's lyric "I'll get you in my dreams" by altering it to "I'll see you in my dreams." They followed with a folked-up version of "Wimoweh," a Zulu chant that turned into one of the first black popular hit records in South Africa, which also went gold.

However, Seeger's politics soon got him into trouble again. In the political hysteria of the time, the Weavers' lyrics to "If I Had a Hammer" were considered so radical that no mainstream music publisher would touch them. In September 1950, President Truman signed the Internal Security Act, authorizing the investigation of, among many other things, "subversive songs." As a consequence, Seeger was subpoenaed to testify before the House Un-American Activities Committee in August 1955. He showed up at the U.S. Courthouse on Foley Square in New York looking like a clown in a plaid shirt, a checked suit, and a garish yellow necktie. Waiving the right to plead the Fifth Amendment against self-incrimination, Seeger battled with his inquisitors for an hour over whether he was a patriot or a subversive, then walked out—for which he was indicted by Congress for contempt. While awaiting trial, he wrote the song "Where Have All the Flowers Gone?"

Seeger's ten-year prison sentence was later overturned, but the Weavers were forced to disband. To make a living, Seeger—dubbed "Khrushchev's songbird" by the right-wing press—sometimes had to sing under an assumed name. Nevertheless, on the left, his reputation for bravery and commitment continued to grow. Seeger taught Martin Luther King Jr. the words to "We Shall Overcome"; he turned the Cuban folk tune "Guantanamera" into a global standard. **If the ethos of cool holds, with Miles Davis, that the notes you don't play are as important as the notes you do, then Pete Seeger could not have been less cool, or less interested in being so. In his idealism, his commitment to change the world through political struggle, and his ambition to sing a better world into existence, he played all the notes. Seeger was "hot." Nevertheless, he took the young Bob Dylan under his wing.**

Just two months after his arrival in New York, Bob Dylan's career took off. His first break came in February 1961, when Gerde's Folk City on West Fourth Street let Dylan play a Monday night "Hoot." By April, he was opening for the Mississippi-born blues champion, John Lee Hooker. In July, he met Albert

Grossman, the portly, driven, thirty-five-year-old Chicago nightclub owner who would become his manager. Then, on September 29, the New York Times's critic Robert Shelton wrote a review of one of Dylan's Folk City gigs, a review that was similar in effect to the rave that Gilbert Millstein had written twelve years earlier for Jack Kerouac and *On the Road*. Within a month, Dylan was signed to Columbia Records by John Hammond, the talent scout who'd been instrumental in the careers of many famous and influential musicians including Billie Holiday. On November 20 and 22, at Columbia Studios on Seventh Avenue, Dylan laid down about seventeen songs in six hours, and his first album, *Bob Dylan*, containing thirteen of those songs, was in the can.

Released March 19, 1962, *Bob Dylan* had a decidedly folkish bent. Dylan performed standards like "Pretty Peggy-O" and "House of the Rising Sun," and blues by Blind Willie Johnson, Blind Lemon Jefferson, and Bukka White. One of the only two originals on the record was the first song that Bob Dylan wrote and performed in public, "Song to Woody." In it, Dylan hails the same men Woody Guthrie sang about in "Pastures of Plenty," using his idol's words, too: "who come with the dust and are gone with the wind." **The special thing about Bob Dylan, though, was the way he sang—ferocious, apocalyptic, possessed. Everyone who heard it—even the people who said that Dylan sounded like a dog with his leg trapped in barbed wire—knew Bob Dylan was a phenomenon.** Still, the record sold less than five thousand copies, and Bob Dylan quickly became known around the Columbia office as "Hammond's Folly."

Between his first and second album, Dylan's girlfriend, Suze Rotolo, seventeen, abandoned him and their tiny walk-up at 161 West Fourth Street for Italy. Their stormy relationship inspired many beautiful songs over the next three years, songs like "Don't Think Twice, It's Alright" and "One Too Many Mornings"—celebrations of tender human feelings tinged with exhausted regret. Those songs, though, were nearly drowned out by the nightmarish visions and stark finger-pointing of songs like "Masters of War" and "A Hard Rain's A-Gonna Fall."

When *The Freewheelin' Bob Dylan* hit the stores in May 1963 and started selling ten thousand copies a week, a reunited Dylan and Rotolo were on its cover, strolling up a slushy Village street arm in arm, in denim and leather. I remember picking up the album for the first time and thinking, enviously,

that they were the first cool couple. But by then Dylan was already involved with Joan Baez, the raven-haired Cambridge folk thrush whose first two million-selling albums had landed her on a 1962 *Time* magazine cover.

For the next year two years, Dylan and Baez reigned as the prince and princess of folk; the two debuted his brand-new "With God on Our Side" at the Monterey Folk Festival in May 1963. In July, Dylan traveled with Seeger and folk-singer Theodore Bikel to Greenwood, Mississippi, to sing a song he'd just finished a few weeks earlier about the man who murdered Medgar Evers, the head of the Mississippi branch of the National Association for the Advancement of Colored People, "Only a Pawn in Their Game."

At the 1963 Newport Folk Festival, Dylan's songs were on everybody's lips, and his skinny, waiflike, tousled image was everywhere. Peter Yarrow prefaced Peter, Paul and Mary's pop hit version of "Blowin' in the Wind" by calling Dylan "the most important folk artist in America today," and the crowd roared. Dylan joined Peter, Paul and Mary; Theodore Bikel; Joan Baez; Pete Seeger; and the Freedom Singers on stage for the grand finale—crossing arms, holding hands, swaying in place, and singing "We Shall Overcome." Dylan publically referred to Seeger as a "Saint." **To Seeger, Dylan must have seemed like Woody Guthrie's true heir, the popular embodiment of Guthrie and Seeger's vision of a politically engaged folk-music. Dylan, though, was finding it increasingly difficult to hew to any political line.**

Dylan first met Clark Foreman through Joan Baez, who brought Dylan to a party at Foreman's Upper West Side apartment after a 1963 concert. As chief of the Emergency Civil Liberties Committee, a veteran group of civil rights and freedom-of-speech defenders, the former Roosevelt New Dealer Foreman had been a courageous foe of Senator Joseph McCarthy. His living room that night was full of old lefties who took the opportunity to inundate Dylan with advice, even insisting at one point that he listen to an audio recording of a speech by the late screenwriter Nedrick Young concerning the social responsibility of writers.

Every year, the Emergency Civil Liberties Committee held a Bill of Rights Day fund-raising dinner at which they honored a public figure with their Thomas Paine Award, named for the Revolutionary War pamphleteer. In 1962, the committee honored the philosopher, mathematician, and anti-

Pete Seeger, 1966.

nuclear activist Bertrand Russell. In 1963, the Committee decided to bestow the Paine Award on Bob Dylan.

The night of the dinner, Dylan showed up at the Americana Hotel in New York late and proceeded to get drunk. When he stumbled to the dais, he looked out across the Grand Ballroom at the fifteen hundred civil libertarians anxious to honor him and—only three weeks after President Kennedy had been assassinated, in the midst of all that raw national political trauma—blurted out that he could identify with Lee Harvey Oswald, the man who had killed the president. "I saw some of myself in him," Dylan mumbled defiantly into a cascade of catcalls and boos, casting his fate with all the other outsiders and outriders who invented cool.

Dylan's third album, *The Times They Are A-Changin'*, released in January 1964, marked the apotheosis of the protest song—from the title track with its ringing invitation, "Come, brothers and sisters throughout the land," to such angry morality dramas as "The Lonesome Death of Hattie Carroll," a song based on the true story of a black maid murdered by a socially prominent Baltimore drunk who got off with a slap on the wrist. Even so, a Dylan backlash among the cognoscenti had begun. The purists at *The Little Sandy Review* back in Dinkytown sounded the warning: *The Times They Are A-Changin'* was "a great disappointment" because "his melodies bear more relation now to popular music than to folk music."

By now it wasn't just folkniks who were listening to Dylan. In May 1964, while on an English concert tour, Dylan was rocked by the buzz around the Beatles, the Rolling Stones, the Hollies, the Kinks, and a dozen other bands. Many of the bands were fans of his, and their fans were his fans, too. The Animals, Eric Burdon's blues band, even performed an electric version of Dylan's take on "House of the Rising Sun" on The Ed Sullivan Show, American TV's premier Sunday night variety venue.

With its slapstick cockiness and oceans of compassion, *Another Side of Bob Dylan* (a title Dylan hated, but which was forced on him by Tom Wilson, his producer) released in August 1964, his third record in little more than a year, was Dylan's first cool album. The song "Motorpsycho Nitemare" is a Harley laying rubber cross a Midwest paralyzed with fear of Fidel Castro's beard. "Now they asked me to read a poem/at the sorority sister's home,"

Dylan whoops in "I Shall Be Free No. 10." "I got knocked down and my head was swimmin'" he goes on, "I wound up with the dean of women." *Another Side* also depicts Dylan growing up—"Ah, but I was so much older then. I'm younger than that now" ("My Back Pages")—and reaching out. In "Chimes of Freedom," a song worthy of Woody Guthrie, Dylan reaches so far out to the psychically dispossessed, the lost, the spaced, the fucked, that he becomes one with them—"the aching ones whose wounds cannot be nursed, the countless confused, accused, misused, strung out ones and worse/and for every hung-up person in the whole wide universe, I saw the chimes of freedom flashing."

At that summer's Newport Folk Festival, Dylan's "topical ballad" workshop drew 5,000 awed, adoring fans. There he debuted "Mr. Tambourine Man" and "It Ain't Me, Babe." Newport '64 also signaled the emergence of a folksong army of guys like David Blue and Patrick Sky, who looked, dressed, slouched, and muttered like Dylan.

At Dylan's solo performance, Ronnie Gilbert, Pete Seeger's old partner from the Weavers, introduced Dylan as Newport's favorite son: "You know him. He's yours." Dylan, however, didn't appear to feel quite that much at home. In *Festival!*, Murray Lerner's Oscar-nominated 1967 film documenting Newport from '63 to '66, there's a scene shot inside a van as it is pulling away after Dylan's workshop. Joan Baez is sitting next to the driver, looking beautiful and self-possessed as she reaches out the window to shake hands with the people lining the roadway, as if she were a candidate or a queen. Dylan, smoking a cigarette, is hunched over, with sunglasses on and his back to the crowd. The star of the '64 Folk Festival was Phil Ochs with his protest songs.

Pete Seeger had helped found the music magazine *Sing Out!* with the simple goal of publishing good songs. Its editor in the early sixties was Irwin Silber, a former employee of Moe Asch at Folkways Records and an early Dylan booster, who printed more songs by Dylan than by anybody else except Woody Guthrie. In November 1964, however, Silber rebuked Dylan in the pages of his magazine. "All of a sudden," Silber addressed Dylan in "An Open Letter To Bob Dylan," "you've become a pheenom, a VIP, a celebrity." **Speaking only as a comrade, simply "out of love and deep concern," Silber warned Dylan that "the American Success Machinery chews up geniuses at a rate of one a day and still**

hungers for more. Through notoriety, fast money and status, it makes it almost impossible for the artist to function and grow." Stay with folk and protest, Silber urged Dylan, or sacrifice your integrity: "stay out in the cold where it's warm."

Meanwhile, Dylan retreated to Albert Grossman's compound in Bearsville, just outside of Woodstock, New York, to write. In January 1965, he started recording again. Back in November 1962, Dylan had tried to transform a bunch of middle-aged Columbia studio musicians into a rock 'n' roll band, but it hadn't worked. With the benefit of hindsight we can see that "Mixed-Up Confusion," the 45 that came out of that session, is the missing link between folk and rock, but for Dylan at the time the title pretty much summed up the recording.

Now Dylan was accompanied by musicians closer to his own age, including John Sebastian, who would go on to start the Lovin' Spoonful, on bass. Among the first songs they recorded was the raunchy, lurching "Subterranean Homesick Blues." Dripping with cool, its antiauthoritarian "You don't need a weatherman/to know which way the wind blows" still rings true. Rerecorded with a full band and released as a single that March, it reached number 39 on the pop charts.

In the middle of the recording sessions, Dylan took off for a last tour with Joan Baez, reprising a set of folk numbers he'd pretty much outgrown. He returned burned-out, telling a journalist that he was sick of preaching to the choir. "Every concert was the same. I'd get standing ovations and they didn't mean anything." Back at his typewriter, Dylan batted out a nameless jumble of words "about ten pages long. It wasn't called anything, just a rhythm thing on paper all about my steady hatred directed at some point that was honest." In mid-June, Dylan went into a New York studio and recorded "Like a Rolling Stone."

Finally, he'd figured out how he wanted to sound. He brought in Mike Bloomfield, the twenty-one-year-old lead-guitar player of the Paul Butterfield Blues Band, which was just beginning to make a name for itself. Harvey Brooks, who with Bloomfield would go on to found the blues-funk big band Electric Flag, played bass. A Tin Pan Alley hipster named Al Kooper was enlisted on the Hammond B3 organ. "Like a Rolling Stone" is a letter from the "mystery tramp," the wised-up hipster, to the Queen of the Scene who's lost everything she'd believed in. "How does it feel?" he demands over and over again; "how does it feel to be on your own, with no direction home, a complete unknown"—just like one of Woody Guthrie's migrant farm hands in "Pastures of Plenty" who "come with the dust and are gone with the wind"—"like a rolling stone."

By 1965, Newport had become the most important folk-music gathering in the United States. That year some two hundred musicians, from clog-dancers and fife and drum corps to hard-working rural professionals like Johnny Cash and Bill Monroe, blues progenitors like Son House, and folk boomers like Judy Collins, Buffy Sainte-Marie, and Joan Baez with her newest protégé, Donovan, on her arm, performed—all for room, board, travel money, and fifty dollars. The opening scenes in *Festival!* make Newport look like the black-and-white Woodstock: a denim-and-Birkenstock-clad horde of humanity swarming across the festival grounds toting bedrolls, bongos, and guitars.

Murray Lerner says 1965 was the first year Newport drew many black kids. Maybe they came to see Howlin' Wolf or his great electric guitar player, Hubert Sumlin. Nineteen sixty-five also marked the first year, according to Lerner, that the audiences danced. The Chambers Brothers and the Muddy Waters Blues Band had brought electric guitars to Newport in 1964, by 1965 Newport was electric.

"There was a weird feeling in the air at Newport" in 1965, Tony Glover writes in his excellent liner notes for the CD set *Bob Dylan Live 1966.* "Fire trucks were stationed at the gates, in case the hoses were needed to quell a riot." In Murray Lerner's film, Pete Seeger in his crew-neck sweater is everywhere: strumming his banjo, leading sing-alongs, exhorting the crowd to make their own music, duetting with Peter, Paul and Mary on "Down by the Riverside" and with Joan Baez on "Go Tell Aunt Rhodie the Old Gray Goose Is Dead."

Trouble erupted even before Dylan's concert. According to Dylan biographer and *New York Times* reporter Robert Shelton in *No Direction Home: The Life and Music of Bob Dylan,* at an afternoon "Bluesville Workshop" hosted by Paul Butterfield's band, Albert Grossman, Dylan's manager and soon to be Butterfield's manager, took strong exception to a patronizing introduction to the band by Alan Lomax, the distinguished twentieth-century musicologist and rediscoverer of Son House, Mississippi Fred McDowell, and Muddy Waters, and wrestled him to the ground before others could separate them.

Tony Glover sensed a restless edginess running through the crowd streaming in for Dylan's performance that evening. No doubt many of them had heard "Like a Rolling Stone" on the radio on their way to the festival. Though it had only been out a few days, the song was already Dylan's first top-ten hit, despite being the longest pop-music hit ever recorded up to that time. It signaled a commercial breakthrough of a kind only Pete Seeger, of all the folksingers, had ever experienced—before it was ripped away from him by anti-Communist politicos. How would Dylan's folk following react?

Nobody outside Dylan's clique knew Dylan planned to show up with a band. Jonathan Taplin, Dylan's road manager at the time, says Dylan's decision to work with Paul Butterfield and Mike Bloomfield and the rhythm section of bassist Jerome Arnold and drummer Sam Lay came at the last moment. Robert Shelton says they stayed up all the previous night rehearsing. Taplin says the only time they had to run through the music was when Albert Grossman cleared the stadium for a sound check right before the show. At the last minute, Grossman sent a private plane to pick up Al Kooper in New York.

Following on the heels of Cousin Emmy's rendition of "Turkey in the Straw," Dylan hit the stage with his scrawny frame draped in "Mod" London's Carnaby Street cool: Cuban heels, tight black slacks, a black leather jacket, and impenetrable Ray-Bans. A black Fender Stratocaster hung from his shoulders. In the stage lights, Dylan's hair rose from his head like flames. The musicians stationed themselves around Dylan like bodyguards, then smashed into "Maggie's Farm," with Bloomfield's whip-thin body leaning in toward Dylan, twisted into the shape of a snake.

Many careful audits of the bootleg tape recorded that night tend to dispel the myth that Dylan was actually booed off the stage. The PA sucked, however; the keyboards were virtually inaudible and vocal and guitar volumes surged and disappeared. Bloomfield had to keep turning his guitar up higher and higher just to be heard. After "Maggie's Farm" made Dylan's point—"I try my best to be just like I am/ but everybody wants you to be just like them"—there was a smattering of boos from the crowd but, as Taplin recollects, "most people just sat on their hands." There were a lot more boos after "Like a Rolling Stone"; somebody screamed "Go back to *The Ed Sullivan Show*." Other people called out for his folk tunes. **"They sounded betrayed," wrote Tony Glover, "angry that Dylan, with his amplified accompanists, seemed to be embracing the world of commercial music they'd made such a conspicuously conscious effort to turn away from." Murray Lerner, who was operating one of the cameras that night, remembers it as "frightening, ominous, dazzling. I didn't know whether it was good or evil. We were entering a whole new world."**

Meanwhile, backstage, the folk-music establishment was coming unglued. After all the years of struggle and oppression, and with all of its new-found popularity and influence over youth, folk music was being challenged by its own favorite son, who had suddenly turned as apolitical as Miles. Paul Rothchild, the producer for Jac Holzman's upstart Elektra Records, was at the mixing board when Seeger demanded that he turn down the sound. Rothchild said no, and Seeger flipped. "Goddamn it, it's terrible!" Seeger bellowed. "You can't understand the words! If I had an ax, I'd cut the cable right now!" He tried to commandeer the board, but Albert Grossman blocked his way. It was as if Grossman and Seeger were wrestling for Dylan's soul.

Taplin says that after "Phantom Engineer," an early version of "It Takes a Lot to Laugh, It Takes a Train to Cry," "a quarter of the people were booing quite loudly." On the tape you can hear Dylan abruptly shout at the band, "Let's go, man. That's all." They duly split, leaving the audience in shock. Dylan brushed past Pete Seeger, who was, by one report, literally weeping in the wings as the stage went dark.

When Taplin rushed backstage he found Dylan "just sitting there on the bottom step with his head in his hands, looking shook" while Peter, Paul and Mary's Peter Yarrow, that evening's MC, begged him to go back out and play. Dylan said he didn't have any more tunes worked up with the band. Yarrow replied "Play acoustic." Johnny Cash, who was scheduled to go on later, "had this jumbo Gibson guitar, and just handed it to him" as Yarrow ran out onstage to urge the crowd "to show Bobby you love him."

When Dylan appeared by himself with Cash's acoustic guitar everybody cheered. "It was like, 'Oh, we won!'" remembers Taplin of the crowd as Dylan launched into "It's All Over Now, Baby Blue," but they were ignoring the tune's explicit message of farewell: "Leave your stepping stones behind, they will not follow you.'" Says Taplin, "I thought it was the perfect way of saying 'fuck you.'" Dylan did one more acoustic tune, "Mr. Tambourine Man"—in which the "vagabond who's rapping at your door . . . standing in the clothes that you once wore" replaces "Like a Rolling Stone"'s "mystery tramp" as Dylan's figure of cool—then walked off the stage, never to return to the Folk Festival, which made it through only two more summers. The two biggest stars at Newport '66 were the hippie San Francisco blues band Big Brother and the Holding Company, featuring Janis Joplin, and Sunset Strip folk rockers the Byrds.

Four years after Newport came Woodstock. Folk became folk-rock and the folk scene became the mass culture. Yet by the turn of the century, Bob Dylan had become a myth, loyal only to his music and the road, a remote and magisterial emblem of cool. The last time I spotted him, he was living in a motor home, a pea-green Cadillac convertible attached to its trailer hitch, parked behind the Sportsman's Lodge in Studio City, California, where his entourage was staying between gigs. I can imagine that whoever occupies the White House in the early years of the twenty-first century would be thrilled to host Bob Dylan and would feel cool for doing it. One of cool's few new rules is to make other people feel cool as well.

John Cassavetes used cool to help get him where he wanted to go, artistically and financially; Andy Warhol reflected cool; Bob Dylan was and remains cool, so cool that he made it possible to be cool and have hit records and money and power. On the wings of the lyrics to "Like a Rolling Stone," cool entered the mainstream and merged with its values. Fifty years after Jack Kerouac described Charlie Parker, Dizzy Gillespie, Miles Davis, and Theolonious Monk, cool's catalysts, as "12th Century monks" or "witch doctors" with their "backs to each other, facing all the winds—bent, miserable, cold," alone with the understanding that "everything belongs to me, because I am poor"—our culture is permeated with cool.

Sporadic attempts have been made to kill cool off with CD titles like *The Death of the Cool*, menswear advertising campaigns trumpeting *The Rebirth of Cool*, or attempts to respell it, à la Kool Keith. Corporations use cool to sell hundreds of products. In our lives, cool has become almost unbearable. A 1998 count by Jerome Weeks of *The Dallas Morning News* turned up 5,704 web sites with "cool" in their titles. That same year, the Virginia Film Festival sponsored the first symposium on cool, which brought together some of cool's leading theoreticians and philosophers, from Robert Farris Thompson to Thomas Frank. Yet, no matter how much cool is abased or debated, it can still be high praise. If cool has been trivialized, it's also been globalized. As English has spread round the earth, so has cool. To use the word "cool" well is to partake of a central ritual of global culture as profound and as universal as a handshake. How important is it to be cool? Well, it's a cool world.

REFERENCES

SELECTED BIBLIOGRAPHY

Abe, Masao, ed. *A Zen Life: D. T. Suzuki Remembered.* New York and Tokyo: John Weatherhill, 1986.

Acker, Ally. *Reel Women: Pioneers of the Cinema: 1896 to the Present.* New York: Continuum, 1991.

Alexander, Donnell. "Are Black People Cooler Than White People?" *Might* 16 (July–Aug. 1997): 46–53.

Allen, Donald ed. *The Selected Poems of Frank O'Hara.* New York: Vintage, 1974.

Allen, Irving Lewis. *New York Life and Popular Speech.* New York: Oxford University Press, 1993.

Amram, David. *Vibrations: The Adventures and Musical Times of David Amram.* New York: Macmillan, 1968.

Anderson, Jervis. *Bayard Rustin: Troubles I've Seen.* New York: HarperCollins, 1997.

———. *This Was Harlem: A Cultural Portrait 1900–1950.* New York: Farrar, Strauss & Giroux, 1982.

Andy Warhol. Exhibition catalogue, Moderna Museet, Stockholm, Boston: Boston Book and Art, 1968.

Artaud, Antonin. *The Theatre and Its Double.* New York: Grove Press, 1958.

Baldwin, Gordon, and Judith Keller, curators. *Nadar Warhol: Paris New York: Photography and Fame.* Exhibition catalogue. Los Angeles: The J. Paul Getty Museum, 1999.

Baraka, Amiri. *The Autobiography of LeRoi Jones.* New York: Freundlich, 1984.

———. *Selected Poetry of Amiri Baraka/LeRoi Jones.* New York: William Morrow, 1979.

Baxter, John. *The Gangster Film.* London: A. Zwemmer, 1970.

Beard, Rick, and Leslie Cohen Berlowitz, eds. *Greenwich Village: Culture and Counterculture.* New York: Rutgers University Press, 1993.

Beaumont, Jennifer. "Interview with Machito (Frank Grillo). *Caribe* (Visual Arts Center, an affiliate of the Phelps-Stokes Fund) (1984), 32–44.

Beck, Julian. *The Life of the Theater.* New York: Limelight, 1986.

Beevor, Antony, and Artemis Cooper. *Paris After the Liberation 1944–1949.* New York: Doubleday, 1994.

Belgrad, Daniel. *The Culture of Spontaneity: Improvisation and the Arts in Postwar America.* Chicago: University of Chicago Press, 1998.

Bender, Thomas. *New York Intellect.* New York: Alfred A. Knopf, 1987.

Benson, Carl, ed. *The Bob Dylan Companion: Four Decades of Commentary.* New York: Schirmer, 1998.

Biner, Pierre. *The Living Theater.* New York: Horizon Press, 1972.

Black, Jack. *You Can't Win.* 1926. Reprint, Kukukuihaele, Hawaii: Omnium, 1992.

Bockris, Victor, and Gerard Malanga. *Up-Tight: The Velvet Underground Story.* New York: Quill, 1984.

Boggs, Vernon W. *Salsiology: Afro-Cuban Music and the Evolution of Salsa in New York City.* New York: Excelsior Music Publishing, 1992.

Bookbinder, Robert. *Classics of the Gangster Film.* Secaucus, N.J.: Citadel Press, 1985.

Bourdon, David. *Warhol.* New York: Harry N. Abrams, 1989.

Boyd, Todd. "A Nod to Cool or the New Blaxploitation?" *Los Angeles Times,* August 7, 1998, 15, 17.

Boyer, Paul. *By the Dawn's Early Light: American Thought and Culture at the Dawn of the Atomic Age, 2nd ed.* Chapel Hill: University of North Carolina Press, 1994.

Boyer, Richard. "Bop: A Profile of Dizzy Gillespie." *The New Yorker,* July 3, 1948, 28–37.

Brando, Marlon, with Robert Lindsey. *Songs My Mother Taught Me.* New York: Random House, 1994.

Breslin, Jimmy. *Damon Runyon: A Life.* New York: Ticknor & Fields, 1991.

Brower, Steven, and John Gall. "Grove Press at the Vanguard." *Print,* March–April, 1994, 24–34.

Brown, Arthur. "What Happened on June 15?" Pamphlet published by the War Resisters League Provisional Defense Committee, 1955. Swarthmore College Peace Collection. Swarthmore College Library, Swarthmore, Pennsylvania.

Broyard, Anatole. *Kafka Was the Rage: A Greenwich Village Memoir.* New York: Vintage, 1997.

Bruce, Lenny. *How to Talk Dirty and Influence People.* 1965. Reprint, New York: Simon & Schuster, 1992.

Bryce-Laporte, Roy Simon. "African Diaspora in the Americas." *Caribe* 6, no. 1 (Spring–Summer, 1982): 15.

Burley, Dan. *Original Handbook of Harlem Jive.* New York: Jive Potentials, 1944. Microfilm.

Burroughs, William S. *The Adding Machine: Selected Essays.* New York: Seaver, 1986.

———. *The Last Words of Dutch Schultz.* New York: Arcade, 1993.

———. *My Education: A Book of Dreams.* Viking/Penguin, 1998.

———. *Naked Lunch.* New York: Grove Press, 1959.

———. *Nova Express.* New York: Grove Press, 1964.

———. *The Place of Dead Roads.* New York: Holt, Rinehart, and Winston, 1983.

———. *Queer.* New York: Viking/Penguin, 1985.

———. *The Retreat Diaries.* New York: City Moon, 1976.

———. *The Ticket That Exploded.* Paris: Olympia Press [1962].

———. *Tornado Alley.* Cherry Valley, N.Y.: Cherry Valley Editions, 1989.

Burrows, Edwin G., and Mike Wallace. *Gotham: A History of New York City to 1898.* New York: Oxford University Press, 1999.

Butterick, George F., ed. Black Mountain College Issue. *Olson: The Journal of the Charles Olson Archives 2* (Fall 1974).

Cage, John. "Empty Words: John Cage Talks Back." In *Loka: A Journal from Naropa Institute.* New York: Anchor/Doubleday, 1975, 96–97.

———. *Silence: Lectures and Writings.* Middletown, Conn.: Wesleyan University Press, 1961.

———. *A Year From Monday: New Lectures and Writings.* Middletown, Conn.: Wesleyan University Press, 1967.

Calloway, Cab. *The New Cab Calloway's Hepster's Dictionary: The Language of Jive.* New York: C. Calloway, 1944.

Carney, Ray. *The Films of John Cassavetes: Pragmatism, Modernism, and the Movies.* Cambridge, Eng: Cambridge University Press, 1994.

———, ed. John Cassavetes Memorial Issue. *Film Comment.* 25 (May–June 1989), 30–49.

Carr, Roy, Brian Case, and Fred Deller. *The Hip: Hipsters, Jazz, and the Beat Generation.* London: Faber & Faber, 1986.

Cassady, Neal. *Grace Beats Karma: Letters from Prison 1958–60.* New York: Blast Books, 1999.

Cohen, Rich. *Tough Jews: Fathers, Sons, and Gangster Dreams.* New York: Simon & Schuster, 1998.

Cohn, Nik. *The Heart of the World.* New York: Alfred A. Knopf, 1992.

Cole, Bill. *John Coltrane.* New York: Schirmer, 1976.

Chauncey, George. *Gay New York: Gender, Urban Culture, and the Making of the Gay Male World, 1890–1940.* New York: Basic Books, 1994.

Charters, Samuel. *Jazz: A History of the New York Scene*. New York: Da Capo, 1996.

Christopher, Nicholas. *Somewhere in the Night: Film Noir and the American City*. New York: Free Press, 1997.

Clark, Tom. *Charles Olson: The Allegory of a Poet's Life*. New York: W.W. Norton, 1991.

———. *Jack Kerouac*. San Diego: Harcourt Brace Jovanovich, 1984.

———. *Robert Creeley and the Genius of the American Common Place*. New York: New Directions, 1993.

Clark, Veve A., Millicent Hodson, and Catrina Neiman. *The Legend of Maya Deren, Vol. 1*. New York: Anthology Film Archives/Film Culture, 1984.

Cohen, John, ed. *The Essential Lenny Bruce*. New York: Ballantine, 1967.

Cohen-Solal, Annie. *Sartre: A Life*. Translated by Anna Cancogni. New York: Pantheon, 1987.

Connor, Marlene Kim. *What Is Cool? Understanding Black Manhood in America*. New York: Crown, 1995.

Crane, Diana. *The Transformation of the Avant-Garde: The New York Art World, 1940–1985*. Chicago: University of Chicago Press, 1987.

Crouch, Stanley. "Bird Land: Charlie Parker, Clint Eastwood and America." *The New Republic*, February 27, 1989, 25–31.

Cubop: The Life and Music of Maestro Mario Bauza. Exhibition catalogue, Caribbean Cultural Center, New York. New York: Caribbean Cultural Center, 1993.

Davies, Philip, and Brian Neve, eds. *Cinema, Politics, and Society in America*. Manchester, Eng.: Manchester University Press, 1981.

Davis, Francis. *Bebop and Nothingness: Jazz and Pop at the End of the Century*. New York: Simon & Schuster, 1996.

Davis, Miles, with Quincy Troupe. *Miles: The Autobiography*. New York: Touchstone, 1989.

Dawson, Fielding. *The Black Mountain Book*. Rev. ed. Rocky Mount, N.C.: North Carolina Wesleyan College Press, 1991.

Day, Dorothy. "Dorothy Day Writes from Jail." *Catholic Worker* 24, no. 1 (July–August 1957): 1, 6.

———. *Loaves and Fishes*. New York: Harper & Row, 1963.

———. *The Long Loneliness: The Autobiography of Dorothy Day*. 2nd ed. New York: HarperCollins, 1997.

———. "Vocation to Prison." *Catholic Worker* 24, no. 2 (September 1957): 1–6.

———. "We Plead Guilty." *Commonweal* 6, no. 7 (Dec. 27, 1957): 330–333.

DeMartino, Richard. "Karen Horney, Daisetz T. Suzuki, and Zen Buddhism" *American Journal of Psychoanalysis*, 51, no. 3 (1991):

Denby, Edwin. *Looking at the Dance*. New York: Popular Library, 1968.

Deveaux, Scott. *The Birth of Bebop: A Social and Musical History*. Berkeley: University of California Press, 1997.

DiPrima, Diane. *Memoirs of a Beatnik*. New York: Olympia Press, 1969.

Douglas, Ann. *Terrible Honesty: Mongrel Manhattan in the 1920s*. New York: Noonday Press, 1995.

Duberman, Martin. *Black Mountain: An Exploration in Community*. New York: E. P. Dutton, 1972.

Duke, Sally Banes. *Greenwich Village 1963: Avant-Garde Performance and the Effervescent Body*. Durham, N.C.: Duke University Press, 1993.

Dumoulin, Heinrich. *Zen Buddhism in the Twentieth Century*. Translated by Joseph S. O'Leary. New York: John Weatherhill, 1992.

Dunaway, David King. *How Can I Keep from Singing: Pete Seeger*. New York: McGraw-Hill, 1981.

Dyer, Geoff. *But Beautiful: A Book About Jazz*. New York: North Point, 1996.

Ellison, Ralph. *Invisible Man*. 1952. Reprint, New York: Vintage, 1972.

———. *Shadow and Act*. New York: Random House, 1965.

Elson, Robert T. *The World of Time, Inc.: The Intimate History of a Publishing Enterprise*. Vol. 2: 1941–60. New York: Atheneum, 1973.

Fariello, Griffin. *Red Scare: Memories of the American Inquisition*. New York: W. W. Norton, 1995.

Fields, Rick. *How the Swans Came to the Lake: A Narrative History of Buddhism in America*. Boulder, Colo.: Shambala, 1981.

Fleming, Richard, and William Duckworth, eds. *John Cage at Seventy-five*. Lewisburg, Pa.: Bucknell University Press, 1989.

Ford, Charles Henri, ed. *View: Parade of the Avant-Garde: An Anthology of View Magazine (1940–47)*. New York: Thunder's Mouth Press, 1991.

Ford, Charles Henri, and Parker Tyler. *The Young and the Evil*. New York: Sea Horse, 1988.

Frank, Thomas. *The Conquest of Cool: Business Culture, Counterculture, and the Rise of Hip Consumerism*. Chicago: University of Chicago Press, 1997.

Furlong, Monica. *Zen Effects: The Life of Alan Watts*. Boston: Houghton Mifflin, 1986.

Gabler, Neal. *Winchell: Gossip, Power, and the Culture of Celebrity*. New York: Alfred A. Knopf, 1995.

Gabriel, Trip. "Cool Is Back, Not Awesome Cool, but Cool Cool." *New York Times*, June 13, 1994, B4.

Gaugh, Harry F. *de Kooning*. New York: Abbeville Press, 1983.

George-Warren, Holly, ed. *The Rolling Stone Book of the Beats*. New York: Rolling Stone Press/Hyperion, 1999.

Geldzahler, Henry. *New York Painting and Sculpture, 1940–1970*. New York: E. P. Dutton, 1969.

Gena, Peter, and Jonathan Brent. *A John Cage Reader*. New York: C. F. Peters, 1982.

Giddins, Gary. *Celebrating Bird: The Triumph of Charlie Parker*. New York: William Morrow, 1987.

Giddins, Gary, ed. "What Was Cool Jazz?" *Village Voice Jazz Supplement*, June 25, 1996, 3–17.

Gillespie, Dizzy, with Al Fraser. *To Be or Not to Bop*. Garden City, N.Y.: Doubleday, 1979.

Gillett, Charlie. *The Sound of the City: The Rise of Rock 'n' Roll*. New York: Dell, 1972.

Ginsberg, Allen. *Collected Poems, 1947–1980*. New York: Harper & Row, 1984.

———. "The Hipsters' Hipster": A Reminiscence of Herbert Huncke. *New York Times Magazine*, December 29, 1996, 39.

———. *Journals: Early Fifties, Early Sixties*. Edited by Gordon Ball. New York: Grove Press, 1987.

Gitler, Ira. *Jazz Masters of the 40's*. New York: Macmillan, 1966.

———, ed. *Swing to Bop*. New York: Oxford University Press, 1985.

Gold, Robert S. *Jazz Talk*. New York: Bobbs-Merrill, 1975.

Goldberg, Joe. *Jazz Masters of the 50's*. New York: Macmillan, 1965.

Goldman, Albert, from the journalism of Lawrence Schiller. *Ladies and Gentlemen—Lenny Bruce!!* New York: Random House, 1974.

Goldsmith, Peter D. *Making People's Music: Moe Asch and Folkways Records*. Washington, D.C.: Smithsonian Institution Press, 1997.

Gooch, Brad. *City Poet: The Life and Times of Frank O'Hara*. New York: Alfred A. Knopf, 1993.

Goodman, Paul. *Growing Up Absurd: Problems of Youth in the Organized System*. New York: Random House, 1960.

Goodman, Paul, and Percival Goodman. *Communitas: Means of Livelihood and Ways of Life*. New York: Vintage, 1960.

Gordon, Max. *Live at the Village Vanguard*. New York: Da Capo Press, 1980.

Gottlieb, Robert, ed. *Reading Jazz: A Gathering of Autobiography, Reportage and Criticism from 1919 to Now*. New York: Pantheon, 1996.

Grauerholz, James, and Ira Silverberg, eds. *Word Virus: The William Burroughs Reader*. New York: Grove Press, 1998.

Greenfield, Jerome. *Wilhelm Reich vs. the U.S.A.* New York: W. W. Norton, 1974.

Gruen, John. *The Party's Over Now: Reminiscences of the Fifties—New York's Artists, Writers, Musicians, and Their Friends*. Wainscott, N.Y.: Pushcart Press, 1989.

Guggenheim, Peggy. *Out of This Century: Confessions of an Art Addict*. New York: Universe, 1979.

Guilbaut, Serge. *How New York Stole the Idea of Modern Art: Abstract Expressionism, Freedom, and the Cold War*. Translated by Arthur Goldhammer. Chicago: University of Chicago Press, 1983.

Guthrie, Woody. *Bound for Glory*. New York: E. P. Dutton, 1995.

Halberstam, David. *The Fifties*. New York: Villard, 1993.

Hall, Lee. *Elaine and Bill: Portrait of a Marriage—The Lives of Willem and Elaine de Kooning*. New York: HarperCollins, 1993.

Hammer, Richard. *The Illustrated History of Organized Crime*. Philadelphia: Courage/Running Press, 1989.

Hanoteau, Guillaume. *L'Age d'Or de Saint Germain-des-Prés*. Paris: Editions Denoel, 1965.

Harris, Mary Emma. *The Arts at Black Mountain College*. Cambridge, Mass.: MIT Press, 1987.

Harris, Oliver, ed. *The Letters of William S. Burroughs, 1945–1959*. New York: Penguin, 1994.

Hawes, Elizabeth. *New York, New York: How the Apartment House Transformed the Life of the City (1869–1930)*. New York: Alfred A. Knopf, 1993.

Hellman, Lillian. *Scoundrel Time*. Boston: Little, Brown, 1976.

Helms, Alan. *Young Man from the Provinces: A Gay Life Before Stonewall*. New York: Avon, 1995.

Hentoff, Nat. "Playboy Interview: Bob Dylan." *Playboy*, March 1966, 41–44, 138–142.

Hess, Thomas. *Willem de Kooning*. New York: George Braziller, 1959.

Hickey, Dave. "American Cool." *Art Issues* (Jan.–Feb. 1999): 10–13.

Holiday, Billie, with William Duffy. *Lady Sings the Blues*. New York: Avon, 1956.

Holmes, John Clellon. *Nothing More to Declare*. London: Andre Deutsch, 1968.

Huncke, Herbert. *Guilty of Everything: The Autobiography of Herbert Huncke*. New York: Paragon House, 1990.

———. *Huncke's Journal*. New York: Poet's Press, 1965.

Hurewitz, Daniel. *Stepping Out: Nine Walks Through New York City's Gay and Lesbian Past*. New York: Owl Books, 1997.

Hurston, Zora Neale. *Mules and Men*. 1935. Reprint, New York: Harper & Row, 1990.

Jackson, Kenneth T., ed. *The Encyclopedia of New York City*. New Haven, Conn.: Yale University Press, 1995.

Jacobs, Jane. *The Death and Life of Great American Cities*. New York: Vintage, 1992.

James, David E. *To Free the Cinema: Jonas Mekas and the New York Underground*. Princeton, N.J.: Princeton University Press, 1992.

Johnson, Joyce. *Minor Characters*. Boston: Houghton Mifflin, 1983.

Jones, Constance. *Karen Horney, Psychoanalyst*. New York: Chelsea House, 1989.

Jones, Hettie. *How I Became Hettie Jones*. New York: Penguin, 1991.

Jones, LeRoi. *Blues People: Negro Music*

in White America. New York: William Morrow, 1973.

Jonnes, Jill. *Hep-Cats, Narcs, and Pipe Dreams: A History of America's Romance with Illegal Drugs*. New York: Scribner, 1996.

Kapleau, Roshi Philip. *Zen: Dawn in the West*. Garden City, N.Y.: Anchor Press, 1979.

Kazan, Elia. *A Life*. New York: Alfred A. Knopf, 1988.

Kazanjian, Dodie, and Calvin Tomkins. *Alex: The Life of Alexander Liberman*. New York: Alfred A. Knopf, 1993.

Kerouac, Jack. *The Dharma Bums*. New York: Viking, 1958.

———. *On the Road*. New York: Viking, 1957.

———. *Some of the Dharma*. New York: Viking Penguin, 1997.

———. *The Subterraneans*. New York: Grove Press, 1958.

———. *Vanity of Duluoz*. New York: Coward, McCann, 1968.

Kingsley, April. *The Turning Point*. New York: Simon & Schuster, 1992.

Kinnaird, Clark, ed. *A Treasury of Damon Runyon*. New York: Modern Library, 1958.

Kirby, Michael, ed. *Happenings: An Illustrated Anthology*. New York: E. P. Dutton, 1966.

Knight, Brenda. *Women of the Beat Generation*. Berkeley, Calif.: Conari Press, 1995.

Kostelanetz, Richard. *Conversing with Cage*. New York: Limelight, 1988.

———. *John Cage (Ex)plain(ed)*. New York: Schirmer, 1995.

Kraft, Kenneth *Zen: Tradition and Transition: A Sourcebook by Contemporary Zen Masters and Scholars*. New York: Grove Press, 1988.

Landesman, Jay. *Rebel Without Applause*. New York: Paragon House, 1990.

Lane, Mervin, ed. *Black Mountain College: Sprouted Seeds: An*

Anthology of Personal Accounts. Knoxville: University of Tennessee Press, 1970.

Lebel, Robert. *Marcel Duchamp*. Translated by George Heard Hamilton. New York: Paragraphic, 1959.

Lehman, David. *The Last Avant-Garde: The Making of the New York School of Poets*. New York: Bantam Doubleday Dell, 1998.

Levy, Julien. *Memoir of an Art Gallery*. New York: G. P. Putnam & Sons, 1977.

Lohr, Steve. "It's Hot, Has Four Letters and Legs." *New York Times*, August 27, 1995, E6.

"The Loneliest Monk." *Time*, February 28, 1964, 84–88.

Lottman, Herbert R. *Albert Camus: A Biography*. New York: Doubleday, 1979.

Lynes, Russell. *Good Old Modern: An Intimate Portrait of the Museum of Modern Art*. New York: Atheneum, 1973.

Mailer, Norman. *Advertisements for Myself*. New York: G. P. Putnam's Sons, 1959.

Major, Clarence, ed. *From Juba to Jive: A Dictionary of African-American Slang*. New York: Penguin, 1994.

Malina, Judith. *The Diaries of Judith Malina, 1947–1957*. New York: Grove Press, 1984.

———. On sharing a jail cell with Dorothy Day. Unpublished transcript of an interview conducted July 8, 1988. Catholic Worker Collection, Marquette University Library, Milwaukee, Wisconsin.

Manso, Peter. *Brando*. London: Orion, 1995.

———. *Mailer: His Life and Times*. New York: Simon & Schuster, 1985.

Marcus, Greil. *Invisible Republic: Bob Dylan's Basement Tapes*. New York: Henry Holt, 1997.

Marriott, Michel. "The 4-1-1 on Urban Cool: Hype or Hope?" *New York Times*, November 5, 1995, Style Section, 53, 56.

Marsh, Graham, Felix Cromey, and Glyn Callingham, eds. *Blue Note: The Album Cover Art.* San Francisco: Chronicle, 1991.

McAuliffe, Kevin Michael. *The Great American Newspaper: The Rise and Fall of the Village Voice.* New York: Charles Scribner & Sons, 1978.

McLuhan, Marshall. *Understanding Media: The Extensions of Man.* New York: McGraw-Hill, 1964.

Mead, Rebecca. "The Beats Are Back." *New York,* 3 May 1995, 31–37.

Meier, August, and Elliot Rudnick, eds. *From Plantation to Ghetto.* 3rd ed. New York: Hill and Wang, 1976.

Mekas, Jonas. *I Had Nowhere to Go.* New York: Black Thistle Press, 1991.

———. ed. "Special Issue: American Directors." *Film Culture* 38 (Spring 1963).

Meltzer, David, ed. *Reading Jazz.* San Francisco: Mercury House, 1993.

Meyerowitz, Joanne, ed. *Not June Cleaver: Women and Gender in Postwar America, 1945–1960.* Philadelphia: Temple University Press, 1994.

Miles, Barry. *El Hombre Invisible: William Burroughs: A Portrait.* New York: Hyperion, 1993.

———. *Ginsberg: A Biography.* New York: Simon & Schuster, 1989.

———. *Jack Kerouac, King of the Beats: A Portrait.* New York: Henry Holt, 1998.

Miller, Arthur. *Timebends: A Life.* New York: Grove Press, 1987.

Miller, William D. *Dorothy Day: A Biography.* New York: Harper & Row, 1982.

Mingus, Charles. *Beneath the Underdog.* New York: Alfred A. Knopf, 1971.

Moore, David G. *Looking Back: Gay and Lesbian Pioneers Before Stonewall: A Chronology.* Los Angeles: One, 1994.

Morgan, Bill. *The Beat Generation in New York: A Walking Tour of Jack Kerouac's City.* San Francisco: City Lights, 1997.

Morgan, Ted. *Literary Outlaw: The Life and Times of William Burroughs.* New York: Henry Holt, 1988.

Morris, Jan. *Manhattan '45.* New York: Oxford University Press, 1986.

Mottram, Eric. *William Burroughs: The Algebra of Need.* London: Marion Boyars, 1977.

Naifeh, Steven, and Gregory White Smith. *Jackson Pollock: An American Saga.* New York: HarperCollins, 1991.

Nash, Jay Robert. *Encyclopedia of World Crime.* Wilmette, Ill.: Crimebooks, 1990.

Neumann, Eckhard, ed. *Bauhaus and Bauhaus People: Personal Opinions and Recollections of Former Bauhaus Members and Their Contemporaries.* New York: Van Nostrand Reinhold, 1970.

Nicosia, Gerald. *Memory Babe: A Critical Biography of Jack Kerouac.* New York: Grove Press, 1983.

O'Brien, John, ed. "The Review of Contemporary Fiction: Grove Press Number." *Review of Contemporary Fiction* 10, no. 3 (Fall 1990).

Odier, Daniel. *The Job: Interviews with William Burroughs.* New York: Grove Press, 1970.

O'Hara, Frank. *Jackson Pollock.* New York: George Braziller, 1959.

———. *Lunch Poems.* San Francisco: City Lights, 1964.

Ollman, Arthur. Introduction to *Arnold Newman: Five Decades,* by Arnold Newman. San Diego: Harcourt Brace Jovanovich. 1986.

Olson, Charles. *Selected Writings of Charles Olson.* New York: New Directions, 1966.

———. *Human Universe and Other Essays.* Edited by Donald Allen. New York: Grove Press, 1967.

Paris, Bernard J. *Karen Horney: A Psychoanalyst's Search for Self-Understanding.* New Haven, Conn.:

Yale University Press, 1994.

Perloff, Marjorie, and Charles Junkerman, eds. *John Cage: Composed in America*. Chicago: University of Chicago Press, 1994.

Phillips, Lisa, with contributions by Maurice Berger and others. *Beat Culture and the New America 1950–1965*. Exhibition catalogue, Whitney Musem of American Art. New York: Whitney Museum of American Art in association with Flammarion Paris, 1995.

Piazza, Tom ed. *Setting the Tempo: Fifty Years of Great Jazz Liner Notes*. New York: Anchor, 1996.

Polizzotti, Mark. *Revolution of the Mind: The Life of André Breton*. New York: Farrar, Strauss & Giroux, 1995.

Quinn, Susan. *A Mind of Her Own: The Life of Karen Horney*. New York: Summit, 1987.

Reich, Wilhelm. *The Sexual Revolution*. 4th edition. Translated by Therese Pol. New York: Touchstone, 1974.

———. *The Mass Psychology of Fascism*. New York: Farrar, Strauss & Giroux, 1970.

Reisner, Robert, ed. *Bird: The Legend of Charlie Parker*. New York: Da Capo Press, 1977.

Revill, David. *The Roaring Silence: John Cage: A Life*. New York: Arcade, 1992.

Rivers, Larry, with Arnold Weinstein. *What Did I Do? The Unauthorized Autobiography*. New York: HarperCollins, 1992.

Roberts. John Storm. *The Latin Tinge: The Impact of Latin American Music on the United States*. Tivoli, N.Y.: Original Music, 1985.

Rogers, W. G., and Mildred Weston. *Carnival Crossroads: The Story of Times Square*. Garden City, N.Y.: Doubleday, 1960.

Rorem, Ned. *Knowing When to Stop*. New York: Simon & Schuster, 1994.

———. *The Paris Diary and the New York Diary, 1951–61*. New York: Da Capo Press, 1998.

Rosenbaum, Ron. "Dan Wolf: Homeric Listener." *New York Observer*, March 11, 1996.

Rosenberg, Harold. *Arshile Gorky: The Man, the Time, the Idea*. New York: Grove Press, 1962.

Rosenthal, David H. *Hard Bop: Jazz and Black Music, 1955–1965*. New York: Oxford University Press, 1992.

Rossett, Barney, ed. *Evergreen Review Reader, 1957–1966*. New York: Blue Moon, 1993.

Rubins, Jack. *Karen Horney: Gentle Rebel of Psychoanalysis*. New York: Dial Press, 1978.

Russell, Ross. *The Life and Hard Times of Charlie Parker*. New York: Charter House, 1973.

Rutkoff, Peter M., and William B. Scott. *New School: A History of the New School for Social Research*. New York: Free Press, 1986.

Salazar, Max. "Machito, Mario, and Graciela: Destined for Greatness." *Latin Beat* 1, no. 6 (June–July 1991): 25–29.

———. "Afro-Cubop History." *Latin Beat* 2, no. 2 (March 1992): 20–25.

———. "Chano Pozo, Part I." *Latin Beat* 3, no. 3 (April 1993): 6–10.

———. "Chano Pozo, Part II." *Latin Beat* 3, no. 4 (May 1993): 22–24.

———. "Noro Morales." *Latin Beat* 6, no. 2 (March 1996): 16–18.

———. "Tribute to Machito." *Caribe* (Visual Arts Center, an affiliate of the Phelps-Stokes Fund). (1984), 32–34.

Sante, Luc. *Low Life: Lures and Snares of Old New York*. New York: Farrar, Strauss & Giroux, 1991.

Sargeant, Winthrop. "Great Simplicity: A Profile of Dr. Daisetz Teitaro Suzuki." *The New Yorker*, August 31, 1957, 34–53.

Sarris, Andrew. *Confessions of a Cultist: The Cinema, 1955–1969*. New York: Simon & Schuster, 1971.

Sawin, Martica. *Surrealism in Exile and the Beginning of the New York School*. Cambridge, Mass: MIT Press, 1995.

Scaduto, Anthony. *Bob Dylan: An Intimate Biography*. New York: New American Library, 1972.

Schechner, Richard. Introductory essay to *The Living Book of the Living Theatre*. Greenwich, Conn.: New York Graphic Society, 1971.

Schick, Frank L. *The Paperbound Book in America*. New York: R. R. Bowker, 1958.

Schickel, Richard. *Brando: A Life in Our Time*. New York: St. Martin's Press, 1993.

Schjeldahl, Peter. "Andy Warhol." Review of Museum of Modern Art Andy Warhol retrospective. *Denver Quarterly* 28, no. 1 (Summer 1993): 108–110.

Schoener, Alan, ed. *Harlem on My Mind: Cultural Capital of Black America, 1900–1968*. New York: W. W. Norton, 1995.

Seeger, Pete. *The Incompleat Folk-Singer*. New York: Simon & Schuster, 1972.

Seitz, William C. *Arshile Gorky: Paintings, Drawings, Studies*. New York: Museum of Modern Art, 1962.

Shahech, Jack, ed. *Nuclear War Films*. Carbondale: Southern Illinois University Press, 1978.

Shapiro, Nat, and Nat Hentoff, eds. *Hear Me Talkin' to Ya*. New York: Rinehart, 1955.

Sharf, Myron. *Fury on Earth: A Biography of Wilhelm Reich*. New York: Da Capo Press, 1994.

Shefter, Martin, ed. *Capital of the American Century: The National and International Influence of New York*. New York: Russell Sage Foundation, 1993.

Shelton, Robert. *No Direction Home: The Life and Music of Bob Dylan*. New York: Ballantine, 1987.

Short, Robert. *Dada and Surrealism*. Secaucus, N.J.: Chartwell Books, 1980.

Smith, Patrick S. *Warhol: Conversations about the Artist*. Ann Arbor, Mich.: UMI Research Press, 1988.

Smith, Robert H. *Paperback Parnassus*. Boulder, Colo.: Westview Press, 1976.

Smith, Wendy. *Real Life Drama: The Group Theatre and America, 1931–1940*. New York: Alfred A. Knopf, 1990.

Snyder, Gary. *The Real Work: Interviews and Talks, 1964–1979*. New York: New Directions, 1980.

Sobieszek, Robert A., curator. *Ports of Entry: William S. Burroughs and the Arts*. Exhibition catalogue. Los Angeles: Los Angeles County Museum of Art; New York: Thames & Hudson, 1996.

Spender, Matthew. *From a High Place: A Life of Arshile Gorky*. New York: Alfred A. Knopf, 1999.

Stearns, Marshall W. *The Story of Jazz*. New York: Oxford University Press, 1956.

Stearns, Peter N. *American Cool: Constructing a Twentieth-Century Emotional Style*. New York: New York University Press, 1994.

Stoehr, Taylor, ed. *Drawing the Line: The Political Essays of Paul Goodman*. New York: Free Life, 1977.

Stokes, Geoffrey, ed. *The Village Voice Anthology (1956–1980): Twenty-five years of Writing from the Village Voice*. New York: William Morrow, 1982.

Suarez, Juan A. *Bike Boys, Drag Queens, and Superstars: Avant-Garde, Mass Culture, and Gay Identities in the 1960s Underground Cinema*. Bloomington: Indiana University Press, 1996.

Sukenick, Ronald. *Down and In: Life in the Underground*. New York: Beech Tree, 1987.

Suzuki, Daisetz Teitaro. *Essays in Zen Buddhism, First Series*. New York: Grove Press, 1961.

———. *Manual of Zen Buddhism*. New York, Grove Press, 1960.

———, with Erich Fromm and Richard deMartino. *Zen Buddhism and Psychoanalysis*. New York: Grove Press, 1963.

Swanberg, W. A. *Luce and His Empire*. New York: Charles Scribner & Sons, 1972.

Tanahashi, Kazuaki, and Tensho David Schneider, eds. *Essential Zen*. New York: HarperCollins, 1995.

Tashjian, Dickran. *A Boatload of Madmen: Surrealism and the American Avant-Garde, 1920–1950*. New York: Thames and Hudson, 1995.

Tate, Greg. *Flyboy in the Buttermilk: Essays on Contemporary America*. New York: Simon & Schuster, 1992.

Taylor, William R., ed. *Inventing Times Square: Commerce and Culture at the Crossroads of the World*. New York: Russell Sage Foundation, 1991.

Thomas, Robert McG., Jr. "Anton Rosenberg, a Hipster Ideal, Dies At 71," *New York Times*, February. 22, 1998.

———. "Harold Fox, Who Took Credit for the Zoot Suit, Dies at 86." *New York Times*, August 1, 1996.

Thompson, Robert Farris. "An Aesthetic of the Cool." *African Arts Mgazine, 7,* no. 5 (Autumn, 1973): 40–43, 64–67, 89–92.

———. *Dancing Between Two Worlds: Kongo-Angola Culture and the Americas*. New York: Caribbean Cultural Center, 1991.

———. *Flash of the Spirit*. Vintage, 1983.

Thurman, Robert. *Inner Revolution*. New York: Riverhead, 1998.

Timmons, Stuart. *The Trouble with Harry Hay: Founder of the Modern Gay Movement*. Boston: Alyson, 1990.

Tomkins, Calvin. *The Bride and the Bachelors: Five Masters of the Avant-Garde: Duchamp, Tinguely, Cage, Rauschenberg and Cunningham*. New York: Penguin, 1965.

———. *Duchamp: A Biography*. New York: Henry Holt, 1996.

———. *Off the Wall: Robert Rauschenberg and the Art World of Our Time*. New York: Penguin, 1980.

Tworkov, Helen. *Zen in America*. San Francisco: North Point Press, 1989.

———, ed. "'Buddhism and the Beat Generation': A Special Section Featuring 'Spontaneous Intelligence,' an Interview with Allen Ginsberg." *Tricycle, the Buddhist Review* 5, no. 1 (Fall, 1995): 58–82.

Tytell, John. *The Living Theatre: Art, Exile, and Outrage*. New York: Grove Press, 1995.

Victoria, Brian A. (Daizen). *Zen at War*. New York: John Weatherhill, 1997.

Von Schmidt, Eric, and Jim Rooney. *Baby, Let Me Follow You Down: The Illustrated History of the Cambridge Folk Years*. 2nd ed. Amherst: University of Massachusetts Press, 1994.

Wainwright, Loudon. *The Great American Magazine*. New York: Alfred A. Knopf, 1986.

Wakefield, Dan. *New York in the Fifties*. New York: Houghton Mifflin/ Seymour Lawrence, 1992.

Watson, Steven. *The Birth of the Beat Generation: Visionaries, Rebels, and Hipsters, 1944–1960*. New York: Pantheon, 1995.

Watts, Alan W. *Beat Zen, Square Zen and Zen*. San Francisco: City Lights, 1959.

———. *In My Own Way: An Autobiography, 1915–1965*. New York: Pantheon, 1972.

Weeks, Jerome. "The Rule of Cool." *Dallas Morning News*, July 30, 1998, 1–2.

Whitford, Frank. *Bauhaus*. London: Thames and Hudson, 1984.

Wilcock, John. *The Autobiography and Sex Life of Andy Warhol*. New York: Other Scenes, 1971.

Willet, John. *The Theater of Erwin*

Piscator: Half a Century of Politics in the Theater. London: Eyre Methuen, 1978.

Williams, Richard. Dylan: A Man Called Alias. New York: Henry Holt, 1992.

Wittner, Lawrence S. Rebels Against War: The American Peace Movement, 1933–1983. Philadelphia: Temple University Press, 1984.

Wolf, Daniel, and Edwin Fancher, eds. The Village Voice Reader: A Mixed Bag from the Greenwich Village Newspaper. Garden City, N.Y.: Doubleday, 1962.

Womack, Bill. "The Music of Contingency: An Interview with John Cage." Zero. 3 (1979).

Woronov, Mary. Swimming Underground: My Years in the Warhol Factory. Boston: Journey, 1995.

Woods, Phil "Bebop." The Note: The Newsletter of the Al Cohn Memorial Jazz Collection 7, no. 5 (May 1995): 1–2.

Zinn, Howard. A People's History of the United States, 1492–Present. Rev. ed. New York: HarperCollins, 1995.

SELECTED FILMOGRAPHY

Bach, Jean, dir. A Great Day in Harlem. ABC Home Video, Stamford, CT, 1995.

Benedek, Laslo, dir. The Wild One. RCA/Columbia Pictures Home Video, Burbank, CA, 1986 [1954].

Brooks, Richard, dir. Blackboard Jungle. MGM/UA Home Video, Culver City: CA, 1989 [1955].

Brookner, Howard, dir. Burroughs, the Movie. Giorno Poetry Systems, New York, 1983.

Cassavetes, John, dir. Shadows. Fox Orion Home Video, Los Angeles, 1996 [1959].

Clarke, Shirley, dir. The Connection. Living Theatre Production. Mystic Fire Video, New York, 1961.

———. The Cool World. Courtesy of the Archive Research and Study Center of the UCLA Film and Television Archive. 1964.

de Antonio, Emile, and Mary Lampson, dirs. Painters Painting. Mystic Fire Video, New York, 1972.

Frank, Robert, and Al Leslie, dirs. Pull My Daisy. Museum of Fine Arts, Houston, 1959.

Frederickson, Bruce, dir. The Song of the Spirit: The Story of Lester Young. Collection Frederickson Willarmine, Minneapolis, 1990.

Fuller, Sam, dir. Pickup on South Street. CBS Fox Video, New York, 1991 [1953].

Guest, Val, dir. The Day the Earth Caught Fire. Thorne EMI Video, London, 1962.

Hawks, Howard, dir. Scarface. MCA Home Video, Universal City, CA [1932].

Hylkems, Hans, dir. Eric Dolphy: Last Date. Rhapsody Films, New York, 1991.

Kazan, Elia, dir. On the Waterfront. Columbia Tristar Home Video, Culver City, CA, 1995 [1954].

———. A Streetcar Named Desire. Warner Home Video, Burbank, CA, 1994 [1951].

LeRoy, Mervyn, dir. Little Caesar. MGM/ UA Home Video, Culver City, CA, 1991 [1930].

MacAdams, Lewis, and Richard Lerner, dirs. What Happened to Kerouac? Vidmark Entertainment, Santa Monica, CA, 1987.

Maech, Klaus, dir. William S. Burroughs, Commissioner of Sewers. Mystic Fire Video, New York, 1991.

Palmer, Robert, dir. The World According to John Coltrane. Tony Byron Multiprises, 1990.

Pennebaker, D. A., dir. Bob Dylan: Don't Look Back. Warner-Reprise Video, Los Angeles, 1967.

Ray, Nicholas, dir. Rebel Without a Cause. Warner Bros. Classics,

Burbank, CA, 1983 [1955].

Schickel, Richard, dir. *Elia Kazan: A Director's Journal*. Castle Hill, 1994.

Siodmak, Robert, dir. *Phantom Lady*. Universal Video, Universal City, CA, 1998 [1944].

Wiede, Robert, dir. *Lenny Bruce: Swear to Tell the Truth*. HBO Documentary Films, New York, 1998.

Zwerin, Charlotte, dir. *Straight, No Chaser*. Warner Home Video, Burbank, CA, 1990.

SELECTED DISCOGRAPHY
[ALL COMPACT DISKS]

Coltrane, John. *Blue Train*. Blue Note CDP 7 460952.

Davis, Miles. *Birth of the Cool*. Capitol Jazz CDP7 928622.

Dylan, Bob. *Another Side of Bob Dylan*. Columbia CK 8993.

———. *Blonde on Blonde*. Columbia CGK 841.

———. *Bob Dylan*. Columbia CK 08579.

———. *Bob Dylan Live 1966: "The "Royal Albert Hall" Concert*. Columbia C2K 65759.

———. *Bringing It All Back Home*. Columbia CK 9128.

———. *The Freewheelin' Bob Dylan*. Columbia CK 8786.

———. *The Times They Are A-Changin'*. Columbia CK 8905.

Gillespie, Dizzy, featuring Charlie Parker. *Groovin' High*. Savoy Jazz/Nippon Columbia SV 0152.

Gillespie, Dizzy, featuring Chano Pozo. *Dizzier and Dizzier*. BMG Media/Victor Jazz 09026-68517-2.

———. *Dizzy Gillespie and His Big Band featuring Chano Pozo*. GNP Crescendo GNPD 23.

Grillo, Frankie "Machito," including Charlie Parker and Chano Pozo. *Afro-Cuban Jazz*. Saludos Amigos/Sarabandas CD 62015.

Kerouac, Jack. *The Jack Kerouac Collection: The Complete Recorded Works*. Rhino Records R-70939.

———. *Jack Kerouac Reads* On the Road. Rykodisc RCD 10474.

Kerouac, Jack, William Burroughs, Lenny Bruce, and others. *The Beat Generation*. Rhino Records R2/R4 7D281.

McLean, Jackie. *Destination Out!*. Blue Note CDP 72438 32087 22.

———. *New Soil*. Blue Note CDP 784013 2.

Monk, Thelonious. *Criss-Cross*. Columbia Legacy CK 48823.

———. *The Best of Thelonious Monk: The Blue Note Years*. Blue Note CDP 7 95636 2.

Monk, Thelonious, featuring John Coltrane. *Live at the Five Spot*. Blue Note D 110 906.

Monk, Thelonious, featuring Sonny Rollins. *Brilliant Corners*. Riverside Jazz Classics OJCCD-026-2.

Morgan, Lee. *The Best of Lee Morgan*. Blue Note CDP 7 911382.

Parker, Charlie. *The Immortal Charlie Parker*. Savoy Jazz/Nippon Columbia SV-0102.

Parker, Charlie, and Dizzy Gillespie. *Bird and Diz*. Verve/Polygram Records 831 133-2.

Powell, Bud. *The Amazing Bud Powell, Vol. 1*. Blue Note CDP 781503 2.

Velvet Underground. *The Velvet Underground and Nico*. Verve/Polygram 5008.

———. *White Light/White Heat*. Verve/Polygram 5046.

Young, Lester. *The Best of Lester Young*. Pablo Records PACD-2405-420-2.

INDEX

Page numbers in *italics* refer to illustrations

PHOTOGRAPHY CREDITS

Art on pages 118, 218, 225, and 230–231 is copyright © Academy of Motion Picture Arts and Sciences.

Art on page 229 is copyright ©Anthology Film Archives.

Art on page 83 is copyright © Archive of American Art, The Smithsonian Institution, Washington, D.C.

Art on pages 177 and 201 is copyright © Archive Photo.

Art on page 254 is copyright © Al Aumuller/Collections of the Library of Congress.

Art on pages 16, 36, 40, 55, and 114 is copyright © Corbis Bettmann.

Art on page 71 is copyright © B.M.I. Archives.

Art on pages 66–67 is copyright © Brown Bros.

Art on pages 102–103 is copyright © Rudy Burckhardt/Tibor De Nagy Gallery.

Art on pages 25 and 169 is copyright © Henri Cartier-Bresson/Magnum.

Art on pages 191 and 217 is copyright © Joan Cohen.

Art on pages 234–235 is copyright © John Cohen, courtesy Deborah Bell, New York.

Art on page 160 is copyright © Corbis.

Art on pages 117 and 151 is copyright © Culver Pictures.

Art on page 258 is copyright © Bruce Davidson/Magnum.

Art on page 84 is copyright © Earl Davis.

Art on page 184 is copyright © Department of Special Collections, University of California Library, Davis, California.

Art on page 26 is copyright © Robert Doisneau/Rapho Paris.

Art on page 147 is copyright © Boris Erwitt/Magnum.

Art on page 93 is copyright © Charles Henri Ford.

Art on pages 110, 123, 124, 128, 132, 138–139, and 198 is copyright © Allen Ginsberg Trust.

Art on pages 21 and 154–155 is copyright © Burt Glinn/Magnum.

Art on page 226 is copyright © Lelia Goldoni.

Art on pages 35 and 48–49 is copyright © William P. Gottlieb.

Art on page 251 is copyright © Daniel Kramer.

Art on page 189 is copyright © Robert Lax.

Art on pages 204–205 and 207 is copyright © The Living Theatre.

Art on pages 163, 243, and 246 is copyright © Gerard Malanga.

Art on page 62 is copyright © Reid Miles.

Art on pages 166–167 is copyright © The Museum of Modern Art/Film Still Archive.

Art on pages 80–81 is copyright © The New York Historical Society.

Art on pages 32, 39, and 57 is copyright © Michael Ochs Archive.

Art on page 96 is copyright © Man Ray/J. Paul Getty Trust.

Art on page 95 is copyright © David Seymour/Magnum.

Art on pages 174–175 is copyright © Gary Snyder.

Art on pages 15 and 23 is copyright © Bill Spilka/Metronome Magazine/Archive Photos

Art on pages 12, 18, 43, and 221 is copyright © Dennis Stock/Magnum.

Art on page 77 is copyright © Time-Life Syndication.

Art on pages 210–211 is copyright © John E. Wulp/The Living Theatre.